Barry Baddock
Horst Messerschmidt
Ulrich Rüffin

Trademark

Neubearbeitung

*Wirtschaftsorientiertes
Englisch für die
berufliche Bildung*

Max Hueber Verlag

Abkürzungen

In diesem Lehrwerk finden folgende grammatische Abkürzungen Verwendung:

n   – noun
adj – adjective
adv – adverb
vb – verb
irr – irregular verb
pl – plural nouns

Verlagsredaktion: Dr. Kurt Bangert, Wolnzach
John Stevens, Hettenshausen
Sprachliche Durchsicht und Beratung: Stephen Fox, München
Umschlaggestaltung und Layout: Erwin Faltermeier, München
Umschlagfoto: Dieter Reichler, München

Ⓡ Dieses Werk folgt der Rechtschreibreform vom 1. Juli 1996.
Ausnahmen bilden Texte, bei denen künstlerische, philologische oder lizenzrechtliche Gründe einer Änderung entgegenstehen.

Das Werk und seine Teile sind urheberrechtlich geschützt. Jede Verwertung in anderen als den gesetzlich zugelassenen Fällen bedarf deshalb der vorherigen schriftlichen Einwilligung des Verlags.

| 3. 2. 1. | Die letzten Ziffern |
| 2001 2000 99 98 97 | bezeichnen Zahl und Jahr des Druckes. |

Alle Drucke dieser Auflage können, da unverändert, nebeneinander benutzt werden.
1. Auflage
© 1997 Max Hueber Verlag, D-85737 Ismaning
Gesamtherstellung: Ludwig Auer GmbH, Donauwörth
Printed in Germany
ISBN 3-19-002477-4

Vorwort zur Neubearbeitung

Trademark ist ein einbändiges Lehrwerk, das auf dem mittleren Bildungsabschluss aufbaut und einen Mindestwortschatz von ca. 1700 Wörtern voraussetzt. Das Lehrwerk ist aus der Unterrichtspraxis entstanden; es richtet sich insbesondere an Schülerinnen und Schüler höherer Handelsschulen (höhere Berufsfachschulen bzw. kaufmännische Berufskollegs).

Die **Neubearbeitung** von *Trademark* berücksichtigt die politischen und gesellschaftlichen Veränderungen der letzten Jahre. Neben zahlreichen aktualisierten Texten und Übungen ("The National Lottery", "The European Union", "The Internet", "National Vocational Qualifications" etc.) wurde das Thema "Graphs, Charts and Tables" völlig neu aufgenommen.

Bei den *Secretarial Activities* finden sich neu "Expressions for the Telephone", außerdem gibt es viele zusätzliche kommunikative Übungen. "Business Communication" wurde durch neue Übungen, z. B. "Contiletters", erweitert.

Trademark besteht aus drei Teilen:

○ **Introductory Course**
Ausgleichen unterschiedlicher Eingangsvoraussetzungen der Schülerinnen und Schüler, insbesondere im grammatischen Bereich; Einführung in wirtschaftsbezogene Themenbereiche.

○ **Main Course**
Ausführliche Behandlung unterschiedlichster Aspekte des internationalen Geschäftslebens; Erarbeitung anderer relevanter Themen wie z. B. "Computerization and Technology" und "Resources and the Environment"; Erörterung häufig auftretender grammatischer Probleme.

○ **Business Communication Course**
Vorbereitung auf die fremdsprachliche Kommunikation im Geschäftsleben (*Secretarial Activities:* "Telephoning in Business", "Visitors to the Company", "Socializing" etc.); Erarbeitung der Formen der modernen internationalen Handelskorrespondenz in englischer Sprache (*Commercial Correspondence:* Geschäftsbrief, Fax etc.).

Der Info-Appendix liefert zusätzlich hilfreiche sprachliche und sachliche Erläuterungen, die die Textarbeit sinnvoll unterstützen. (Aussprachehilfen, Nachschlagegrammatik, "commercial terms", "dispatch documents", gängige Abkürzungen).

Diese Aufteilung ermöglicht eine flexible Handhabung des Lehrwerks, denn die einzelnen Teile können – nach den Bedürfnissen der jeweiligen Lerngruppe – unterschiedlich gewichtet werden.

Die Texte zu den einzelnen Themenbereichen sind vielfältig (fachliche Darstellungen und Erörterungen, zum Teil mit Grafiken; Geschäftsbriefe, Werbetexte, Zeitungs- und Zeitschriftenartikel, Interviews). Jede Lektion bietet abwechslungsreiches Übungsmaterial (Fragen zum Text, Einsetzübungen, Zuordnungsübungen, Hörverständnisübungen). Die Übungen sind so angelegt, dass kooperative Arbeitsformen (z. B. Partnerarbeit) im Unterricht verwirklicht werden können. Der Übungsapparat von *Trademark* berücksichtigt die in den Lehrplänen geforderten Fertigkeiten Hören, Sprechen, Lesen, Schreiben und Übersetzen, wobei auf der schriftlichen Äußerungsfähigkeit ein besonderer Schwerpunkt liegt. Die Lehrbuchtexte, die mit dem Symbol gekennzeichnet sind, finden sich auf der Textkassette (Hueber-Nr. 2.2477). Zur weiteren Schulung des Hörverständnisses wurde eine spezielle Kassette mit Übungen entwickelt (Hueber-Nr. 3.2477), auf die im Lehrbuch ebenfalls mit dem Symbol verwiesen wird.

Trademark bereitet die Schülerinnen und Schüler auf ihr späteres Berufsfeld sprachlich vor. Sie erlernen und üben u. a. die Techniken "note-making" (text- oder gesprächsvorbereitende Notizen) und "note-taking" (text- oder gesprächsprotokollierende Notizen), sie üben das Übersetzen von Fachtexten und den Umgang mit Fachvokabular, sie schreiben nach Diktat und trainieren die Textproduktion z. B. in Form von "letter writing".

Verfasser und Verlagsredaktion

Contents

INTRODUCTORY COURSE

Unit	Theme/Text(s)	Skills	Grammar/Vocabulary	Page
1	***Technologies Mean Opportunities*** M & C – Young but Successful An Office Conversation	Reading comprehension Note-making Listening comprehension Note-taking	Present simple vs. present progressive	*10*
2	***A Company in the Making*** An Interview with M & C	Reading comprehension Listening comprehension Note-making/note-taking	Present progressive vs. Present perfect progressive	*14*
3	***A Business Career*** Jean Mace's Boss – Jean Mace	Reading comprehension	Past simple vs. Present perfect simple	*17*
4	***The Computer – a Man-Made Device*** Computers Never Fail?	Reading comprehension Note-making	Past simple vs. Past perfect simple	*20*
5	***Opening Up New Markets*** Going Continental	Reading comprehension Listening comprehension Note-making/note-taking	Will-future vs. Going to-future	*23*
6	***Applying for a Job*** A Job Interview	Reading comprehension Listening comprehension Note-making/note-taking	Conditional clauses: types 1 and 2	*26*
7	***Technologies in Everyday Life*** Paying Digitally – Phonecard Phones Drawing Cash Digitally – Cash Dispensers	Reading comprehension Note-making	Passive voice	*29*
8	***Planning One's Career*** Action for Jobs	Reading comprehension Note-making	Adjectives vs. adverbs Position of adverbs	*32*

MAIN COURSE

Unit	Theme/Text(s)	Skills	Grammar/Vocabulary	Page
1	***Banking and Savings*** Small Savers Banks and the Letter of Credit	Text production Reading comprehension Listening comprehension	Auxiliaries (part I) Vocabulary practice	*38*
2	***Investment and the Stock Exchange*** Letter from a Broker Types of Business	Reading comprehension Text production	Reported speech Verbs + that-clause Verbs + noun/pronoun + infinitive Verbs + gerund Vocabulary practice	*47*

Contents

Unit	Theme/Text(s)	Skills	Grammar/Vocabulary	Page
3	***Advertising and Publicity*** Advertising Techniques Advertising Standards	Reading comprehension Listening comprehension Text production	Comparison of adjectives and adverbs Vocabulary practice	*55*
4	***Credit*** Live Now, Pay Later Opening a Credit Account: "Do's" and "Don'ts" Protecting the Consumer	Reading comprehension Note-taking Listening comprehension Text production	Expressions of quantity Mass and count nouns Vocabulary practice	*64*
5	***International Trade Organizations*** The European Union Incoterms	Reading comprehension Listening comprehension Note-taking Text production: essay writing	Conditional clause: type 3 Vocabulary practice	*74*
6	***Computerization and Technology*** The Internet The Rise of Big Blue	Reading comprehension Text production	Gerunds and infinitives	*82*
7	***The Development of a Product*** Developing "Stardrive" Distribution of Goods	Reading comprehension Text production	Auxiliaries (part II) Vocabulary practice	*87*
8	***Employment and Unemployment*** Newspaper Article New Industries for Old The Youth Training Scheme	Reading comprehension Listening comprehension Note-taking	Reporting verbs Vocabulary practice	*95*
9	***Resources and the Environment*** Water, Water Everywhere Green Belts	Reading comprehension Text production	Pronoun use Vocabulary practice	*104*
10	***Graphs, Charts and Tables*** Stardrive: Current Sales Report The Growth of Part-time Working	Reading comprehension Communication practice Listening comprehension Note-taking Report writing	Tenses for graphs, charts and tables Vocabulary practice	*111*

MAIN COURSE

Contents

BUSINESS COMMUNICATION COURSE

Secretarial Activities

Unit	Theme/Text(s)	Skills	Grammar/Vocabulary	Page
1	*Telephoning in Business*	Reading comprehension Text production: acting out	Phrases for making telephone calls	*122*
2	*Appointments*	Text production: dialogue completion / letter writing	Phrases for making appointments	*126*
3	*Travelling Arrangements*	Text production: letter writing	Phrases for making travelling arrangements	*129*
4	*Room Reservations*	Text production: letter writing	Phrases for making room reservations	*132*
5	*Invitations*	Text production: text expansion /letter writing Reading comprehension	Phrases for making invitations	*134*
6	*Visitors to the Company*	Text production: acting out	Phrases for receiving visitors	*136*
7	*Socializing*	Text production: acting out	Phrases for socializing	*138*

Commercial Correspondence

Unit	Theme/Text(s)	Skills	Grammar/Vocabulary	Page
1	*English – the Language of Business Communication*	Reading comprehension Note-making	Vocabulary connected with English as the language of international business	*140*
2	*Layout of the Business Letter*	Reading comprehension Text production: text reorganization	Terms regarding the layout of a business letter	*142*
3	*Enquiry*	Reading comprehension Note-making Text production: letter writing / contiletter Listening comprehension Note-taking	Useful words/phrases for – pointing out the intention of the business letter – the specific content of the business letter Structures common in business letters	*145*
4	*Offer*			*154*
5	*Order*			*163*
6	*Acknowledgement of Order*			*171*
7	*Delay in Delivery*			*178*
8	*Complaints and their Adjustments*			*185*
	Translation Exercises	German – English		*193*

Contents

I Language Section — 202
  1. Basic Grammar — 202
  2. Important Irregular Verbs — 213
  3. Pronunciation Guide — 215

II Correspondence Section — 216
  1. List of Intentions — 216
  2. Commercial Terms — 219
    a. Terms of Delivery — 219
    b. Terms of Payment — 219
    c. International Dispatch Documents — 221
  3. Abbreviations — 222
    a. Common English / American Abbreviations — 222
    b. Abbreviations of English Counties and American States — 224

Vocabulary: Unit by Unit — 225

Alphabetical Vocabulary List — 245

ℝ

Introductory Course

Unit 1 — Introductory Course

Technologies Mean Opportunities

A. Text

1. M & C – Young but Successful

Most people have heard of Silicon Valley, in California. And most people know how Silicon Valley got its name: from computers. Silicon Valley is the home of the American computer industry. It has been a big success story, with small companies booming into worldwide corporations within the space of only a few years.

The secret of success in Silicon Valley in the early years was often brilliant ideas rather than financial strength. But there are people with good ideas all over the world, and, therefore, successful computer companies, too. One of them is M & C, which stands for Mace & Clark Advanced Computer Technol-

Silicon Valley – the centre of American computer technology

ogy, a small specialist company in Birmingham, England. The secret of M & C's success is their tailor-made software. M & C specializes in computer solutions for small businesses. Their customers are bakers, plumbers, decorators, small builders and so on. But M & C does not only supply software, it offers and sells hardware, too.

M & C is run by Jean Mace and Stephen Clark. They own the company as co-partners and share responsibilities. Jean Mace looks after sales management and is the financial director, while Stephen Clark deals with the technical side.

You will learn more about M & C during the course of this book.

Understanding the text

a. How do Jean Mace and Stephen Clark share responsibilities in their company?
b. What do you need, besides money, to run a successful business?
c. Why has the company been named M & C Advanced Computer Technology?
d. What is "Silicon Valley" famous for?
e. For what reasons would a company contact M & C?

2. An Office Conversation

It's a Friday afternoon. Jean Mace rushes into Susan Leonard's office. Susan is M & C's secretary.

J Tell me, Sue, what are you doing at the moment?
S I'm typing some confidential letters for Mr Clark.
J How long will that take? You see, I'm having some trouble with this contract proposal for Williams and Co.
S What's the matter?
J Well, there are some last-minute changes. It's very urgent; their agent is waiting for it, and I promised he would have it by Monday at the latest.
S Well, I know Stephen's just preparing for his interview with those newspaper people on Monday. So perhaps his letters can wait.
J I'll ask him. (*Dials a number on the telephone. Then:*) Hello, Stephen! I'm afraid we've got an emergency here. It's about this proposal for Williams and Co. As you know, we've got to get it to them by Monday. So I need Susan's help! How desperately are you waiting for those letters? ... It'll be all right to have them ready on Monday? OK, thank you, Stephen. Bye for now!
S So – another long Friday!

Understanding the text

a. Why is Jean Mace asking for Susan's help?
b. Can Susan help her at once?
c. How does Stephen react when Jean phones him?
d. Describe how Susan feels after the phone call.

Unit 1 — Introductory Course

B. Talking grammar: present simple vs. present progressive

> Most people *know* how Silicon Valley got its name.
> M & C *stands* for Mace & Clark.
> M & C *doesn't* only *supply* software.

The *present simple tense* is used to describe situations, habits and facts which are true at the time of speaking or writing. They are seen as a state of affairs, not temporary events. It does not matter whether the state of affairs is also true of the past or the future. Remember that questions and negative forms are formed with do/does/(not).

> I'*m* typ*ing* some confidential letters for Mr Clark.
> What *are* you do*ing* at the moment?

The *present progressive tense* is used to describe processes or actions which are taking place at the moment of speaking or writing. They are taking place here and now and are temporary events, not permanent states.

C. Practice

1. Find the simple and progressive forms

Have a close look at texts A 1 and A 2 again and find examples of present simple and present progressive forms.

2. Office activities

Here is a list of activities the M & C people have to do almost every day.

a. Susan types letters.

b. Jean reads contracts.

c. Susan and Jean talk to each other.

d. Stephen dictates letters.

e. Jean phones important customers.

f. They all have lunch.

g. Stephen receives visitors.

h. Stephen and Jean talk about offers.

i. Susan does photocopying.

j. Jean plans her activities for the following day.

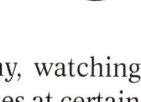

You are a visitor to the company, watching the M & C people in their activities at certain times of the day. Describe what they are doing, like this:

a. It's twelve minutes past eight now and Susan is typing letters.

3. Complete

The following sentences describe both actions and habits. Choose the proper form.

a. Susan usually reads the newspaper in the morning, but today (she/hurry/to the bus) because she's late.
b. It's Friday evening, and Susan is still working in the office. Normally (she/leave/the office) at 5 p. m.
c. Jean is looking for her glasses, as (she/never/work) without them.
d. In the evening (Stephen/watch/TV), but tonight (he/read/offers).
e. On Fridays (the M & C people/usually/make plans) for the week to come.
f. Susan (often/type/letters) for Stephen, but at the moment (she/help/Jean).
g. Almost every day (they all/have lunch) together. This is impossible today, as (Jean and Stephen/receive/visitors).
h. On weekends (Jean/spend/her spare time) at the seaside, while (Stephen/play/tennis).
i. It's four o'clock already. (Jean/get/nervous) because (the agent/wait for/the contract).
j. Susan is getting angry. (She/look for/an important letter). (She/always/keep/them) near her typewriter, but now (it/not/be/there).

4. What about you?

Report to your classmates what you do every day.

5. What's happening now?

What is going on in your classroom right now? Describe it.

6. Do, don't, does or doesn't?

(a) M & C stand for "Miller & Clark"? – No, it (b). "M" stands for "Mace", not "Miller".
(c) big corporations buy M & C's products? – No, they (d).
Who (e) M & C sell to, then? – Small businesses, like plumbers and decorators.
(f) plumbers and decorators need computers? – Well, why not?
(g) Jean and Stephen just run the company for someone else, or (h) they own it, too? – I (i) know.
(j) they both look after the financial side, or (k) just one of them do it? – Jean (l).
What (m) Stephen do then? – He deals with the technical side.
And who makes the coffee, the secretary? – No, they're an emancipated company, they all (n).

7. Make sentences

Use the correct form.

a. Susan (not have) time to read the newspaper at lunchtime, so she (not take) it with her to work.
b. When (the M & C people/have lunch)?
c. When (Jean/make plans) for the next day?
d. She and Susan (not make plans) now because they (work) on the contract proposals.
e. Stephen (not need) his letters before Monday; he (prepare) for his interview now.
f. Nobody at M&C (like) long Fridays.

Follow-up exercises: *Arbeitsbuch*, pp. 6 and 44.

A Company in the Making

A. Text

An Interview with M & C

Stephen Clark is in his office, talking to George Robertson, a local newspaper reporter.

R How long has your company been in the computer business, Mr Clark, and what exactly do you do?
C Well, we started in 1991 and we've been doing more or less the same kind of business the whole time. The only difference is that, at the beginning, we did more hardware business, but now the focus is very much on software. At the beginning, for example, we bought components, assembled them here and sold our own computers, but for some years now we've been importing other people's products and marketing them as our own. We'll continue to do that as the hardware side of our business, but we're mainly concentrating on software now, as I said.
R Where do you buy this hardware?
C We've been purchasing from Japan, Korea, Europe and the USA. The most important aspects we look for are quality, high technological standards which fit our line of production, and, last but not least, price. Just recently suppliers from the Far East have been making most favourable offers.
R Ah, ha. And why is M & C increasing software activities?
C Well, practically all small businesses can afford their own equipment nowadays, and of course they want applications software. The software market has been expanding rapidly. Our experts try to develop solutions which will meet the specific demands of the particular business.
R And can you tell me where your markets are, exactly?
C Of course, M & C has mainly been selling on the British market, but we're increasingly looking for new markets in Europe.
R Isn't this difficult for a company of your size?
C Certainly, it's not easy. But recently we've been establishing contacts with several foreign companies who might act as possible partners.

R Oh, that's very interesting… can you tell me anything more about it?
C I'm sorry, but I'm afraid I can't, just at the moment. Why don't we look around the building instead? Would you come this way, Mr Robertson?

Understanding the text

a. What's the reason for George Robertson's visit to M & C?
b. What have M & C's activities been since 1991?
c. Where do they buy hardware from?
d. What are the points M & C is most interested in when they buy computers?
e. Why is the software market expanding?
f. What are the aims of M & C's software development?
g. Why do you think Stephen is unwilling to talk about M & C's contacts with several foreign companies?

B. Talking grammar: present progressive vs. present perfect progressive

> We're concentra*ting* on software now.
> We*'ve been* do*ing* the same kind of business the whole time (and will continue to do so).
> We*'ve been* purchas*ing* from Japan, Korea, Europe and the USA (but now we've changed exclusively to a Far East supplier).

The *present progressive* describes processes and actions taking place here and now. The *present perfect progressive* describes processes and actions that began in the past and have continued up to now. Sometimes the sentences give information about the beginning or the duration of the process or action.

> We've been dealing in computers *since* Jean and I decided to work together.
> We've been dealing in computers *for* several years.

The beginning point of the process is indicated by *since*. The duration of the process is indicated by *for*. *For* corresponds to German *seit* or *lang*.
Note: … *for* five years = *seit* fünf Jahren *or* fünf Jahre *lang*.

C. Practice

1. Make sentences using present perfect progressive

The sentences in column A describe what people are doing now. Change these sentences by adding what is in column B. At the same time, decide whether to use *since* or *for* with the information in column B. Change the verb forms as necessary.

Unit 2 Introductory Course

A	B
a. Stephen is waiting for George Robertson.	thirty minutes
b. George is looking for Stephen's place.	9 o'clock
c. Our company is doing this kind of business.	1991
d. We are importing other people's products.	several years
e. M & C is mainly concentrating on software.	the last six months
f. Suppliers from the Far East are making most favourable offers.	they entered into mass production
g. M & C is increasing software activities.	a lot of businesses bought their own computer
h. They are looking for new markets.	quite a long time now
i. Small businesses are demanding applications software.	they learned how to deal with it

2. How long *or* since when?

When asking about present activities you can ask about:
– their duration   (= how long)
– their beginning point (= since when)

M & C is not the only thing in the lives of Jean Mace and Stephen Clark. Besides their work, they have their hobbies and private interests, and have had most of them for many years now. Have a look at the following lists:

Jean Mace:

a. learn German (two years)
b. travel abroad (many years)
c. drive sports cars (1991)
d. go to theatre (beginning of her studies)
e. drink champagne (her holiday in France)

Stephen Clark:

f. take diving lessons (last summer)
g. play with model railways (his childhood)
h. paint (more than five years)
i. read computer magazines (he left school)
j. collect classical records (a couple of years)

Now ask questions and answer them.

Example: go to the same pub (he moved to Birmingham)

Since when has Stephen been going to the same pub?
(He has been going to the same pub) since he moved to Birmingham.

Follow-up exercises: *Arbeitsbuch,* pp. 7 and 44.

A Business Career

A. Text

Jean Mace's Boss – Jean Mace

Being independent has always been a very important thing in Jean Mace's life. Even when she went to school, she dreamt of a career in a business of her own. With M & C
5 this dream has come true, although she had to work a lot to be successful in the end.
Even during her time at Wolverhampton Grammar School, she was interested in economics, which, as she soon found out, involved knowledge of other school subjects, 10 too. When she left school, she was quite sure she would take up a business career. In order to learn about the financial side, she successfully applied for a training course as a bank clerk with Lord's Bank in Wolverhampton. It 15 was there she came across computer technology for the first time when the bank management decided to introduce computer com-

munication systems. Ever since then, she has kept a keen eye on the progress in that field. In 1987, she went to Wolverhampton Polytechnic to read economics. In addition, she attended courses in computer science. It was during one of these courses that she met Stephen Clark, who was more technically-minded. They soon found out that they had similar interests which might prove a suitable basis for a business partnership.

They started M & C in 1991. At first it was just the two of them, Jean and Stephen. They had to work very hard – 11 hours a day, 7 days a week, and with no time for holidays. But today they've made it.

The biggest question at first was money, of course. Thanks to her old connections with Lord's Bank, Jean managed to solve this problem within a surprisingly short period. As far as the technical side of the business is concerned, she has always relied on Stephen as the technical expert. But she has the financial side of things well under control.

So far there has not been the slightest doubt for Jean Mace as to whether she has made the right decision – despite the long hours and all the work. Whatever problems and risks the future may have in store – her dream has come true!

Understanding the text

a. How long has Jean Mace been interested in business?
b. Why did she apply for a training course as a bank clerk? Was she accepted?
c. Why do you think the bank management decided to introduce advanced communication systems?
d. How did Jean manage to get enough money to start M & C?
e. Even in today's world, some of Jean's business partners are surprised to meet a female financial director. She and Stephen don't think there's anything unusual about that. Do you?

B. Talking grammar: past simple vs. present perfect simple

> Jean Mace *attended* courses in computer science.
> (i. e. she doesn't attend them any longer)

The past simple is used to describe situations, habits and facts which are finished now.

> a. Ever since then, she *has kept* a keen eye on the rapid progress in that field. (i. e. she still has a keen eye on that progress)
> b. Today they *'ve made* it.

a. The *present perfect simple* is used to describe situations, habits and facts which were true in the past and still are at the time of speaking and writing.
b. It is also used to describe an action which took place in the past, but the result of which is important at the moment of speaking or writing.

C. Practice

1. Sentence switchboard

Make meaningful sentences by choosing one element from each of the columns below.

A	B	C
Jean Mace	applied	interested in economics.
Susan Leonard	has always shown	working as a secretary with M & C in 1993.
Stephen Clark	started	founded in 1991.
M & C	were	an interest in technology.
Computers	have shared	much more expensive ten years ago.
The two partners	have been	responsibilities for many years now.
	was	in this business since 1991.
	has been	for a training course as a bank clerk after
	has always been	leaving school.

2. Complete

Each of the following sentences contains both a situation / habit / fact which is finished and a situation / habit / fact which was true in the past and is now.
Complete the sentences using the right tense of the verbs in brackets.

a. The teacher (give) us a new text yesterday, but so far I (not have) time to read it.
b. We (order) the goods last Friday, but they (not arrive) yet.
c. Jean and Stephen (own) M & C since they (start) their business partnership in 1991.
d. Jean (be) interested in economics since she (be) a schoolgirl.
e. She and her old classmates (not see) each other since they (leave) school.
f. Computers (change) many jobs drastically, especially since they (be) introduced in offices.
g. Modern technology (make) more things possible than people (think) even ten years ago.
h. Britain (be) a member of the EU since she (join) in 1973.
i. The Japanese (develop) a new chip which will be on the market soon, although they only (start) working on it less than one year ago.
j. They (go) to Spain for a holiday last month. As far as I know, they (not return) yet.
k. I (not hear) from him since he (phone) me last November.
l. 10 days ago, someone (steal) Stephen's car; the police (not find) it yet.
m. In 1969, Neil Armstrong (be) the first man to land on the moon. Since then, scientists (gain) more detailed knowledge of it.
n. Industrialization (begin) in the 19th century and it (not end) yet.

Follow-up exercises: *Arbeitsbuch*, pp. 7 and 45–46.

Unit 4 — Introductory Course

The Computer – a Man-Made Device

A. Text

Computers Never Fail?

The principle of life-long learning was stretched to its limits at Worthington Primary School yesterday.
77-year-old Betty Wilson perplexed teachers and headmistress alike, demanding a primary school place – not for her grandchild but for herself!

Charles Brewer

Back to School for Grandma

How could it happen? As is usual every year, the Worthing Education Authority had sent computerized information sheets to the parents of five-year-old children in the area. Among those parents was Samuel Wilson, 99. He was very surprised when he read the letter informing him that his daughter Betty was to start primary school and giving him a list of schools in the area to choose from. Soon he found the reason for this strange demand. The computer had worked out every detail properly, except for one: it had recorded Betty's year of birth as 1991 instead of 1919. Of course the easiest thing would have been to inform the Authority. But this wasn't like Betty. She had always suspected that machines were less reliable than humans. Therefore she decided to play a trick on the Authority's computer, which had offered her the unexpected chance to make her distrust publicly known.

So when the first day of term came, things had been well arranged. Betty had bought a school uniform, although it had been difficult to get one her size. She had persuaded her father to accompany her to school. Most important of all, Betty had informed the local press of what was to happen. As far as Betty was concerned, things could take their course.

20

Understanding the text

a. Why was Samuel Wilson surprised to find that his daughter was to start primary school?
b. Why didn't Betty inform the Authority?
c. What made it difficult for Betty to find a school uniform?
d. How had Betty arranged for the public to be informed about what was to happen?
e. Computers never fail. What do *you* think?

B. Talking grammar: past simple vs. past perfect simple

> So when the first day of term *came*, things *had been* well *arranged*.

Both the *past simple* and the *past perfect simple* tenses are located in a past time frame. They describe situations, habits and facts which were true at a certain point of time in the past (... when the first day of term *came* ...) and before that (... things *had been* well *arranged*.). Their relation is the same as that of the present and present perfect tenses which, however, are located in a present time frame.

C. Practice

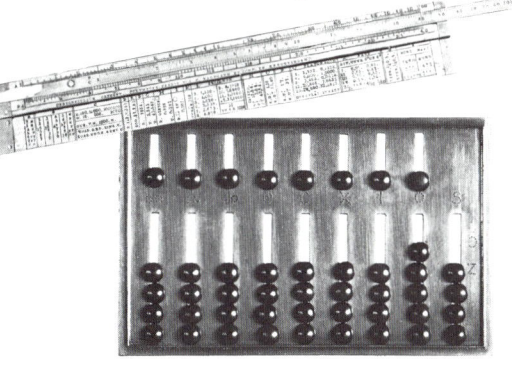

1. Before the computer came

The first digital computer was completed in 1944. Up to that time:

a. people /use/ their fingers or mechanical devices to count or calculate
b. letters /be/ written on mechanical typewriters
c. secretaries /not have/ the possibility to correct texts immediately
d. companies /store/ information on large quantities of paper
e. information /be/ exchanged by mail or phone
f. office clerks /process/ information quite slowly
g. people /not have/ big problems with data protection

h. technical progress /not be/ as rapid as it is nowadays
i. blue collar workers /not need/ any computer knowledge
j. industrial productions /require/ far more labour
k. only a few people /consider/ the development of "intelligent" machines possible

Make sentences like this: Up to that time, people had used their fingers or mechanical devices to count or calculate.

2. The man who made the mistake

Do you remember Betty Wilson's story? Of course, the computer could only do what it had been told to. And computers are always told to do things by human beings – like James Croft, who is in charge of Worthing Education Authority's computer. The day he fed his computer was not his day because almost everything went wrong:

a. he /wake up/ late
   he /forget/ to set his alarm clock (because)
b. the train /leave/
   he /arrive/ at the station (when)

So he took a taxi.

c. the taxi driver /drop/ him at the office
   he /find out/ he /forget/ his money (when)
d. he /have to/ borrow some from his colleagues
   he /always dislike/ the idea on principle (although)

This was a case of emergency, of course.

e. he /sit down/ in front of his computer
   he /notice/ that it /already be/ operated before (when)
f. there /be/ no other expert in the office
   he /wonder/ who /be able to/ run the program (as)
g. the secretary /confess/ she /try/ her luck
   he/ be/ absent (that, while)
h. it /take/ him a couple of hours to rearrange everything
   she /leave/ a considerable mess (as)

However, he succeeded in the end.

i. he /can't help/ giving her a lecture
   she /mean/ well (although)
j. he /read/ the newspaper article a few days later
   he /have to /admit/ nobody /be/ perfect (when, that)

not even James Croft.

Tell James Croft's story by linking the sentences with the words in brackets. As you tell the story, the basic tense is the past simple – however, there are events which took place earlier.

Follow-up exercises: *Arbeitsbuch*, pp. 8 and 45–46.

Opening Up New Markets

A. Text

Going Continental

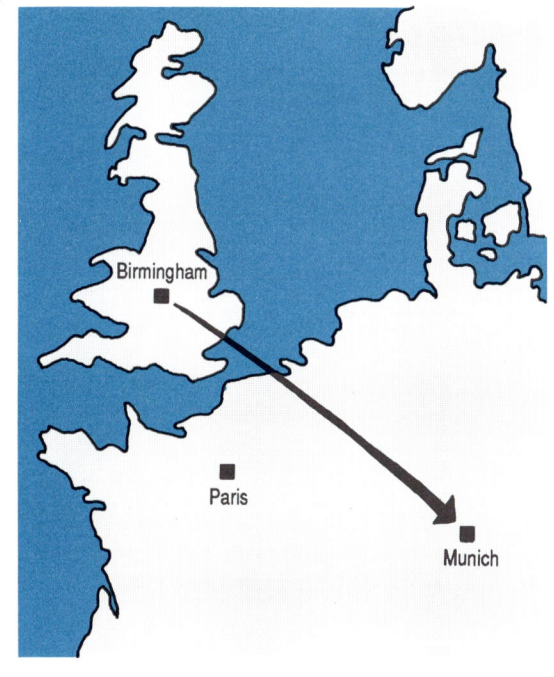

In order to find new markets abroad, M & C has got in touch with the German firm Ingrid Bilker KG, Munich. Bilker deals in office communication systems. Now Jean Mace and Stephen Clark are planning Jean's first visit to Munich.

S When is the meeting taking place?
J At 11.30 tomorrow. Susan has booked the 7.30 flight. Ingrid Bilker is going to meet me at the airport personally.
S Oh, is she?
J Yes, now can we go through our checklist just to make sure I haven't forgotten anything important.
S OK. Good idea.
J Right. First: how will our products and services fit into the German market?
S Yes, and don't forget to find out whether we will have to make any changes to our software to meet any specific demands over there. We also, of course, need information on products already on the market.
J I'm going to talk about our likely competitors anyway. I expect we'll meet some keen competition, but we'll have a fair chance of doing well, according to Bilker. They're going to present their latest market research figures, which are rather promising – so Mrs Bilker told me on the phone.
S OK. And as regards quantities and terms, I suppose you've already got that sorted out in your mind, financial director!
J Don't be silly, Stephen, of course I have. I've also got some questions about their sales set-up, outlets, etc., so I think I know what I need to ask there.
S Fine. Anything else then?
J Well, yes. One of the essential questions is whether we're going to sell M & C or BILK products.
S What do you mean?
J Oh, Stephen! Have you forgotten? Surely you remember Bilker wasn't happy about acting as our agents merely representing

our name. They'll insist on selling under their own name.

S I can't see any difference – quality will always succeed, if you ask me.

J Basically you're right. Nevertheless, selling products also means selling names. Whichever market we're going into, M & C should stand for quality, if you ask me.

(*looking through her list*) There's another point. Have you got the paper about our production facilities with all the technical details Bilker asked for?

S Of course; you know I'm just as efficient as our computers. But seriously now, don't forget to ask the Bilker people about any regulations of the German Telekom our hardware will have to comply with. Also, what about their storage capacity: will they have to expand it?

J (*making a note*) Okay. I'll keep that in mind. Now, there's nothing else I want to mention. What about you?

S I think that's it. Have a nice trip, look after yourself and good luck!

Understanding the text

a. What makes Bilker appear interesting as a partner for M & C?
b. Is Bilker optimistic about M & C's sales in Germany?
c. Under what circumstances will it be necessary to modify M & C's hardware?
d. Why do you think a product's name is an important matter to deal with?
e. What are the reasons for Stephen's interest in Bilker's storage capacity?

B. Talking grammar: will vs. going to

> I think we'*ll have* a fair chance of doing well.
> They'*re going to present* their latest market research figures.

Both *will* and *going to* describe future intentions and activities. *Going to* is used (a) when the speaker has already decided (before speaking) that his intention will almost certainly be carried out or (b) when the speaker is sure that a future action will take place whether the speaker has any influence on the matter or not. If he is not certain, or when he makes up his mind at the moment of speaking, *will* is used. Often it is possible to use both forms.

C. Practice

1. Will *or* going to?

Examples:

Stephen: What did Susan get those papers from my desk for?

Jean: We (check) last month's sales figures. (We're going to check last month's sales figures.)
(= We had intended to do so before you asked me.)

Stephen: I think last month's sales figures should be rechecked.
Jean: You're right, I (do) it. (I'll do it.) (= I've just decided to do it.)

Note that in some sentences both forms are possible.

a.
S Did you remember to send the order to Smith & Co?
J Oh no, it has completely slipped my mind. Susan (post) it today.

b.
S Why haven't you sent a reply to their offer yet?
J I don't quite like their terms of payment. I've just phoned them. They (write) a new offer.

c.
J Last week's incoming orders have placed us in a difficult position.
S I know. I think we (have to) have an extra shift on Saturday.

d.
J I expect the number of incoming orders (decrease) in the winter.
S Are you sure? Don't forget our new model (be) on the market in autumn.

e.
S If business keeps growing like that, we (have to) take on new staff.
J Don't let's rush into anything! Nobody knows what the situation (be) like in a couple of months.

2. Planning an office party

Susan Leonard and Max Brown of M & C's assembly shop have been asked to plan their yearly office party, which is to take place after Jean's return from Germany.
Complete with *will* or *going to*.

M Have they decided on a day yet?
S Yes, Jean thinks next Friday afternoon (a/fit) best because we (b/not work) on that Saturday, they've decided.
M I see, and how many people (c/be) there?
S As far as I know, all the staff but two (d/take part). Some local press representatives (e/come), too. Stephen hopes they (f/write) some short articles about us.
M Um, where do you think we should have the party?
S That depends very much on the weather. If Thursday's weather report says it (g/rain), we (h/arrange) for it to take place inside, in the canteen. But I'd prefer to have it outdoors, so let's hope the weather (i/be) fine.
M What shall we do about the food and drinks? I suggest we have the same arrangement as last year. I (j/take care of) the food if someone else looks after the drinks.
S That's what I thought. In fact, I've already spoken to Angela Smart. She (k/attend to) the drinks. I've told her how much she can spend.
M Good.
S Do you think we (l/need) some decorations to make the place look less factory-like than last year?
M I suppose so. I hadn't really thought of that. Let's try one of the shops in town that runs a party service then.
S That's a good idea. I (m/phone) right now. (*returns some minutes later*) I've found someone. They (n/be) here by Friday morning and (o/look after) everything.
M Fine. All problems solved then. Let's hope Miss Mace's trip to Munich is a success and we (p/have) something to celebrate …

Follow-up exercises: *Arbeitsbuch*, pp. 8–9 and 47–48.

Applying for a Job

A. Text

A Job Interview

Today Martin Briggs, 16, is a bit nervous. He's going for a job interview at M & C's. Entering the office, he addresses Susan Leonard, the secretary.

M Good morning! Er, can you help me, please? I've an appointment with Miss Mace at 9.30.
S Then you must be Martin Briggs. I'm afraid Miss Mace is still in the assembly shop at the moment.
M If it's inconvenient now, I'll come later.
S No, I don't think that will be necessary. It'll only take a few minutes. You can wait in her office. This way please!
   (*a few minutes later Jean Mace enters*)
J Hello, Martin, I'm sorry to keep you waiting.
M That's all right.
J So, about this office job. The application you sent looks rather promising. But do you mind if I ask a few questions?
M No, of course not.
J Well, what made you decide to apply for this job in particular?
M Two reasons, basically. First, I'm interested in working with other people and organizing things. I've been on the committee of our youth club since I was 14. Second, I like working with computers and I think computers make office work much more interesting. So I think if I can work with a computer company, then I'll be able to use modern, up-to-date equipment and combine my present interests.
J Tell me about your experience with computers.
M Well, I've got a personal computer and I took application courses at school which showed me how useful a computer can be.
J If you weren't right, we wouldn't have so many customers! But I'm happy to say we have. In fact, sometimes our customers expect us to work practically round the clock, so we have to be very flexible about our working time. In other words, if we asked you to work overtime and the occasional Saturday, would you be willing to?
M That's alright with me, provided public transport will allow it.
J (*Looking through the papers*) Let's see. You live in Walton. That means if you take the 8.15, you can be here by 9. If we ask you to start earlier or stay longer in

the evening, we'll have to make sure that fits in with the timetables. (*Putting the papers aside*) Well, I've no more questions. Now you know roughly what the job involves; pay, holidays and so on were in our advertisement. Is there anything else you would like to know?

M Just one question really. When will I know whether you are able to offer me the job?

J It'll take a few days because we are still interviewing, but so far you're quite high on my list. If you ring next Friday, we should be able to say. Anyway, I very much hope we'll meet again.

M Thank you very much, Miss Mace. Goodbye.

J Goodbye, Martin.

Understanding the text

a. Why is today different for Martin Briggs?
b. Why can't he talk to Miss Mace straightaway?
c. What led him to apply to M & C?
d. What kind of working hours can he expect?
e. What chance does Martin Briggs have of getting the job?

B. Talking grammar: conditional clauses

A conditional clause is a logical connection of *condition* and *result* (*if/given that ... then ...*). It is not important whether the condition or the result is specified first.

> a. If I *can work* with a computer company, I*'ll be* able to use modern, up-to-date equipment.
> b. If we *asked* you to work overtime, *would* you *be* willing to?

a. Conditional clause, type 1 (if-clause: present simple, main clause: future): The *result* is possible or even likely to come about.
b. Conditional clause, type 2 (if-clause: past simple, main clause: conditional): In this case the *result* is possible, the *condition*, however, is not real at the moment of speaking.

Note: Both types refer to the present.

C. Practice

1. Complete

After the job interview Martin is dreaming about his future.
Choose a suitable verb form in each of the following sentences:

a. If I was in the manager's position, I (accept) no other application but Martin Briggs'.
b. If I (get) the job, I will earn my first wages.
c. Unless I spend all the money, I (be able to) buy a bike.

d. If they (give) me a chance, I would convince them of my abilities.
e. If M & C does not accept my application, I (try) somewhere else.
f. My parents would be happy if I (succeed).
g. If Miss Mace asked my teachers at school, they (recommend) me.
h. If the computer industry (expand) rapidly, I'll be sure of a successful career.
i. If I go by what Miss Mace said, they (react) positively.
j. Unless I ring up next Friday, I (probably lose) the job.

2. Youth unemployment

The following phrases are about the serious problem of youth unemployment. Use them to form conditional sentences which describe possible situations:

Example: If I didn't get a job after school, I'd make a plan of how to proceed.

a. not get a job after leaving school/make a plan of how to proceed
b. the situation not improve/developing new ideas become even more important
c. not be lucky straightaway/write dozens of applications and go to as many job interviews as possible
d. hang around at home/be bored
e. be unemployed/need the help of parents and friends
f. not know what to do about the situation/have to look for government programmes
g. not find a job in the desired field/review one's preferences
h. join a government programme/be able to improve one's qualifications
i. not inform oneself enough/not know about the current trends in the job market

3. On a separate sheet, complete the following sentences with meaningful phrases

a. If you plan your future after school, …
b. You will have to look for work facilities in other towns if …
c. If you do well in your exams, …
d. If you knew someone in your field of interest, …
e. You would have to think about some alternatives if …
f. A job applicant will have a good chance if …
g. If companies did not ask for skilled labour, …
h. If a worker isn't interested in life-long learning, …
i. If automation continues to develop so rapidly, …
j. Unless you prepare yourself properly for a job interview, …

Follow-up exercises: *Arbeitsbuch*, pp. 9 and 47–48.

Technologies in Everyday Life

A. Text

1. Paying Digitally – Phonecard Phones

Phonecard phones are widely available. However, these phones can only be used if you have a special card which may be bought at various values from Post Offices and shops displaying the "Phonecard" sign. Any number of calls can be made up to the value of the card, whenever you wish, without the need for cash.

The procedure is as follows. First, you insert the card. The credit limit will be checked automatically. Then listen for the dial tone and dial the number. The connection will be made in the usual way. Your card will be returned with the credit reduced at the end of the call.

Payphones that accept credit cards such as Visa, Mastercard, Diners Club, etc., have also been installed in some places. Instructions are given on notices next to these phones.

Understanding the text

a. What do you need to use this type of phone?
b. Where can you buy phonecards?
c. A friend planning a trip to London has heard about phonecard phones. (S)he asks you how they work. Please help her/him.
d. What other type of phonecard phone exists?

2. Drawing Cash Digitally – Cash Dispensers

Cash dispensers operated by servicecards have been widely introduced in GB. In most cases, they are outside bank branches and can be used when the bank is closed. Usually

5 they are located inside branches and can be used as a way of avoiding writing cheques or standing in queues to withdraw money. They are often installed in big shops and department stores.

Servicecards can be applied for only by hold- 10 ers of accounts. But before you receive one, you will be notified of your personal number, which has only four digits. So it's easy to remember, but should not be written down or told to anyone. 15

To use your servicecard, insert the card in the slot, then key in your personal number. The amount of money you want to withdraw has to be keyed in, too, of course. Seconds later, your card will be returned to you, followed 20 by your cash.

Understanding the text

a. Where can cash dispensers be found?
b. What advantages do they offer?
c. Who is allowed to use them?
d. How does the system work?

B. Talking grammar: passive voice

> The credit limit *will be checked* automatically.
> Cash dispensers *are located* inside branches.

The passive is used when the target of an action or the action itself is the main focus of the statement. Often the agent or "doer" is not mentioned at all.

C. Practice

1. Complete

Complete the following sentences (taken from different operating instructions) by using a passive construction. Also, try to find out whether the sentence refers to a radio, a bicycle, a TV set, a coffee machine, an electric shaver or whether it can refer to all of these.

a. Buttons 1–6 (to be used) for choosing the frequency.
b. When the carafe (to be removed), the filt-

er swings upwards and dripping (to be prevented) automatically.
c. Each of our products (to be checked) carefully before leaving the factory.
d. The long-hair trimmer (to be designed) to trim your beard.
e. The sound (to be switched on) if the green button (to be pressed) again.
f. To prevent overheating, make sure that the ventilation holes (not to be covered).
g. Claims (not to be accepted) if our guarantee conditions (not to be observed) carefully.
h. During the connection of earphones, the built-in loudspeaker (to be switched off) automatically.
i. A perfect shave (to be obtained) if you take good care of the cutting parts.
j. Few tools (to be required) to adjust the saddle position and fix the pedals.
k. Any damage should (to be reported) immediately to the retailer from whom the product (to be purchased).

"Listen! What was that? My beeper, my wrist-watch alarm, your microwave, our telephone or a telephone on TV?"

2. Britain's economy

Complete the following text by putting the verbs in brackets into the passive. Pay attention to the tenses!

During the last century, Great Britain (a/to be recognized) as the leading trading and commercial power. The reasons for this (b/to be found) in the first industrial revolution, in Britain's export facilities and, of course, in its colonies. But gradually this position (c/to be endangered) by other industrializing nations and political events like the two world wars and countries moving towards independence.

More and more British products (d/to be confronted) with foreign competitors. The traditional Commonwealth market lost its former importance as former colonies gained their independence. However, necessary changes in the classic industries (e/not to be made).

The British economy (f/to be offered) new opportunities when Britain joined the Common Market in 1973. Exports to the other countries of the community (g/to be increased) since then. Traditional industries like steel or textiles (h/to be replaced) by the service sector. London (i/to be made into) one of the most important financial centres of the world. In order to cope with the future, many steps (j/to be taken). Private initiatives (k/to be supported) by the Government. State-owned companies (l/to be changed) into joint-stock companies. New, technology-oriented industries (m/to be established) in areas of high unemployment. Public financial support (n/to be granted) for promising economic enterprises. Rationalization and modernization (o/to be considered) as adequate preparation for the needs of the future.

Follow-up exercises: *Arbeitsbuch*, pp. 10 and 48–49.

Planning One's Career

A. Text

Action for jobs

Action for jobs

Decisions about jobs and training are among the most important you're ever likely to take. So before you make any, you need to make sure you've got all the necessary facts and are fully aware of all the opportunities. Whatever your personal circumstances, your experience or your ambitions, you'll find some really useful signposts here to set you off on the right road.

Check

your individual circumstances first. Ask yourself these basic questions:

- what are your likes/dislikes?
- which are your strong/weak subjects at school?
- are you more practically or theoretically minded?
- what are your spare-time activities?
- do you like working at regular times/in the same place?
- do you prefer working together with other people to working alone?

Of course the job you have in mind will impose some extra requirements. Certain school-leaving qualifications might be needed; with technology developing extremely rapidly, the question arises whether the job you may be interested in faces an uncertain future. Finally, the financial side should be looked at as well as the attractions of different careers.

Contact

as many people as possible as soon as possible. Take advantage of as many sources of information as possible, such as:

- people already working in "your job"
- job advertisements in newspapers/magazines
- your local jobcentre
- trade associations/unions
- information brochures published by authorities/organizations/companies

Choose

the possibilities which sound right for you. But be aware of the fact that there are "dream jobs" which almost everyone wants to get. Limiting yourself to just one job possibility might prove dangerous. Avoid being inflexible, think in terms of alternatives – this will certainly improve your chances.

Understanding the text

a. Why is it necessary to plan one's working life?
b. How can you find out about your personal situation?
c. To what extent are other people's experiences important for your decisions?
d. What is to be understood by the term "dream jobs"?
e. Which of the aspects mentioned in the text are relevant to your personal situation? Give reasons.

Unit 8

B. Talking grammar: adjectives vs. adverbs

> Check your *individual* circumstances first.
> Avoid being *inflexible*.
> Choose the possibilities which sound *right* for you.

Persons and things (= nouns) are described by means of *adjectives*.

> a. This will *certainly* improve your chances.
> b. *Finally*, the financial side should be looked at.
> c. You'll find some *really* useful signposts here.
> d. Technology is developing *extremely* rapidly.

When describing what is not a person or thing, *adverbs* should be used (for example, when referring to: a. verbs, b. whole sentences, c. adjectives, d. adverbs).

C. Practice

1. Holiday jobs – collecting more than money

The adjectives in brackets should be added to the text if they fit. Those which don't fit should be changed to adverbs.

If your pocket money won't stretch as far as buying a (1/special) bike or a holiday which will allow you to lie (2/lazy) in the sun, don't get (3/nervous). (4/Calm) reflect on the fact that there are (5/various) ways of taking a break. Who likes to lie on the beach all day long? Not when you could get the chance of earning (6/useful) money, meeting (7/interesting) people and having a (8/good) time by (9/enjoyable) working your way through the vacation. In addition to money, you might even pick up some (10/useful) experience which you will (11/probable) need when the time comes for job hunting.

First decide what you (12/real) want from your holiday. Are you (13/simple) interested in the money? Do you want (14/physical) work after (15/academic) school life? Do you prefer (16/social) work, would you like to come into contact with (17/practical) working life, or are you looking for (18/suitable) opportunities to make new friends? Your range of interests may be (19/extreme) (20/wide). But be careful, don't (21/automatic) plump just for the money. Think of other aspects, too, like gaining (22/valuable) work experience or (23/simple) improving your knowledge. A (24/useful) way of doing this is to find a job near where you live. Try asking, phoning or writing to companies or organizations that might need help during the holiday, like stores, restaurants, factories, newspapers. You might have a good chance if you apply (25/early) enough. Try your local Jobcentre, study job offers in your newspaper (26/careful), and be prepared to work (27/hard).

33

2. Saying or writing it differently

Form new sentences (without changing the meaning) by replacing adverb-constructions with adjective-constructions, or the other way round. Make any other grammatical changes necessary.

Example:
We expect our order to be executed satisfactorily.
We expect a satisfactory execution of our order.

a. The new clerk is working diligently.
b. All of the applicants have written unsatisfactory replies.
c. We will give your application serious thought.
d. I am well qualified for this position.
e. She has good writing skills in French.
f. Does her pronunciation sound correct?
g. This job will mean hard work for you.
h. Is his keyboard speed fast enough?
i. You will be paid an attractive salary.
j. Our new staff member is expected to do extensive work with high-tech equipment.

D. Talking grammar: position of adverbs

> Martin answered the job advertisement *quickly*.
> He took a programming course *at school last year*.

Adverbs are most commonly placed at the end of a sentence (in the order "manner – place – time" when there is more than one).

> Martin *often* thinks about his future.
> He has *always* wanted to work with computers.

One important exception is the group of adverbs which includes: always/never, usually/hardly ever, sometimes/often, etc.
They go before a full verb, after an auxiliary.

> Martin *gladly* agreed to work overtime.

Many adverbs of manner can also take this position.

> M & C's job offer sounds *really* good.
> M & C has been expanding *extremely* rapidly.

Adverbs precede adjectives and adverbs they modify.

34

> We sell computers *internationally*.

Adverbs of manner can be placed at the end of a sentence for emphasis.

E. Practice

1. Complete

The following sentences are taken from all kinds of advertisements. Put the adverbs in brackets in their correct place.

a. Save with Lord's Bank! After a short period you will receive substantial interest. (surprisingly)
b. Our company has been interested in young staff members. (always).
c. I'm used to working. (independently)
d. We hope to receive your completed application. (soon)
e. We don't ask for a medical examination. (normally)
f. You'll get no better offer. (surely)
g. Our programs integrate several functions. (automatically)
h. Our clerks are trained to answer your questions. (specially)
i. You don't have to be a customer of our company. (necessarily)
j. Costs have increased, but not our prices! (dramatically)

Example:
We sell computers. (internationally)
We internationally sell computers. *Or:*
We sell computers internationally.

Follow-up exercises: *Arbeitsbuch*, pp. 11 and 48–49.

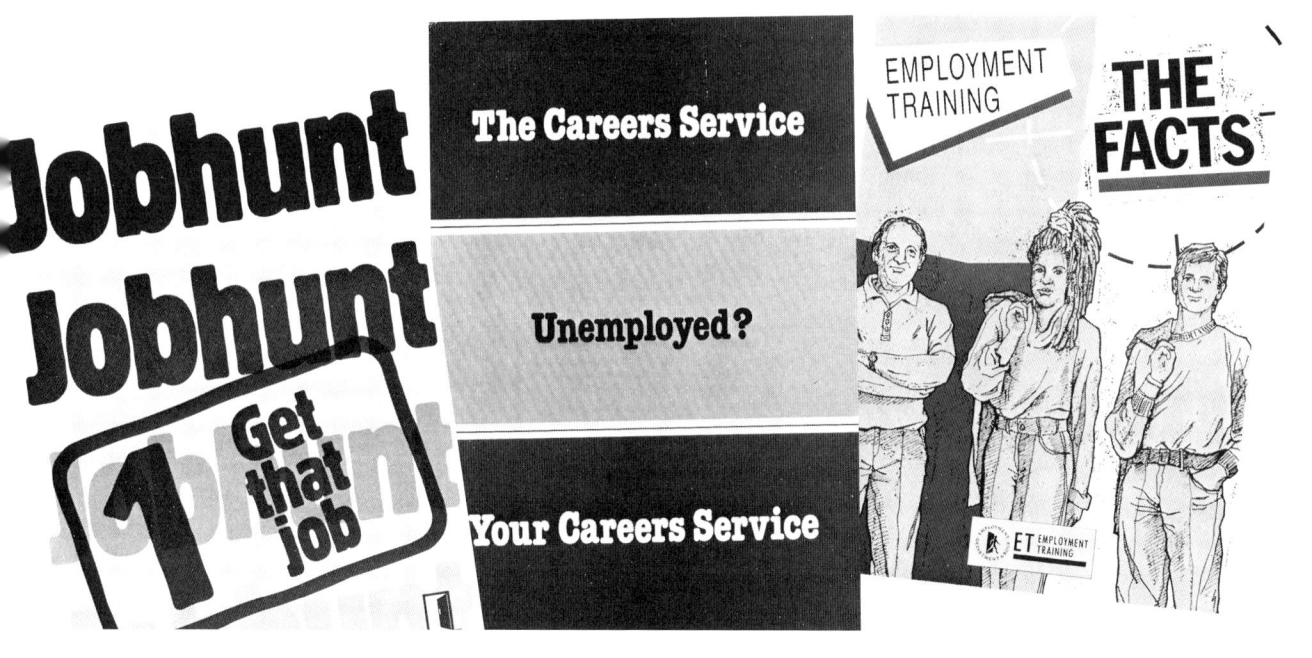

Ⓡ
Main Course

Unit 1 | Main Course

Banking and Savings

A. Lead-in

Think about your spending and saving habits. First, write down how much pocket money and/or wages you get (income). Then calculate how you normally spend the money (expenditure):

For example, how much do you spend on …?
– cosmetics
– hairdressing
– disco
– cinema
– playing sport
– watching sport
– records and tapes
– books
– gifts
– food
– clothes
– transportation
– travel
– other items (be specific)

If your expenditure exceeds your income, you can forget about savings! But, if your income exceeds your expenditure, then you probably are – or could become – a "small saver".

B. Text

Now read this information leaflet from the Bank Savings Association:

Small Savers

"Small Savers" in Britain

Tens of millions of people in Britain, just as in Germany, are "small savers" – individuals who keep some money in a safe place where it will earn some interest. In Britain, most small savers put their money into a bank or a so-called building society. Branches of banks and building societies can be found in every city and town.

The Government also runs a savings bank, called the National Girobank. Its services are operated by the thousands of post offices up and down the country.

"Current Account" and "Deposit Account"

Let us suppose you are living in Britain, and you have a bank account there. As in Germany, you choose from two types of bank account:

- a current account: little or no interest is paid on current accounts, but you may take out (that is, withdraw) your money at any time. Also, with a current account, you can pay bills by cheque, instead of cash – a great convenience for many people.

- a deposit account: you will receive higher interest on your deposit account, but you have to inform the bank some time in advance before you can withdraw your money. This time period ("notice of withdrawal") might be anything from 7 days to several months.

Other Services Offered

Of course, banks and building societies offer more services than just saving their customers' money. To take just one example, your regular bills can be paid quickly and automatically through your current account. You could instruct the Electricity Company to send your monthly bill directly to your bank, which will pay the bill and debit (that is, deduct the money from) your current account. This is called "direct debiting".

Small Fees Only

For these services and for taking care of your money, you will have to pay the bank a small fee (a "flat charge") every quarter year: And you have to pay an "entry charge" for every transaction, or movement of money into or out of your account. But as long as the "balance" (or final total) of your current account shows that it still contains <u>some</u> money, then you are "in credit". Of course, the bank is happy to make use of your money. So it may give you a small amount of money in return (known as an "allowance"), but not as much as the interest you would get on a deposit account.

For further reading on building societies and interest rates, see *Arbeitsbuch*, pp. 64–65.

C. Comprehension and analysis

1. Answer these questions on the text

a. Comparing current accounts and deposit accounts, what is the main disadvantage of each?

b. We have seen that electricity bills can be paid for by direct debiting. Can you think of 2 more items that can be paid for in this way?

c. Would you be willing to give your bank the responsibility to pay your regular bills through direct debiting? Or do you prefer to control your financial affairs directly by paying all bills yourself?

2. A Statement of Account

This statement shows all the transactions into and out of Jean Mace's current account:

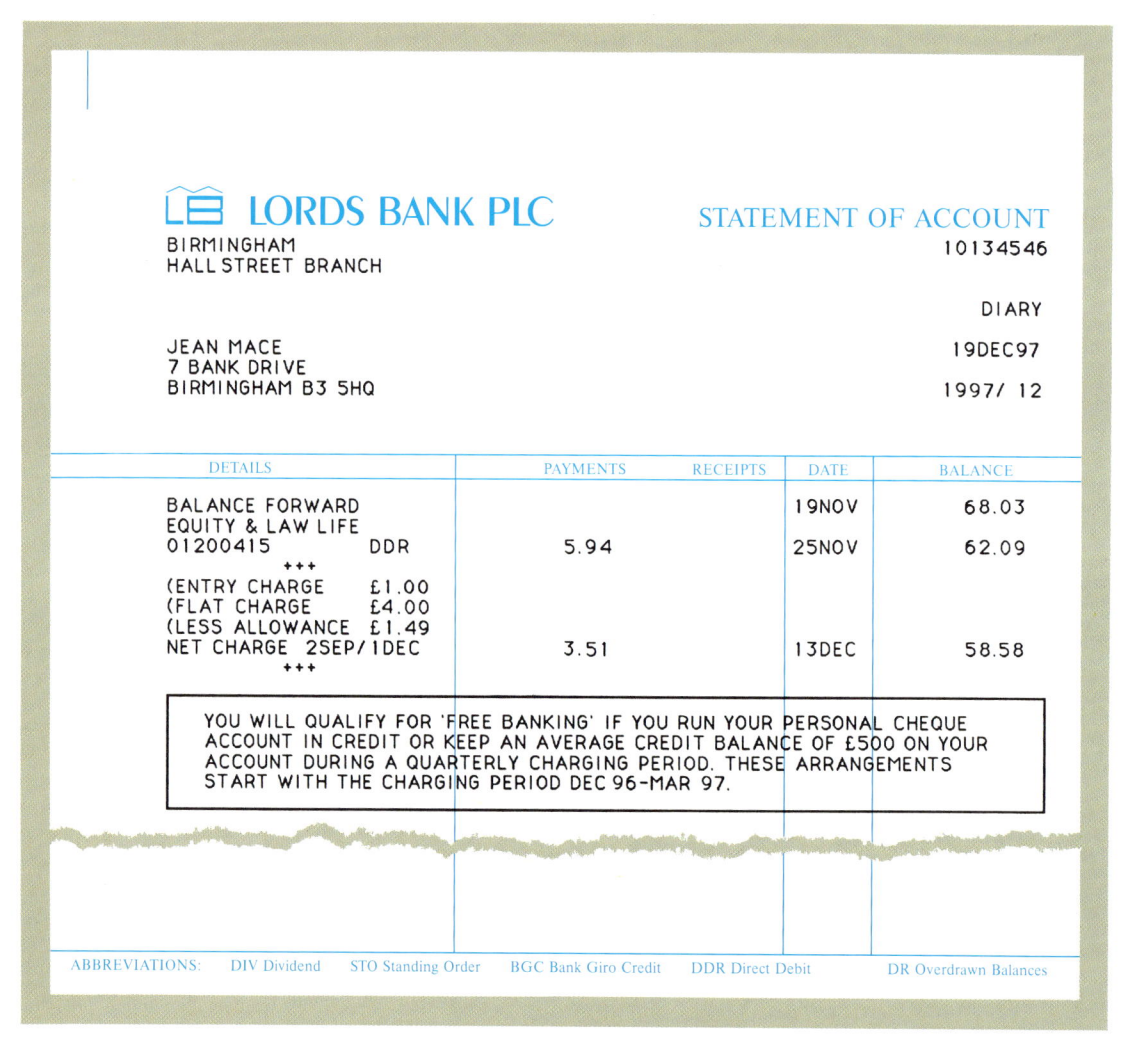

LORDS BANK PLC
BIRMINGHAM
HALL STREET BRANCH

STATEMENT OF ACCOUNT
10134546

JEAN MACE
7 BANK DRIVE
BIRMINGHAM B3 5HQ

DIARY
19DEC97
1997/ 12

DETAILS	PAYMENTS	RECEIPTS	DATE	BALANCE
BALANCE FORWARD			19NOV	68.03
EQUITY & LAW LIFE				
01200415 DDR	5.94		25NOV	62.09
+++				
(ENTRY CHARGE £1.00				
(FLAT CHARGE £4.00				
(LESS ALLOWANCE £1.49				
NET CHARGE 2SEP/1DEC	3.51		13DEC	58.58
+++				

YOU WILL QUALIFY FOR 'FREE BANKING' IF YOU RUN YOUR PERSONAL CHEQUE ACCOUNT IN CREDIT OR KEEP AN AVERAGE CREDIT BALANCE OF £500 ON YOUR ACCOUNT DURING A QUARTERLY CHARGING PERIOD. THESE ARRANGEMENTS START WITH THE CHARGING PERIOD DEC 96-MAR 97.

ABBREVIATIONS: DIV Dividend   STO Standing Order   BGC Bank Giro Credit   DDR Direct Debit   DR Overdrawn Balances

a. It shows that £5.94 was paid to Equity and Law Life Insurance Company. How was it paid?
   – the bank sent an international money order;
   – the bank paid it automatically, without asking Jean;
   – Jean sent a cheque to the insurance company;
   – Jean paid it in cash.
b. How much did Jean receive from the bank in return for keeping money in her account?
   £1.00; £4.00; £1.49; £3.51
c. What period is covered by the statement?
   19 Nov–13 Dec; 19 Nov–19 Dec; 25 Nov – 13 Dec; 2 Sep–1 Dec
d. How much did Jean pay into her account during this period?
   Nothing; £5.94; £9.45; £68.03
e. If Jean transfers £500 from her deposit account to her current account and keeps it there, which items will not appear in her next statement?
   – Balance forward
   – Entry Charge + Flat Charge + Net Charge
   – Flat Charge + Allowance + Net Charge
   – Entry Charge + Allowance + Net Charge
f. Look at this cheque. Will it later appear as a transaction on Pankhurst Decorators' account, on Jean Mace's or on both?

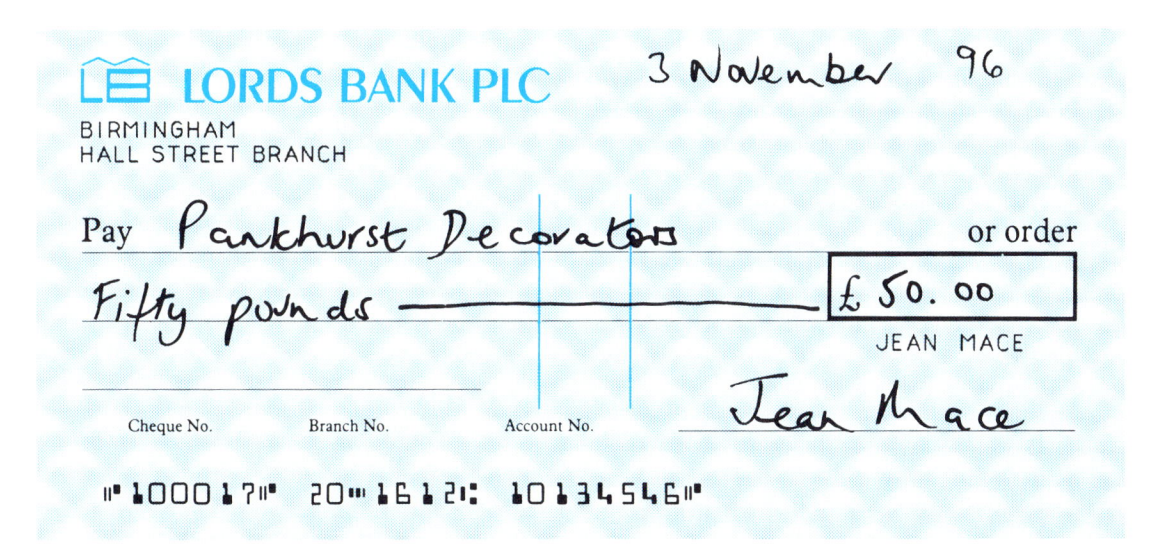

D. Talking grammar: auxiliaries (part I)

For more help on this grammar point, refer to *Modale Hilfsverben* in **Basic Grammar**, pp. 206–07.

> The verbs *will/would, can/could, may/might* indicate *attitudes*.
> They have no -s or *ing* form and are always followed by an infinitive.

Unit 1 — Main Course

These sentences show some of their common uses:

will
future time: You *will* receive higher interest on your deposit account.

would
willingness (similar to *will*): I *would* (will) be glad to help you.
conditional situations: You do not get as much interest as you *would* get on a deposit account.

can
ability (= "be able to"): With a current account, you *can* pay bills by direct debit cheque.
permission: You have to inform the bank before you *can* withdraw your money.

could
ability in the past (= past tense of *can*): Before the price rise, you *could* travel quite cheaply.
conditional (= ability to do something in certain circumstances): With a current account, you *could* instruct the Electricity Company to send bills direct to your bank.

may
permission: You *may* take out your money at any time.

might
possibility: This time period *might* be anything from 7 days to several months.

Match the following expressions with the blanks in the cartoon captions:

– might think   – can cash   – could see
– may … speak

"Ted? He (a) you in five minutes. He's just having a shower."

"You mean you (b) it only if I steal the cheque card, too?"

"(d) I … with the dog of the house?"

"If you shaved, put on a clean shirt and polished your shoes, the neighbours (c) you were going to a fancy dress party!"

Follow-up exercise: *Arbeitsbuch*, p. 50.

Unit 1 — Main Course

E. Vocabulary

Read the following letter which Jean sent her bank manager. Then match the blanks in the letter with the expressions which follow.

Dear Manager,

I am writing about my account (number 101345546) at your (a) in Hall Street.

I have signed a contract with a building company and will soon move into a new house which will require extensive decorations. This means I will have to write a large number of (b) for small (c) over the next 18 months. So I would be happy if you would send me a (d) every month instead of every quarter, until further notice. This will help me to keep a check on my finances and to make sure that my current account remains (e).

Furthermore, to help pay my decorating bills, I will have to take some money from my deposit account. Would you please let me know how much (f) I should give you before doing this.

Yours faithfully

Jean Mace

Jean Mace

Choose from

- savings
- interest
- transaction
- amounts
- statement of account
- notice
- branch
- cheques
- in credit
- balance

F. Communication practice

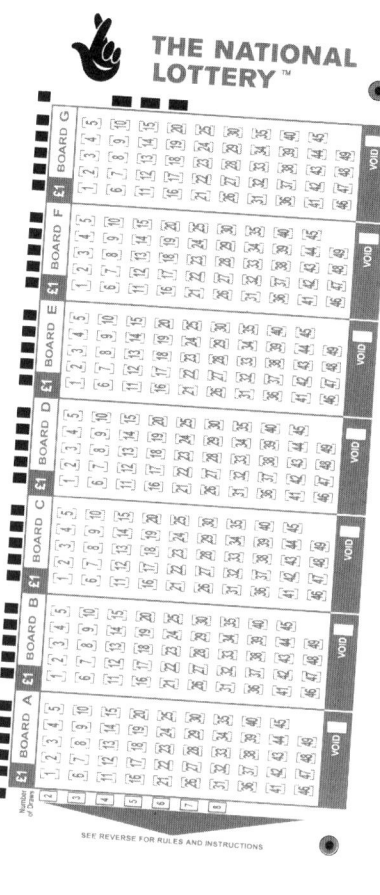

1. The National Lottery was introduced in Britain in 1995. It was based on the public *Lotto* in Germany.
2. Read this short description of the rules:

The National Lottery

With a minimum of £1, you can take part in the National Lottery.

For £1 a board, you can play as many boards as you like.

For each board you play, you should select 6 numbers (between 1 and 49).

On each draw date, 6 main numbers and 1 bonus number (between 1 and 49) will be drawn at random.

If you have selected all 6 main numbers on one board, you win (or share) the *jackpot prize*.

If you have selected the bonus number and 5 of the main numbers on one board, you win a *bonus prize.*

You should claim your prize within 180 days.

Each week, the total prize money must be at least 45% of the total amount paid into the lottery.

The National Lottery is intended to produce financial support for charities, cultural institutions (such as theatres), and sports organizations.

3. This letter, sent from Britain to a German student, contains three mistakes. Find them!

> Dear Claudia,
> I was interested to read about the class report you're preparing on Britain's National Lottery. Yes, I can give you some information about it. I believe it works very much like the lottery you're familiar with in Germany. Each week, you can pick groups of 6 numbers. Then there's a draw, and you can win a so-called "jackpot" if you pick 6 correct numbers. And, at any time, you can reclaim the money you've paid in.
> To take part, I think you have to pay a pound every week. So in theory, you could win the "jackpot" every week. If you do win, you have 180 days to claim your prize. How much can you win? Well, the prize money varies each week. So it really depends on how much is paid into the lottery that week. But the organizers do have to pay out exactly 45% of the money they get in.
> Well, I hope that's helpful. Give my regards to Dan.
> With best wishes
> Brian

G. Further reading

Banks and the Letter of Credit

One of the banks' most vital international services is to supply letters of credit. Without these documents, international trade would be almost impossible. A letter of credit guar-
5 antees payment by a buyer in one country to a seller in another. Often, the letter is "irrevocable". That is to say, no-one – neither the payer nor the bank – can change their minds later and not pay. Because an irrevocable let-
10 ter of credit cannot be cancelled, the seller can be sure of getting his money.
Imagine an automobile manufacturer in Germany who wants to pay an Australian supplier for some spare parts. The manufacturer
15 will fill in a form asking his bank to open a credit in his favour (that is, enter a sum of money into his account). After doing this, that bank will contact the seller's bank. The seller's bank will then issue a letter of credit
20 and send it to the seller. The letter will list the papers which he must give his bank before it will pay him.

Of course, both of the banks concerned will charge a fee for their services. But their letter of credit protects both the buyer and seller in 25 international trading practice. The buyer can be sure that payment will not be made until all necessary papers are in order. And the seller can be sure he will be paid immediately after the goods have been delivered. So the 30 letter of credit provides a safe and trusted method of payment between importer and exporter.

Answer the following questions:

a. What is the advantage to the seller of an irrevocable letter of credit?
b. How does a letter of credit protect the buyer?
c. "Without these documents, international trade would be almost impossible". Can you think of difficulties that would arise if banks were unable to give letters of credit?

Follow-up exercise: *Arbeitsbuch*, p. 13.

Main Course / Unit 2

Investment and the Stock Exchange

A. Lead-in

Look at these illustrations. Try to find out what they have in common.

What is the man in picture 1 doing?
What could "oil shares" in picture 2 mean?
What do you think is going on in picture 3?

The answers all have a connection with the title of this unit.
They will be revealed one by one during the unit!

B. Text

Letter from a Broker

A friend advised Stephen Clark to "invest in shares". So Stephen wrote to his broker to find out more about it.
Here is the reply he received:

Dunn & Lambert
Brokers and Insurers

24 Wren Buildings
Birmingham B5F 3GH

28 March 1997

Dear Mr Clark,

Many thanks for your letter enquiring about investments. As we were recently discussing savings, perhaps I should make clear the difference between savings and investments.

You can save money in order to spend it later, or simply to have it handy in case of emergency. As you know, you can lend these <u>savings</u> to a bank, a building society or even to the Government.

You could use your savings to buy something which will produce an income or some other benefit for you. This is known as <u>investment</u>. For example, you could save through a building society, then use your savings to help buy a house. This house becomes your investment because it can be used to produce income if the property increases in value.

A very popular form of investment nowadays is shares. You can buy a small part (that is, one or more "shares") of a company, and this makes you a part owner of the company. As a shareholder, you receive a part of the company's profits (known as "dividends") each year. And you are free to sell your shares at any time.

If you are a shareholder in a successful company, your dividends will increase every year - this is regular "income". But also the selling price of your shares will increase - this is known as "capital growth". But buying shares always carries a certain risk. The money you spend on them is known as "risk capital" because it is always possible that the company will fail. If this happens, you may lose all your original investment and receive nothing.

Instead of buying shares, you could invest without risk in "gilt-edged securities". Basically, these are loans to the Government, and offer total security. However, with investments, there is generally a relation between the risk and the reward. Investing in something as safe as "gilts" is unlikely to produce spectacular profits for you.

I hope this information is helpful. I suggest that you think about it and then phone me if you are still interested in the idea of investing. I advise you to delay any investment decisions until then.

With very best wishes,

Peter Lambert
Peter Lambert

Summary

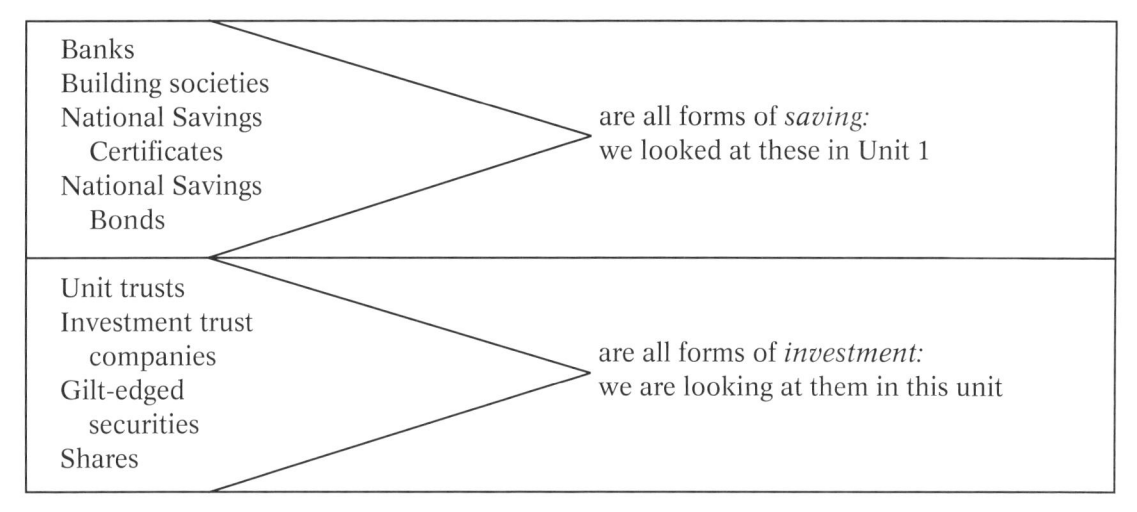

Banks Building societies National Savings Certificates National Savings Bonds	are all forms of *saving:* we looked at these in Unit 1
Unit trusts Investment trust companies Gilt-edged securities Shares	are all forms of *investment:* we are looking at them in this unit

Brokers, like Mr Lambert, buy and sell shares, and give professional advice on investments. The broker in picture 1 on page 47 is watching movements in share prices, and telephoning up-to-date advice to one of his customers. Each day, newspapers report the share prices of important companies and goods – as in picture 2 on page 47.

Changes in these prices are mainly the result of busy – sometimes hectic – daily trading at London's Stock Exchange (picture 3), the world's main share-trading centre.

C. Comprehension and analysis

Mr Lambert's letter contains seven paragraphs. Each paragraph develops one main point. Match the paragraph summaries on the left-hand side to the paragraphs indicated on the right-hand side:

summary of paragraph	paragraph beginning
a. gives 2nd example of investment	1. Many thanks for …
b. defines investment	2. You can save money …
c. explains the purpose of the letter	3. You could use …
d. develops 1st example of investment	4. A very popular …
e. gives 1st example of investment	5. If you are a …
f. closes with offer and advice	6. Instead of buying …
g. defines savings	7. I hope this …

D. Talking grammar: reported speech

For more help on this grammar point, refer to *Indirekte Rede* in **Basic Grammar,** pp. 208–09.

1. Look at these ways of reporting what someone has said. In particular, study the tense changes.

direct statement	reported statement
He said, "I will go by bus."	He said (that) he *would* go by bus. or He told me (that) he *would* go by bus.
He said, "I am expecting a letter quite soon."	He told me (that) he *was expecting* a letter quite soon.

direct question	reported question
He asked, "Where is Mr Lambert's office?"	He asked *where* Mr Lambert's office *was*.
He asked me, "What are you writing?"	He asked me *what* I *was writing*.

Using the patterns above, change the following sentences into reported speech. Begin: He said ... *or:* He asked ...

a. "What do you think about investing?"
b. "I'll send you our publicity brochure tomorrow."
c. "We won't take any action before July."
d. "Where can we get advice on share purchases?"
e. "The manager will reply personally to your letter."
f. "Who is the new manager?"
g. "We have been looking for a suitable partner for some time."

2. Look again at this advice from Mr Lambert's letter

> I advise you to delay any investment decisions until then.
> (Note: *advise* + noun/pronoun + infinitive)
> I suggest that you think about it.
> (Note: *suggest* (or *recommend*) + *that*-clause)
> The main verb (*advise, suggest, recommend*) is followed by an -ing verb if the person receiving the advice or suggestion is *not* mentioned:

> He advised delaying any investment decisions until then.
> (Negative: They advised me not to buy ordinary shares.
> Also: They advised against buying ordinary shares.)
>
> I suggest putting half the money into savings.
> He suggested buying gilt-edged.
> (Negative: He suggested not buying gilt-edged.)
>
> He recommends waiting for a change in the economic climate.
> I recommend investing in plastics.
> (Negative: I recommend not investing in plastics.)

> Note, too, the use of conditional *would:* I would suggest/advise/recommend, etc. This is less direct, more tactful than I suggest/advise/recommend ... It is often used diplomatically: I would advise you to pay the bill immediately. It is now 3 weeks overdue.

Mr Lambert is writing again to Stephen Clark, concerning his investment possibilities.

Dunn & Lambert
Brokers and Insurers

24 Wren Buildings
Birmingham B5F 3GH

6 April 1997

Dear Mr Clark,

Further to my letter last week, I would like to send some more suggestions and advice for you to consider. I feel sure they will help you with your investment plans.

First of all...

Now complete Mr Lambert's letter for him, as follows. First, rewrite the following 6 sentences, using the verb phrases shown:

a. Make an investment plan. (advise)
b. Select your purchases carefully. (would recommend)
c. Don't sell shares except when you badly need the money or a sharp fall in share prices seems possible. (would advise against)
d. Keep records of all your investments, as you will need them for income tax purposes. (also suggest)
e. As a general rule, review your investments at least twice a year. (recommend)
f. Don't use newspapers except as a guide to share prices. (suggest ... not)

Now read the following additional sentences g–k:

g. Give careful thought to your needs for income compared with capital growth, and to the amount of risk you are willing to take.
h. You should watch for any changes in the economy and keep a watch, too, on the company you have invested with.
i. You should never rush into an investment decision.
j. It is wise to keep all your records in one place, and to list all interest and dividends as you receive them.
k. And remember that your investment aims will not always remain the same: be flexible and think ahead.

Arrange the 11 sentences into the following 3 paragraphs, in order to complete Mr Lambert's letter:
– things to do before buying shares
– things to do while holding shares
– general advice
End the letter: With very best wishes, ...

Follow-up exercise: *Arbeitsbuch*, p. 51.

E. Vocabulary

Match the expressions on the left-hand side with the meanings on the right. You know some of them already.

expression	meaning
a. Investment Trust Company	1. A form of collective investment. Some investors pool their money to form a central fund which buys shares in various companies. Each investor holds a number of "units" in proportion to his original investment.
b. The Stock Exchange	2. A form of lending to the Government – practically a no-risk investment. Originally the certificates had gold edges.
c. Unit Trusts	3. These give the holder a part of the company's earnings after all other payments have been made.
d. Ordinary Shares	4. With these, each holder receives a fixed dividend. He will get paid before "ordinary" shareholders if the company gets into trouble or goes bankrupt.
e. Gilt-edged Securities	5. A public company with shares which can be bought and sold. It has the freedom to invest widely, for example, in the shares of other companies.
f. Preference Shares	6. The organization which brings together people who are looking for capital and people who want to invest. It can be seen at work in picture 3 on page 47.

Follow-up exercise: *Arbeitsbuch*, p. 75.

F. Communication practice

1. "That money talks, I'll not deny.
   I heard it once. It said goodbye."

The possibility of profits makes people willing to invest. Risk makes them reluctant to invest. Since starting this unit, are you more willing to invest your (perhaps imaginary!) capital, or less willing?

2. Imagine you have £500 to spend on a holiday in 12 months' time. Of course, you would like more. So how will you make your money work for you in those 12 months?
In pairs, discuss the following possibilities. Then choose *one*, and explain the reasons for your decision. At the end of the exercise, your teacher will tell you how much you profited from your decision after the 12 months!

a. A safe account at Ironclad Bank, guaranteeing 2% interest per year.
b. Shares in Icarus Airlines, a new company whose share price has increased by 120% in 8 weeks, and is still rising. Icarus has started a number of early morning "businessmen's" flights between European capital cities. Your broker warns you that the major airlines are now trying to offer the same service more cheaply – which could lead to a big fall in the value of any Icarus shares you buy.
c. Shares in Exkreta Fertilisers, an old and well-known company. Their shares have not made any profits for a year. But they've marketed a new potato spray, which might sell well. "As a result," your broker says, "shares bought now could perhaps be sold at 20% profit later. The prospects look quite good."
d. Gilt-edged securities at 9% interest. However, these securities are not payable for another 7 years. So, in 12 months' time, the best you could do is to sell them for whatever price you can get. Your broker thinks you might be able to sell them at a profit of 4% to 5% next year.

For your discussion, here are some phrases you can use to express opinions:

What I think is …
I feel that …
In my view …
In my opinion …

G. Further reading

Types of Business

In Britain, a *public* limited company – "plc" for short – is a company whose shares anyone can buy. You don't have to work for the company or have any other connection with it. If you own shares, you own a piece of the company and regularly receive a part of the company's profits, known as your "dividend".

A public limited company must have at least 2 members, but may in fact have several thousand shareholders. If any individual bought more than 50% of the shares, he would automatically be able to control the company.
Once such a company has started business, you don't buy more shares by investing more money in it. Instead, you buy shares from existing shareholders. In a public limited

company, you can buy and sell these shares openly and freely, generally through a Stock Exchange.

In a second type of business – a *private* limited company – a shareholder can only sell shares if all the other shareholders agree. Such companies have between 2 and 50 shareholders, and the company's name includes the word "Limited" (or the abbreviation "Ltd"). In both these types of business, shareholders are "liable" for the company's debts only up to the value of their shares. This means that if the company goes bankrupt, you (as a shareholder) will only lose your shares – nothing more.

But let us imagine you own a British business which is *not* limited. Maybe you are a "sole proprietor" (i. e. the only owner) or you are in a "partnership" (a business owned by between 2 and 20 people). Then you have unlimited liability for your company's debts. This means that if the company goes bankrupt, you may even have to sell your personal possessions (car, furniture and so on) in order to pay the company's debts. If your partners don't play any active role in the running and the work of the business, they are known as "sleeping partners". But they share the profits with you and run the same risks if the company fails.

Similar to a limited company in Britain is the type of organization in the United States known as a corporation. Like a British limited company, it has a board of directors (led by a chairman), who are often the major shareholders and who make the important decisions on company policy. The board normally employs a president and a number of vice presidents to execute this policy and to run the company's day-to-day business. In some corporations, the chairman of the board and the president are one and the same person.

Answer the following questions:

a. In what kind of company do you have to get other people's permission if you want to sell your shares?
b. Why is it better to be in a limited, rather than an unlimited, company if it goes bankrupt?
c. If you were one of 20 people wishing to start a business, which of the following types of company would you be allowed to form: a public limited company; a private limited company; a partnership?
d. Have you ever thought of starting a business on your own or with partners? What kind of business? What kind of problems would you expect at the start?

Follow-up exercise: *Arbeitsbuch*, pp. 14–15.

Main Course   Unit 3

Advertising and Publicity

A. Lead-in

1. Advertising slogans

Can you complete these slogans with the following words:
whitest, better, more, finest, day, cigarettes, stream.

- "Start your (a) the EasyGleam way" (toothpaste)
- "Get (b) with D 4" (perfume)
- "Goodtime (c) are fresher tasting"
- "Cool as a mountain (d)" (cigarettes)
- "Turgil washes (e)" (washing powder)
- "Beanso gives you (f) coffee"
- "This wonderful coat is made from the (g) Kerry wool"

2. Questions in advertisements

For each of the following headings, try to decide what product or service is being advertised, choosing from the list at the bottom of the page.

A BIT BREATHLESS?

Leaving the UK?

Are you legal, decent, honest and truthful?

LOOKING OLDER?

Need Help Getting Up?

In the race for foreign investment, who overtook the competition?

advertising control	language school	building society	financial advice
taxi service	running shoes	airline	plastic surgery
furniture removal	heart medicine	tennis lessons	
face cream	grasscutting service	alarm clock	

55

B. Text

Advertising Techniques

Advertising has long had a powerful influence in the United States. The world's biggest advertising industry is to be found on Madison Avenue, New York, and its techniques are imitated everywhere. Take, for example, the use of people in adverts.

A picture showing a group of well-dressed, elegant individuals shows you that this product is chosen only by the most sophisticated people (and that is why it is more expensive than other, similar products). Automobiles, perfumes, liqueurs are often advertised in this way. Often, the advertisers are aiming such adverts at the not-so-rich, who would like to identify with the people in the picture. Or the advert can show young people having a party, laughing, singing, having a lovely time – and using the product. It is easy to think of certain international drinks or cigarettes which are presented in this way. The product is shown to be as desirable as youth itself. Or the advert shows people – sometimes alone in the wilderness – enjoying excitement or contentment, far from the hassles of the city. This technique is most commonly used to advertise cigarettes, which then seem like a "passport" to such an escape.

Or maybe the advertiser wants to show that the product is "the latest thing" – a new, sensational breakthrough. This impression can be reinforced if the product is presented by a serious-looking man in a white coat – obviously a scientific expert – who describes the product's technical qualities.

Or well-known people, like sports stars or TV personalities, can be shown using the product. The reader, respecting the celebrity, will respect his or her opinion about the product. Who, in Germany, has not seen the familiar faces of professional footballers or tennis stars endorsing goods from fruit drinks to hi-fi equipment?

Pictures of babies and little children can create a pleasant, sentimental effect which makes the product desirable. Of course, they play their part in baby product adverts. But they appear with even greater frequency in adverts for insurance and house-purchase!

But the type of person most featured in advertisements is the attractive young woman. In the case of "male" products (say, shaving cream or men's clothes), her picture makes the product appealing to men, through association. But such pictures work even more effectively in adverts for "female" products (women's magazines or perfume, for example). This, say Madison Avenue psychologists, is because women consumers would like to be as young and attractive as the woman in the picture, and so they are tempted to buy the product.

C. Comprehension and analysis

1. Answer these questions on the text

a. How do adverts showing babies or happy children appeal to people?

b. An advert will often feature affluent people in expensive surroundings. Is the advertiser trying to show that the product is so expensive that it belongs in expensive homes, or what?

c. Why do advertisers feature women in adverts, regardless of whether the advert is directed at men or women or both?

d. Think of some particular advertisements in papers, magazines and/or the cinema which have attracted *your* attention. Do you think they helped to persuade you to spend money?

2. **Read and think**

Look at these holiday advertisements, and answer the questions which follow:

Germany

- Germany can turn a holiday into a romantic experience in so many different, enjoyable ways.
- Its quaint medieval towns. Its rolling, wooded hills topped by fairytale castles, sweeping down to the winding valleys of Germany's majestic Rhine, Moselle, Weser and Neckar rivers. Its bustling cities, with their fascinating mixture of old and new architecture, great shopping, excellent restaurants with local wines, pavement cafés and exciting nightlife.
- Whether you travel by air, by sea and rail, or bring your car there's a holiday to suit every taste. Indeed, the choice is wider than ever before, and tremendous value too – like the special offer we've highlighted here.
- Why not send for our brochures and discover just how Germany can turn a holiday into a romantic experience.

Discover its romance

Please send me a free colour brochure and details of the many holiday offers available in the Federal Republic of Germany, plus details of German Federal Railways 9 and 16 day rail-rover Tourist Card.

To: German National Tourist Office, 61, Conduit Street, London W1R 0EN.

Name_____

Address_____

SE2

Unit 3 — Main Course

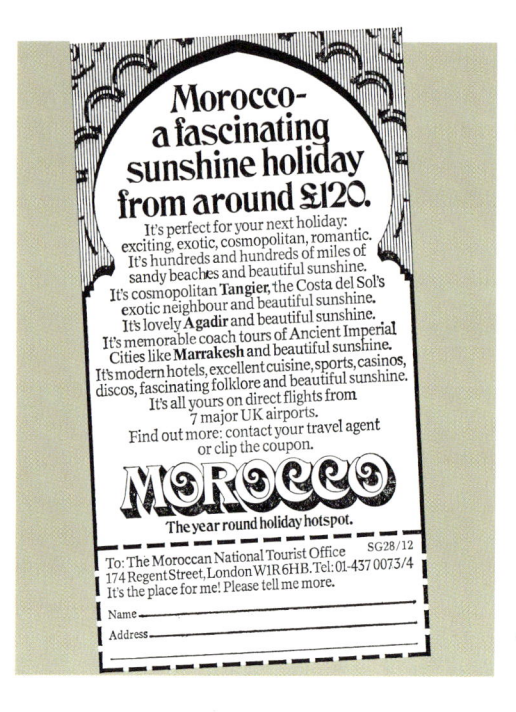

Morocco – a fascinating sunshine holiday from around £120.

It's perfect for your next holiday: exciting, exotic, cosmopolitan, romantic. It's hundreds and hundreds of miles of sandy beaches and beautiful sunshine.
It's cosmopolitan **Tangier**, the Costa del Sol's exotic neighbour and beautiful sunshine.
It's lovely **Agadir** and beautiful sunshine.
It's memorable coach tours of Ancient Imperial Cities like **Marrakesh** and beautiful sunshine.
It's modern hotels, excellent cuisine, sports, casinos, discos, fascinating folklore and beautiful sunshine.
It's all yours on direct flights from 7 major UK airports.
Find out more: contact your travel agent or clip the coupon.

MOROCCO
The year round holiday hotspot.

To: The Moroccan National Tourist Office SG28/12
174 Regent Street, London W1R 6HB. Tel: 01-437 0073/4
It's the place for me! Please tell me more.
Name
Address

a. Which words in the slogans especially attract the reader's attention?
b. These words are used in the small print of the advertisements: exotic / excellent / fascinating / romantic/romance / discover/discovery / exciting / bustling. What kind of readers do you think such words appeal to? What kind of readers will they *not* appeal to?
c. Ideally, a holiday advertisement will (i) attract readers' attention and interest, and (ii) provide some "hard" information (price range, length of holiday, method of travel, how to make a booking and so on).
Does the Germany advertisement concentrate mainly on (i) or (ii)? Or does it successfully combine both? Does the Morocco advertisement?
d. Both adverts describe a country. Say which you think is the better-written description, and why.

D. Talking grammar: comparison of adjectives and adverbs

For more help on this grammar point, refer to *Adjektive – Adverbien* in **Basic Grammar**, pp. 209–11.

1. Note

The endings -*er* and -*est*	
The words *more* and *most*	are used to make comparisons.

adjectives

comparative	superlative
They appear with even great*er* frequency in adverts for insurance and house-purchase. That is why it is *more* expensive than other, similar products.	The world's *biggest* advertising industry is to be found in Madison Avenue. This product is chosen only by the *most* sophisticated people.

-er, -est endings are normally used with

a. one-syllable adjectives: big, bigger, biggest
b. two-syllable adjectives ending in -y, -ow, -le, -er:
   lively, livelier, liveliest
   narrow, narrower, narrowest
   little, littler, littlest
   clever, cleverer, cleverest

   (Note the changes in spelling.)

Look at these irregular forms:
bad, worse, worst
good, better, best
far, further/farther, furthest/farthest

All other adjectives take *more/most*:
expensive, more expensive, most expensive

adverbs

Adverbs work in a similar way to adjectives:

comparative	superlative
We'll arrive home soon*er* than you. Such pictures work even *more* effectively in adverts for "female" products.	You should apply on the soon*est* possible date. This technique is *most* commonly used to advertise cigarettes.

Note these irregular forms:
well, better, best
badly, worse, worst

2. Rewrite the following sentences, changing the adjectives into their correct form as indicated

Example:
Mintchew – the (fresh) mint of all. (superlative)
Mintchew – the freshest mint of all.

a. What could be (exotic) than a holiday in Tahiti? (comparative)
b. Glubbs – the (good-tasting) toothpaste in the world. (superlative)
c. See the world's (fascinating) places at the world's (low) prices – with JetTours. (superlative)

3. Rewrite the following sentences, changing the adjectives into *adverbs*, as indicated

Example:
We check all of our products (rigorous). (superlative)
We check all of our products most rigorously.

a. No brake linings are tested (careful) than Oldhams'. (comparative)
b. Leading experts agree that engines run (well) on Stewpot Grade A Motor Oil. (comparative)
c. Of all the world's health drinks, milk is developed (natural). (superlative)

Follow-up exercise: *Arbeitsbuch*, pp. 52–53.

E. Vocabulary

1. Study this list of advertising expressions. We have used some of them already. The definitions are correct – except that *two* of them have been paired wrongly.
Find the two, and make a note of their correct definitions.

advertising agency – a company that plans and does advertising for other companies

brand – a line of products by a particular company

code of practice – a set of rules for fair and decent advertising methods

commercial (noun) – a radio or TV advert

consumer – a registered name or logo, signifying a particular product

image – the idea that people have of a product

medium – a method of getting information to the public (e.g. newspapers, radio, TV)

slogan – a few words, easily remembered, which often appear in large print in adverts

sponsored – recommended, supported or paid for by someone for publicity purposes

trademark – a person who buys products or pays for a service

2. Listen to the following dialogue, an interview between a newspaper reporter and a committee member of Torrenton, a local football club.
Then write a short newspaper article about the advertising scheme they are discussing. Don't simply copy the words of the interview. Invent a suitable title and use these notes to help you organize your article:

advertising scheme / new Youth Team
men's games at weekends / youth games mid-week
new floodlights / fund-raising / local businesses / £50 for name / 10 years / help Youth Team

JARGON JUNGLE
Cooling off is an important bit of financial consumer protection. When you buy an investment product – unit trusts, life insurance or a pension plan – you have a 14-day 'cooling off' period in which to change your mind and ask for your money back.

F. Communication practice

1. What do *you* think?

Consider the following statement: "Advertising does more harm than good".
Now look at the arguments (*for* and *against*) which follow. For each one, give a score of 1 to 5, as shown here:

I disagree with this point totally.	(1)
I think this is not very convincing.	(2)
I am not sure about this point.	(3)
I feel this is true to a great extent.	(4)
I agree with this point totally.	(5)

for

a. In content and form, adverts are not different from propaganda.
b. They make people want things they don't really need; this makes people greedy.
c. Many adverts are silly, dishonest or insulting to readers' intelligence.
d. The cost of advertising adds to the cost of the goods and services advertised.
e. Adverts are immoral because they make use of people's jealousy, fears, etc.
f. Advertisers influence opinions and reports in newspapers and on TV – a serious limit to freedom of expression in the media.

against

a. Adverts give information (including technical facts and pictures of products) which helps people to choose; without them, people simply wouldn't know what is available on the market.
b. Adverts keep prices down because they create large-scale demands.
c. Adverts make life colourful, interesting and attractive; without them, streets, buildings, newspapers would be dull and grey.
d. The income from adverts helps keep down the cost of things like newspapers and magazines.
e. People don't have to read adverts if they don't like them – they are still free to enjoy their TV programme or newspaper.
f. Advertising leads to more open competition, and so to more efficient production and lower prices.

2. Discuss

Get into pairs and compare your scores. Discuss particularly those points where your scores differ widely. Try to convince each other of your point of view! In your discussion, use the following expressions:

agreeing

I couldn't agree more.
That's just what I think.
That's right.
You've got a point there.
I'd go along with that.

disagreeing politely

I take your point, but ...
I see what you mean, but on the other hand ...
I'm not so sure about that.
You said that ... but it seems to me that ...
Yes, but surely ...

3. Write a summary of both sides of the argument, expressing your own point of view at the end. Find a suitable title.

G. Further reading

Advertising Standards

In exercise A, page 55, we saw an advertising slogan in the form of the question "Are you legal, decent, honest and truthful?" Taken from an advert produced by Britain's Advertising Standards Authority, it is addressed to British advertisers in general. It is a warning that their adverts have to maintain certain standards in order to be publishable.

By contrast, the United States have several "watchdog" organizations safeguarding the standards of the huge American advertising industry. For example, the Federal Communications Commission controls advertising in broadcasting through its power to grant licences for TV and Radio stations; the Post Office Department keeps a check on mail advertising; and so on. An important development came in 1911, when the Associated Advertising Clubs of America, at their annual convention, adopted the motto "Truth in advertising" and established a National Vigilance Committee to police advertising. Since then, advertising standards have improved little by little as a result of the efforts of the various professional groups in the advertising industry.

As in other countries, the main aim has been to eliminate objectionable or untruthful advertising. The most common claims that have to be dealt with are false and misleading comparisons of price and quality, exaggerated claims about quality, and "bait" advertising (quoting a ridiculously low price for a product which is not really for sale, in order to attract customers to a store). And since the early 1970s, when the women's rights movement gathered strength, sexism in advertisements has become a very frequent cause of complaints.

This concern about advertising standards is, of course, a sign of the size and importance of the advertising industry. In a large, free-enterprise country like the United States, it is vital to economic life. Or, to put it another way, doing business without advertising is very much like winking at someone in the dark. You know what you are doing, but nobody else does.

> **Are you legal, decent, honest and truthful?**
>
> Advertisers have to be.
>
> The Advertising Standards Authority
> Write to The Advertising Standards Authority
> Brook House
> 2/16 Torrington Place
> London WC17HN

Answer the following questions:

a. What is one of the differences between the controls on advertising in Britain and the United States?
b. Exactly what do advertising standards organizations aim to do?
c. What might women find objectionable in an advertisement?
d. Are there any advertisements which you find offensive? Why? What is the best way to deal with them, in your opinion?

Get rolling

SIR – As the Government health warning does not appear on pipe tobacco the obvious thing to do is to roll one's cigarettes from this substance.

We would do well to remember that the tobacco plant is one of God's gifts to men, and if used wisely can do no harm.

JOHN GERRARD
London, N.W.2.

EVERY PACKET CARRIES A GOVERNMENT HEALTH WARNING
MIDDLE TAR As defined by H.M.Government.

Warning: The Surgeon General Has Determined That Cigarette Smoking Is Dangerous to Your Health.

e. Do you consider Government warnings on cigarette packets necessary and/or useful?

Follow-up exercise: *Arbeitsbuch*, pp. 16–17.

Unit 4   Main Course

Credit

A. Lead-in

Look at this collection of headlines. Clearly, credit cards – known also as "plastic money" – make news.

- The trend is toward more use of credit cards – but at a price
- **The plastic revolution rolls on**
- Why the credit card deck is stacked
- The debt you owe your credit card
- Keep your borrowing in check
- **How to avoid being a creditaholic**
- COVER STORY: The credit-card boom

a. Can you think of any examples of "plastic money" which you have seen in your own country?
b. An alcoholic is someone who can't give up drinking. Exactly what problem do you think a "creditaholic" has?
c. A set of playing cards (i. e. a deck of cards) is "stacked" if they have been unfairly arranged. One headline-writer suggests credit cards are "stacked". How? (Look at the other headlines for a clue.)
d. The situation shown in this cartoon would not take place in real life. But what particular problem of credit card use does it point to?

Let's look more closely at credit cards, their benefits and disadvantages.

"We're from the friendly loan company. It's about your repayments."

B. Text

Live Now, Pay Later

In Charles Dickens' novel *David Copperfield*, written in the 19th century, a character called Mr Micawber expresses a philosophy which few people would have disagreed with in those days:

"*Annual income twenty pounds, annual expenditure nineteen pounds and six, result happiness. Annual income twenty pounds, annual expenditure twenty pounds nought and six, result misery*".

Although Britain's money system has changed somewhat since then, Mr Micawber's arithmetic still makes sense today!

His point, of course, was that we should live within our means and not spend more than we earn – that is, not get into debt. But is debt such a bad thing? Probably not. Even Mr Micawber himself might have been willing to go into a small amount of debt as long as he knew his expenditure was less than his income. "Result happiness".

But the philosophy of "live now, pay later" is nowadays regarded as quite normal and respectable, compared with Mr Micawber's time. Banks and other financial institutions are willing to lend money – or "extend credit", as it is known – to individuals and companies. There has been particularly rapid growth in consumer credit – that is, lending to people so they can buy things if they promise to repay the money later.

The main vehicle for this growth has been the credit card – "plastic money", as it is known. Back in 1950, an American entrepreneur had the embarrassing experience of dining at a restaurant, then finding he hadn't enough money to pay the bill. So he launched Diners Club – issuers of the world's first credit card, usable only in certain restaurants. American

65

Express arrived eight years later, and is today a world leader among credit card companies. Nowadays, many supermarkets, hotels and petrol stations issue their own cards to credit-worthy customers. In Europe, the use of "plastic money" is growing as the EU moves towards the goal of a shared currency. With the disappearance of currency exchange charges, spending on credit around Europe will be easier and cheaper.

Text 2

Opening a Credit Account: "Do's" and "Don'ts"

16-year-old Martin Briggs is considering opening a credit account with a big department store. Therefore he has been collecting information about credit, and, with the help of his computer, he has made a list of "do's and don'ts", as follows:

DO'S	DON'TS
DO check the Annual Percentage Rate (APR) when you open a credit account. This is the total cost of the credit, expressed as an annual rate. The lower the APR, the better the credit offer. If you do not see the APR, ask.	DON'T just ask: "Can I afford the monthly payments?" when you open a credit account in order to buy something. A more important question is: "Is this the cheapest way to borrow?". Compare the value of different credit facilities.
DO take a personal loan from a high street bank to pay particularly large bills. Their APR is usually a couple of per cent lower than credit card companies'.	DON'T be tempted to borrow more than you can manage to repay. If you have to borrow in order to repay earlier loans, you're in trouble. Remedy: spend less!
DO pay your credit card account at the end of the month – otherwise you will find yourself paying more fees.	DON'T start with the biggest debts if you ever have to attack your debts one by one – start with the most expensive, i.e. those charging the highest interest.
DO try to keep paying at least something regularly if you have trouble keeping up payments. In the meantime, write to the creditors and explain your problem. Very often, they will ease your payments for a while in these circumstances.	DON'T stop payments, no matter how hard-pressed you are. If the goods prove faulty, tell the supplier at once.
DO keep any letters you have in connection with a loan in case you have a dispute or a difficulty.	

C. Comprehension and analysis

1. Answer the following questions

a. What is the difference between the attitude to debt in Mr Micawber's time and now?
b. What is the difference between spending money and buying with a credit card?
c. How would a common European currency affect the use of credit cards?
d. How would/do *you* deal with the danger of overspending with credit cards?

2. Listen and take notes

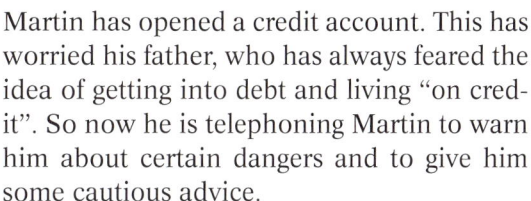

Martin has opened a credit account. This has worried his father, who has always feared the idea of getting into debt and living "on credit". So now he is telephoning Martin to warn him about certain dangers and to give him some cautious advice.

As you listen to the conversation, decide which items Martin has already noted. Also write down the extra pieces of advice from his father which he has *not* yet noted.

D. Talking grammar: expressions of quantity

1. "some" and "any"

> Do try to keep making *some* payments regularly. (a positive sentence)
> Don't borrow *any* sum of money which it will be difficult to repay. (a negative sentence)
> Can you think of *any* examples of "plastic money" which you have seen in your own country? (neutral *yes-no*-question)

Generally, *some*-words (somebody, somewhere, etc.) are used in positive statements; *any*-words are used after negatives and in neutral *yes-no*-questions.

> Note: A sentence may even have a negative sense without a word like "no" or "not":

> He refused to accept *any* help. (a negative sentence)
> He agreed to accept *some* help. (a positive sentence)
> They were too poor to have *any* holidays. (a negative sentence)
> They were well-off enough to have *some* holidays. (a positive sentence)

> If we ask a *yes-no*-question expecting a *yes*-answer, we use a *some*-word. Compare:

> Did *anyone* call last night? (I don't know if anyone did; that's why I'm asking.) (neutral *yes-no*-question)
> Did *someone* call last night? (I was expecting a call from a friend.) (question expecting a *yes*-answer)

Unit 4 — Main Course

Summary

	examples	these normally appear
some- words	somebody, somewhere, something, some, etc.	– in positive sentences – in *yes-no*-questions expecting a *yes*-answer
any- words	anybody, anywhere, anything, any, etc.	– after negatives – in neutral *yes-no*-questions

2. Choose "some" or "any"

ENTERPRISE

Loan Guarantee Scheme

Need a loan for your small business?

The Loan Guarantee Scheme makes it easier for you to get a loan quickly and without fuss.

Does your small business need (a) financial support? The Loan Guarantee Scheme makes it easy for you to get a low-interest loan quickly and without (b) fuss. (c) businesses qualify for loans as high as £75,000.

○ Is (d) business eligible?
▷ Most new or existing small businesses are eligible. But (e) evidence of business know-how and good planning is required.

○ Are there (f) costs involved?
▷ If you receive a loan, you must pay the first 2% of interest on it. (g) types of business have to pay 3%.
○ Do I have to fill in (h) special application forms to find out more about the scheme?
▷ No. Just call or visit your local tax office. Why not do it today?

3. Mass and count nouns

Look at these sentences:

with *count nouns*	with *mass nouns*
We don't have many customers.	We don't have much trade.
May I see you for a few minutes?	Could I have a little of your time?
Most banks can give you investment advice.	Most investment carries a certain risk.
There will be fewer mechanical typewriters in future.	There will be less paperwork in future.
Of all countries, we have the fewest export problems.	We haven't the least idea how we can help you.

Count nouns are seen as individual units, e. g. people, minutes, problems.
Mass nouns are seen as a collective whole, e. g. trade, investment, paperwork.

Note how expressions of quantity are used:

	with *count nouns*	with *mass nouns*
a large amount	many (formal)	much (formal)
	a lot of (informal)	a lot of (informal)
not a large amount	not many	not much
	few	little
a small amount	a few	a little
comparatives & superlatives	more/most	more/most
	fewer/fewest	less/least

Notes: a. *A lot of* is more common – and less formal – than *many/much*. It can be used instead of *many* or *much*:

formal:	informal:
There is much room for growth.	There is a lot of room for growth.
They will have many opportunities to expand.	They will have a lot of opportunities to expand.

b. Notice the difference between *little* and *few* with or without *a*:

There would be *little* (or *not much*) profit in trying to persuade more people to use credit cards. (So let us try something else.)

Unit 4 — Main Course

> There would be *a little* profit in trying to persuade more people to use credit cards. (So we should go ahead and try it.)
>
> Mr Micawber expresses a philosophy which *few* (or *not many*) people would disagree with in those days. (There was almost no disagreement.)
>
> Mr Micawber expresses a philosophy which *a few* people would disagree with in those days. (There was some disagreement.)

Therefore, *little* and *few* (without *a*) and *not many/much* have a negative sense.

Follow-up exercise: *Arbeitsbuch*, pp. 53–54.

4. Find the correct word

Use each of these words once for the blanks in the text which follows:
fewer, little, a little, less, least, much, a lot of, most

LORDSCARD...
For the Traveller

There is (a) point in taking cash or travellers cheques when you go with LORDSCARD.

Here's why.

The (b) attractive aspect of LORDSCARD is that you can get cash with it almost anytime anywhere. Of all the countries in Western Europe, North and South America, the Middle and Far East, (c) than 10 are outside the LORDSCARD banking network.

When you are so far from home, you may find that you have to dip into the red for a few days. We don't mind - and we don't charge you (d) interest. We charge you exactly for those days - no more.

If you happen to lose your LORDSCARD, it cannot be used by anyone else without knowledge of your personal number. (Note: Because of search and handling costs, we would have to charge (e) more than your original application fee in order to issue your replacement LORDSCARD).

Many people feel that the low end-of-month charges are the (f) attractive aspect of having a LORDSCARD. Accounts which keep a minimum balance of £100 are charged 2% (g) than the normal bank charges. Doesn't it make (h) sense to travel with LORDSCARD?

For further reading about this kind of card, see *Arbeitsbuch*, p. 109.

E. Vocabulary

Anyone looking for credit should "shop around", because it comes in various shapes and sizes – not only in the form of credit cards. Here is a list of some other *types of credit*. Match them with the *definitions* which follow.

types of credit
a. hire purchase

definitions
1. These are money co-operatives run by people with something in common. Members may live in the same street or work at the same firm. By

types of credit	definitions
	saving with the co-operative, they can get low-cost loans to help pay bills.
b. finance company personal loans	2. These can be a good method of paying for a big item (like a new home) which requires a long-term loan. The company who lend you the money may ask you for security. (i. e. evidence that you will be able to repay the loan finally).
c. bank overdrafts	3. With this form of credit, you can take the goods straight away by paying a deposit. You then pay at weekly or monthly intervals. If you fall behind with the payments, the goods can be taken back, because you do not own them until you have made all the payments.
d. credit unions	4. If you have a current account, your bank will normally let you overdraw it up to an arranged limit. You have to pay a fixed rate of interest for this form of credit.
e. digital cash dispensers	5. This allows you to draw money from your bank account at any time of the day or night. You can overdraw up to a limit agreed with your bank.

For further reading about forms of credit, see *Arbeitsbuch*, p. 112.

F. Communication practice

1. Reading and discussion

As we have seen above, digital cash dispensers are another type of credit. They are machines which issue cash to you immediately. Your bank later charges you for this service.

Lords Bank has a cash dispenser on the second floor of Floggers' food store. But on the very day you get your new card, Floggers close their second floor – and the cash dispenser – for six months for renovation. You are annoyed because you bought your card only in order to go shopping there. Lord's Bank is sympathetic, but can do nothing.

In pairs, discuss what you would write in a letter of complaint to Floggers. You can use these expressions for making suggestions:
Let's say/ask/suggest .../What about ...? / I wonder if we could ... / I'd like to suggest ...

2. Writing

Write the letter of complaint, using some of these expressions:
I am writing about .../I was most surprised to find .../Surely, you do not expect your customers to .../In the circumstances, I suggest that you .../If you do not ..., I shall have to ...

G. Further reading

Protecting the Consumer

Millions of ordinary people in Britain can, if they wish to, immediately acquire credit from a number of shops and department stores, just by filling in some simple forms. One problem is, as we have seen, that people can be tempted to overuse their credit so that they are faced with enormous debts later. How can this problem be solved – or, better, avoided?

One answer would be a National Credit Register, which would collect information about individuals' debt records and their ability to repay loans. At present, there are a number of "credit reference agencies" which attempt to do this. Their purpose is to supply a "credit rating" (that is, an assessment of someone's ability to repay) to, for example, a bank which is considering that person's application for a loan. In this way, fewer people who are "bad risks" would receive credit. But many British people are unwilling to have their personal details recorded and stored in this way. They say it is an "invasion of privacy" – quite apart from the danger of such information being misused.

What seems more acceptable to the general public is a system of consumer protection – ways of giving advice and legal help concerning individual rights regarding credit matters. There is in Britain a network of Consumer Protection Departments and Consumer Advice Centres which investigate misleading descriptions or charges. And there is an Office of Fair Trading, a Government department which keeps watch on trading matters and protects both consumers and businessmen against unfair practices. For example, this office will check on the fitness of traders who provide credit or hire goods to individuals, and helps provide protection under a law called the Consumer Credit Act. The Office of Fair Trading can also resolve disputes about the accuracy of personal information stored by credit reference agencies.

Answer the following questions:

a. What is the main danger of easily obtainable credit?
b. What would be the advantage of a National Credit Register?
c. Why are people reluctant to have a National Credit Register?
d. Is "consumer protection" really necessary, in your opinion? What form should it take?

Follow-up exercise: *Arbeitsbuch*, pp. 18–19.

International Trade Organizations

A. Lead-in

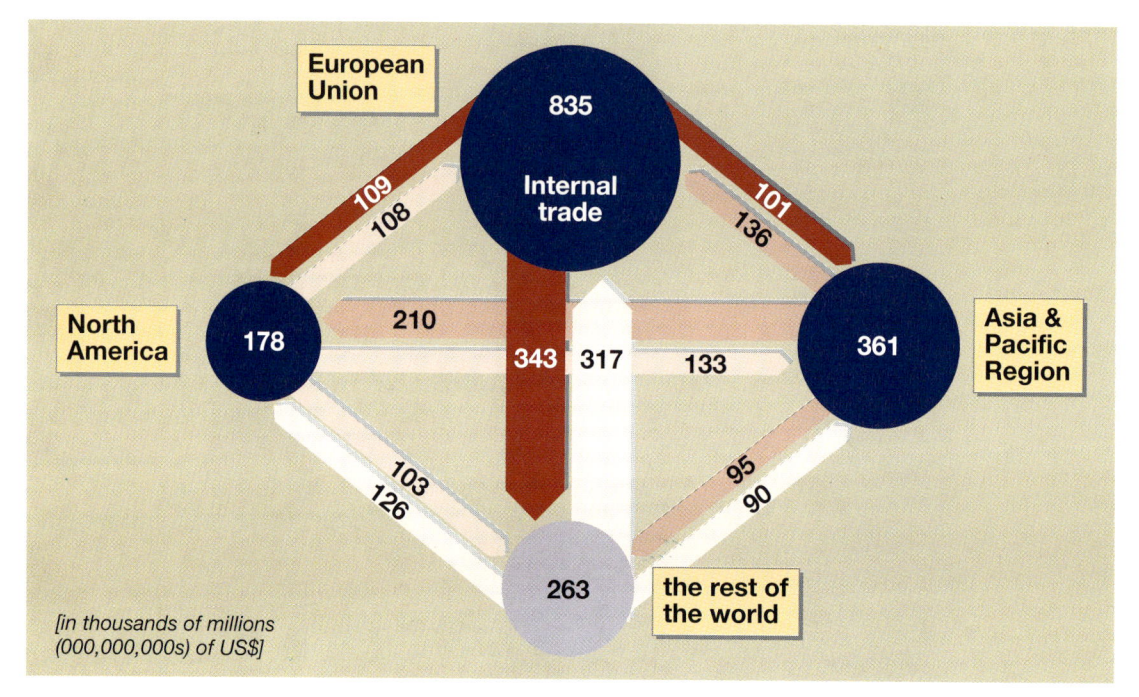

European Union: 835 Internal trade
- EU ↔ North America: 109 / 108
- EU ↔ Asia & Pacific: 101 / 136
- EU ↔ rest of world: 343 / 317

North America: 178
- North America ↔ Asia & Pacific: 210
- North America ↔ rest of world: 103 / 126

Asia & Pacific Region: 361
- Asia & Pacific ↔ rest of world: 133 / 95 / 90

the rest of the world: 263

[in thousands of millions (000,000,000s) of US$]

1. The diagram shows what volume of trade the main regions of the world have with each other.
   a. Which region provides the main buyers for North American exporters?
   b. Which is the greater – EU imports from, or exports to, the Asian and Pacific countries?
   c. Which region provides most of the EU's trade?

2. What do you know about international trade? Read the following statements. Which of them is false? Discuss them with a partner.

   a. No nation is self-sufficient – even the huge United States relies on imports for almost all of its nickel, tin and platinum.
   b. Highly industrialized nations like Great Britain and Germany can produce only a part of the food and raw materials they need, and so they specialize in manufacturing and exporting machinery and equipment.
   c. Some nations have got together to form clubs – or international trade organizations – in order to increase and improve their trade with other countries.

d. NATO – the North Atlantic Treaty Organization – is an example of an organisation devoted to increasing imports and exports between its member states.

e. Usually, the member states of a trade organization abolish or reduce the tariffs, or import duties, on goods traded between them.

B. Text

The European Union

The European Union (EU) is the name of an organization of European states who have decided to co-operate in three broad areas:

- economic and monetary union
- foreign and security policy
- justice and home affairs

In practice, this co-operation shows itself in a great number of ways – from recognizing each other's school diplomas to exchanging criminal records; from allowing EU citizens to seek work in each other's countries, to giving loans and grants to help underdeveloped regions.

Of course, some EU policies have progressed faster than others. For example, a tariff-free trading zone and the shared agricultural market were established many years ago. But it has proved more difficult to establish a currency union, although plans have now been laid to establish a single European currency from the end of the century onwards.

As far as trade is concerned, the EU is the most powerful organization in the world. EU member states are involved in 20% of the world's trade. In the last 30 years, the EU's trade with countries outside the Union has increased more than three and a half times over. But the increase in trade among the EU member states themselves has been a much more important advantage of membership. This trade has increased eightfold in the same 30-year period.

The advantages of EU membership are also very great as far as jobs are concerned. The number of unemployed in Germany alone might have increased by 7 million if the country had not been in the EU. (Furthermore, an EU fund exists to help deal with unemployment in the Union. In 1996, 9.9% of people in the EU were unemployed. The rate in Germany alone was 9.1%.)

Scotland is a good example of the way the EU helps underdeveloped regions. If the European Coal and Steel Community Fund had not directed modernization grants of £120 million there, those two Scottish industries would have collapsed completely. Another £170 million was given in direct non-repayable grants to the Scotland Development Department and to Scottish Regional Authorities to help build up the infrastructure, and create and safeguard jobs. And special loans and grants went to Scottish energy industries (particularly oil, which Europe desperately needs).

C. Comprehension and analysis

1. Answer these questions on the text

a. What two main advantages of EU membership does the author point to?
b. Why is Scotland featured in the text?
c. In what ways do you think *you* have benefitted from EU membership?

2. Listen, read and take notes

We have seen some arguments in favour of the European Union.
You will now hear an interview with Arthur Shaw, an Englishman opposed to membership of the EU.
Before listening, study the following arguments. Which of them does Mr Shaw use in the course of the interview? Take notes on them.

a. Union members give favourable trading terms to each other, and this provokes outside states to cut their trade with the Union.
b. The Union has too many members, and is impossible to co-ordinate.
c. Member states have given up part of their political independence, and can no longer control their own affairs.
d. The Union consists of competing states, all working for their own interests, so unity is fundamentally impossible.

e. It is hard for the Union to force individual member states to obey all the rules.
f. In joining the Union, a member state may have to abandon former trading partners who remain outside the Union.
g. Membership is expensive, and there is no guarantee that each member gets out as much as it puts in.

3. Essay writing

After rereading the points for and against membership of the EU, express (in writing) your own opinion and the main reasons for it.

D. Talking grammar: conditional clause: type 3

For more help on this grammar point, refer to *Bedingungssätze* in **Basic Grammar**, pp. 207–08.

1. Read and study

> The number of unemployed in Germany alone might have increased by 7 million if the country had not been in the EU.
>
> If the European Coal and Steel Community Fund had not directed modernization grants of £120 million there, those two Scottish industries would have collapsed completely.

> These are type 3 conditional sentences: each one shows how a *result* in the past or present depends on a *condition* in the past. We cannot change that condition (or its result), so condition type 3 is sometimes called an *impossible condition*.

There are 2 kinds:

if-clause	*main-clause*
past perfect	perfect conditional
If you had asked me earlier, I would have brought some money. I wouldn't have invited the Bakers if you had told me they drink so much.	
if-clause	*main-clause*
past perfect	present conditional
If you had taken the medicine when the doctor told you, you would be well again. She'd be rich now if she had invested that money in oil.	

Unit 5 Main Course

The if-clause can come at the start or the end of the sentence:

> I'd have told you if I had received the money.
> or
> If I had received the money, I'd have told you.

(Note the punctuation).

Follow-up exercise: *Arbeitsbuch*, p. 55.

2. Complete the following

On a separate sheet, make these into type 3 conditional sentences:

a. If we had got here in time ...
b. If he had taken my advice ...
c. You would not have stomach ache if you ...
d. If I had forgotten ...
e. Would you have changed your plans like that if ...?
f. They would have been absolutely delighted if ...

3. Cartoon captions

Complete the verbs in brackets so that the captions make sense:

a. I ask for mercy, judge – I (would not rob) the house if I (know) it was yours!

b. If you (not yawn) when I tried my smash, this (would not happen)!

c. If I (know) that it would cause all this trouble, I (would not ask) for a rise!

d. You (would meet) a tall handsome man if you (not come) in here!

78

E. Vocabulary

1. Matching

Match up the following expressions and definitions:

expressions	definitions
a. trading partner	1. a tariff – or tax – paid on goods coming into a country
b. industrialised country	2. one of two or more countries which agree to buy, sell and exchange products among each other
c. goods and services	3. a country which can provide its needs without buying goods from abroad
d. developing country	4. things produced or work done which can be sold
e. self-sufficient economy	5. a country that is able to produce and manufacture a lot of goods
f. import duty	6. a type of money that can be freely exchanged for other types of money
g. balance of payments	7. the difference between expenditure on imports and income from exports
h. convertible currency	8. a poor country that is trying to become richer and to improve the living conditions of its people

2. Find the correct word

Use each of the expressions from the above box once for the blanks in the following text:

Few nations can boast a (a). Consequently, virtually every nation has to engage in international trade. Put simply, it has to sell the (b) it can offer in order to buy those it needs. This is equally true whether the nation in question is an (c) or a (d). Ideally, a country's economy will be sound enough to support a (e), which is certainly the basis for a healthy (f). So the country will not feel the need to protect its home industries by imposing any (g) on the products of any (h) with whom it does business.

F. Communication practice

The languages of the EU

Like most international organizations, the EU has two sorts of languages: *official languages* and *working languages*. Official languages are used for official public documents, especially those with legal value. Working languages are the languages used internally. All languages with official legal status in one or more member countries should be official EU languages as well. This means there are now 11 official EU languages – all of them considered equal in every way. But in practice, the EU has limited much of its internal translations to German (which has the highest number of native speakers in the EU), French and English. Some informal meetings do not have interpreters at all, and are conducted in English entirely.

Native language speakers in the EU (in millions of inhabitants)

German (88.8 in Germany, Austria, Belgium, Italy and Luxembourg)
French (63.3 in France, Belgium, Italy and Luxembourg)
English (60.0 in the UK and the Republic of Ireland)
Italian (56.4 in Italy)
Spanish (39.2 in Spain)
Dutch (21.1 in the Netherlands and Belgium)
Greek (10.3 in Greece)
Portuguese (9.8 in Portugal)
Swedish (9.0 in Sweden and Finland)
Danish (5.2 in Denmark)
Finnish (4.7 in Finland)

In pairs, discuss and make notes on the following questions. Then present your opinions to the class, so that they can be discussed openly.

a. What kinds of problems can result from having so many official EU languages?
b. Are there any ways of dealing with these problems?
c. Given the importance of the EU, which languages should be taught in school in the various member states?

In your report, use some of these expressions for changing the subject:

Now the next point is …
I'd like to move on now to …
Now I'll say a few things about …
At this stage, we'd better look at …
Now, concerning …

For further reading on languages in the EU, see *Arbeitsbuch*, p. 110.

G. Further reading

Incoterms

Whether we like it or not, documentation is a large and necessary part of international trade. The International Chamber of Commerce (ICC) exists largely in order to make this documentation easier and more efficient. More exactly, they have established trading principles and rules for international usage,

Incoterms

EXW	ex works	ab Werk
FAS	free alongside ship	frei Längsseite Seeschiff
FOB	free on board	frei an Bord
FCA	free carrier	frei Frachtführer
CFR	cost and freight	Kosten und Fracht
CIF	cost, insurance, freight	Kosten, Versicherung, Fracht
CPT	carriage paid to	frachtfrei
CIP	carriage and insurance paid to	frachtfrei versichert
DES	delivered ex ship	geliefert per Schiff
DEQ	delivered ex quay	geliefert ab Kai
DAF	delivered at frontier	geliefert Grenze
DDP	delivered duty paid	geliefert verzollt
DDU	delivered duty unpaid	geliefert unverzollt

which are regularly reviewed so as to take account of new methods of transport and documentation.

Out of this have come "Incoterms" – a set of handy trade terms established through wide acceptance and use over several decades. Buyers and sellers worldwide have come to accept this uniform set of trading expressions, which allows them to determine easily the costs of an international transaction. Incoterms make explicit the obligations of both buyer and seller and concentrate on the most important trade terms. They take the form of 3-letter abbreviations, for example, FOB – "Free on Board". This means the goods are to be placed on board a ship by the seller at a port of shipment named in the sales contract. The risk of loss or damage to the goods is transferred from seller to buyer when the goods pass the ship's rail.

So, instead of spelling everything out in detail, buyer and seller can use a standard set of terms that allows them to incorporate pre-established rules into their contract. If both buyer and seller agree to adopt these terms and rules, they are binding. So, of course, it is necessary that they know exactly how this or that term works before they enter into a contract. For, in the increasingly complex world of international trade, using exact terms with exact meanings is of vital importance.

Answer the following questions:

a. What kind of changes make regular revision of ICC rules necessary?
b. What difficulties will be experienced by international traders who do not use Incoterms?
c. Can you think of any other agreed codes or sets of expressions which are used for international communication? (Do not think only of international trade.)

Follow-up exercises: *Arbeitsbuch*, pp. 20–23.

Unit 6 — Main Course

Computerization and Technology

A. Lead-in

The Internet is an electronic system by which people all over the world can communicate with each other, via their computer screen.

Smileys have become popular among Internet-users. A smiley is a combination of punctuation marks that repesents a facial expression

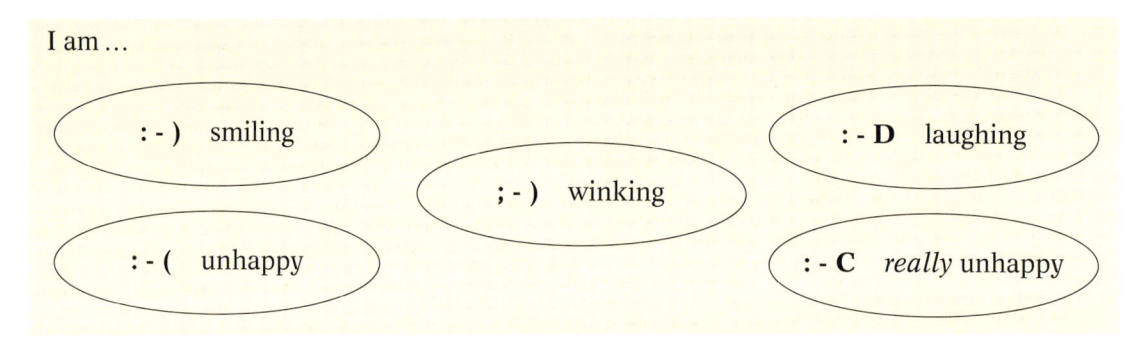

I am…

- : -) smiling
- ; -) winking
- : - D laughing
- : - (unhappy
- : - C *really* unhappy

Here are five more smileys. Try to match them with the words:

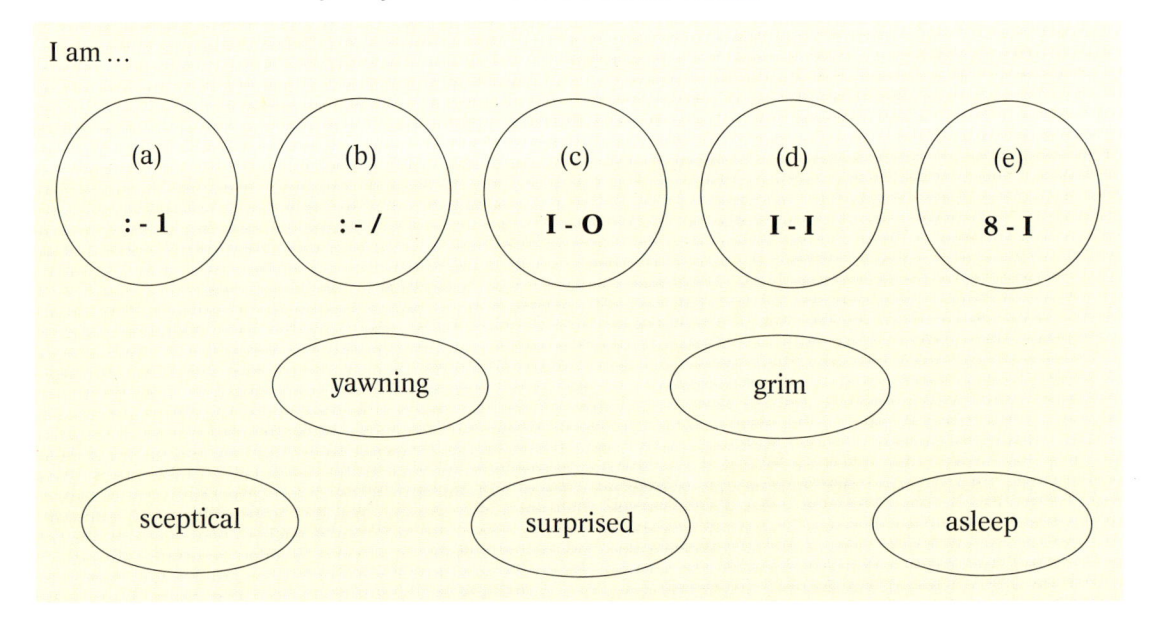

I am…

(a) : - 1
(b) : - /
(c) I - O
(d) I - I
(e) 8 - I

- yawning
- grim
- sceptical
- surprised
- asleep

B. Text

The Internet

The Internet was originally conceived back in the 1960s, as a military security network. But right from the beginning, people saw the Internet's potential for doing high-speed and efficient business. It steadily developed into a huge global market. But, for the Internet marketplace really to work, something else was needed – a system of electronic money. This would allow bills to be paid instantly. It would also allow credit to be stored easily – and there would be no need to pay bank fees. To succeed, though, electronic money had to be user-friendly and familiar to ordinary people. So a number of electronic money systems have been developed that closely resemble cash. One of these systems works like the cash dispenser we discussed earlier. First, an account is set up for the user. Then, when the user wants to withdraw an amount of cash, he or she requests it from his or her bank, via the Internet. The bank then downloads money to his or her personal computer.

Suppose the user then orders some books, through the Internet. When asked to pay, he or she has to confirm the purchase, and then his or her software transfers the required amount to the bookseller. This electronic money system goes one step beyond the cash dispenser: it is, basically, a method of "messaging" money. It also allows trade all over the globe, since money can be deposited in any currency. Paying in electronic cash cuts out expensive currency conversions for both customers and businesses. And, on top of this, electronic money is more secure than older methods of holding money.

But, when all is said and done, the big brake on the development of electronic money – or any other technology – is the customer's trust. Inventors nowadays are careful to avoid making the old mistake of believing that technology drives people. Ultimately, people themselves decide to accept a new technology – or to reject it. So an electronic money system can only succeed if it adapts to the needs of its users.

C. Comprehension and analysis

Answer these questions on the text

a. What, according to the author, are the advantages of "electronic money"?
b. Why is it impossible to introduce and use an electronic money system quickly?
c. Arrange the following parts into their correct order, so that it describes the method of "messaging" money:
   1. user's software transfers correct money to the seller
   2. user requests cash from bank, via Internet
   3. user's account is set up
   4. user confirms the purchase
   5. bank downloads money to user's personal computer
   6. user is asked to pay
   7. user orders a product or service on Internet

D. Talking grammar: gerunds and infinitives

For more help on this grammar point, refer to *Infinitiv-Gerundium* in **Basic Grammar**, pp. 211–12.

1. Look again at this sentence, which contains two verbs.

> Inventors nowadays are careful to *avoid making* the old mistake of believing that technology drives people.
>
> The form of the second verb, ending with *-ing,* is called a *gerund* (a verb used as a noun).

From the following notes, build six complete sentences, adding words as necessary. In each sentence, change the second verb into a gerund.

a. Concentrated on – listen to the lecture.
b. Was afraid of – move to a new school.
c. Interested in – join the computer course?
d. Succeeded in – get an interview for the job.
e. Apologize for – arrive late for the conference.
f. Insisted on – stay till the end of the film.

2. Look again at this sentence. It also contains two verbs.

> Ultimately, people themselves *decide to accept* a new technology.
>
> Here, the form of the second verb, together with the word *to,* is called an *infinitive.*

Rewrite the following six sentences so that the second verb is an infinitive (with *to*). Make any other necessary changes, too.

a. This is not the program which will solve our problem.
b. Simmons was the first applicant who failed the test.
c. This is the generator you can use in case of emergency.
d. We hired a secretary who would handle the complaints.
e. We need the manual which will show us how to proceed.
f. There is nothing we can do but wait for advice. (We will have …)

Follow-up exercise: *Arbeitsbuch*, pp. 56–57.

E. Vocabulary

Combine these words into six pairs, and match the pairs with the six definitions.
They have all to do with uses of computer technology.

| video | page | desktop | micro | electronic | conferencing |
| weather | processor | satellite | publishing | home | mail |

Definitions

a. a combination of computer and laser printer which allows books, magazines, etc. to be made in the office or at home
b. the central chip in a small computer which controls most of its operations
c. a system for sending written messages without the use of paper
d. a method of enabling people in different cities to see each other and have a discussion
e. a man-made object which moves around the Earth, transmitting information about winds, storms, snowfalls, and other climatic events
f. a location in the Internet run by a particular individual or organization, usually to give information about itself

F. Communication practice

Project

Prepare a report to the class about a new technical invention, product or service you have read about or seen recently:

What does it do?
Who can use it?
What does it cost?
Why is it a good/bad idea?
etc., etc.

Use some of these summarizing expressions:

In brief...
To sum up...
All in all...
In short...
On the whole...
To put it in a nutshell...

"The shop assistant said any child could read this manual. Get my daughter, Susi, on the phone, will you, Mrs Denby."

G. Further reading

Read this article from the magazine *Business and Technology News*.

The Rise of Big Blue

In 1987, IBM (International Business Machines) became the biggest and most powerful company in the world, measured in terms of share-trading on New York's Wall Street Stock Exchange. Known as "Big Blue" (due to the colour of its advertisements and commercial image), IBM was born early in this century, thanks largely to a young American called Thomas Watson. The son of poor immigrant farmers in New York State, Watson completed a course in business school before trying his hand briefly at bookkeeping. Then he discovered his real talent: selling. Working for the national Cash Register Company, he learned some aggressive techniques aimed at pushing rivals out of business. He then moved to a business in which he soon took control of a group of tabulating and recording machine companies.

These companies owned a patent on record machines which used punch-cards (cards with tiny holes which could be "read" by a machine). These – the world's first computers – had been invented by Hermann Hollerith, the son of a German immigrant family. In fact, in Germany in 1910, Hollerith had founded a company called Dehomag (Deutsche Hollerith Maschinen Gesellschaft mbH) a whole year before Thomas Watson formed the group which later became IBM.

Mainly by making his customers dependent on the products and services of IBM, Watson managed to capture a huge 90% share of the rapidly expanding computer market. His methods continued to succeed, even during the risk-filled period of the 1950s, when technological development was rapid. 1953 saw the introduction onto the market of IBM's first electronic calculator. And by 1956, the company had 85% of America's business market, mainly because (as Watson had planned) so many U.S. businesses were already dependent on IBM punch-card machines.

So "Big Blue" has continued to grow through the last three decades, always adapting quickly to changes in technology.

Answer the following questions:

a. What role was played by German-born Hermann Hollerith in the development of IBM?
b. Describe Watson's method of giving IBM a hold on the U.S. market.
c. "Big Blue" continually adapted to changes in technology in order to keep up with competitors. Think of some examples of changes they had to adapt to – or future changes they may have to adapt to.

Follow-up exercise: *Arbeitsbuch*, pp. 23–24.

The Development of a Product

A. Lead-in

These figures show what percentages of young people (aged 16–19) in Britain spend part of their leisure time in sports activities.

	males	females
outdoor games		
football	21	1
rugby	4	–
golf	4	1
cricket	4	–
tennis	4	3
other sports		
athletics	7	4
swimming (indoor)	13	15
swimming (outdoor)	8	7
horse riding	1	4
bicycling	6	4
darts	20	7
billiards/snooker	36	8
tenpin bowling	2	1

Do any of the figures surprise you?
How many of these sports have you participated in yourself?
Which are not at all popular in Germany?
Which are well-known in Germany?
Which sports popular in Germany have little or no popularity among young people in Britain?
Sun Athletics is an American manufacturer specializing in highly colourful sports goods for young people (both sexes). Which game do you think offers the best possibility for that firm on the British market? Why?

B. Text

Developing "Stardrive"

One August morning, the Management team of Sun Athletics met to consider a report from their Market Research section. They knew they would have to make a major decision that morning: whether to launch a colourful new tennis racket onto the very competitive sports goods market in Britain. They had already met with some success in Germany, with their brightly-coloured "Sun" basketball, but the British sports scene was different. The company's Market Research section had reported a strong growth in British youngsters' spending on tennis equipment. In their sales forecast, they estimated that the teenage market there seemed ready for a new kind of tennis racket. "The new model", they said, "does not have to be cheaper than rackets already available. But, to appeal to young people, it must not be produced in old-fashioned, conventional colours. We must aim for something new and daring."

So the Engineering and Design section was set to work. With the main outdoor season due to begin in the spring, there was no time to be lost. Soon, they had come up with several very colourful new models. These were studied by the Planning and Control section who, cooperating closely with Financial Control section, finally chose a yellow and red model called "Stardrive". Soon after, Financial Control sent in their budget report on "Stardrive", with estimates of the production, publicity and distribution costs of the new model.

By Christmas, production deadlines had been decided on. The necessary materials were ordered from the Stores and Purchasing section, and the Shop Floor (where the rackets were actually to be made) received their production orders. It was made clear to everyone involved in production that they should tell no-one about the new product. Until "Stardrive" was officially launched in Britain, neither the public nor the company's rivals were supposed to know about it.

C. Comprehension and analysis

1. Study this flow chart of Sun Athletics' production process. What are the missing labels in boxes A, B and C? Use the text to guide you.

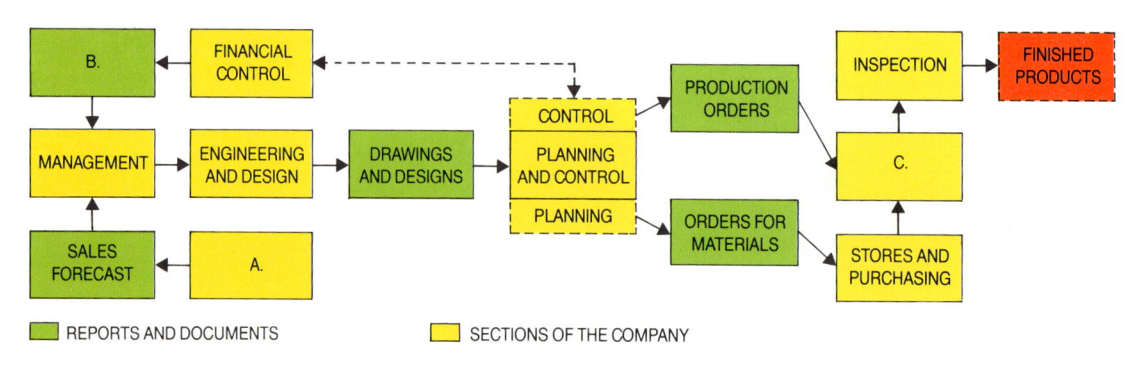

2. If you were planning to launch a new product, what would you do before deciding for or against the plan?

D. Talking grammar: auxiliaries (part II)

For more help on this grammar point, refer to *Modale Hilfsverben* in **Basic Grammar**, pp. 206–07.

1. Uses

Look at the use of the verbs in italics in these sentences:

> They *should* tell no-one about the new product.
> We *must* aim for something new and daring.
> They would *have to* make a major decision that morning.
> The new model *does not have to* be cheaper than rackets already available.
> It *must* not be produced in old-fashioned conventional colours.

Let us examine some of these (auxiliary) verbs:

a. *should + ought to*

> *obligation*
>
> In *should*-sentences, the speaker recognizes an obligation, but it isn't necessarily fulfilled:

> You should be courteous to strangers (but I don't know if you are).
> They should tell no-one about the new product (but perhaps some of them will).
> I should go to football practice tonight (but I'll go to the cinema instead).

> *advisability*

> You should leave now if you want to catch the 5.30 train.

> *strong probability*

> The job is well paid – it should be easy to find someone for it.

89

Ought to has much the same meaning as *should*. But notice the difference in form:

I should I ought to	go to my French class.
I should I ought to	finish the work tonight. (We will probably finish it *or* we have an obligation to finish it.)

b. *must + have to*

obligation

Must is also similar to *should*. But, while *should* indicates an obligation which may not be fulfilled, *must* indicates one which the speaker intends to fulfil. Look at these differences:

> I should go to football practice tonight, but I'm going to the cinema instead.
> I must go to football practice tonight – that's why I can't go to the cinema.

necessity

Sometimes an obligation is so strong, we can regard it as a necessity:

> We must aim for something new and daring.
> The emergency exit must be kept clear at all times.

inference

Sometimes, *must* shows that the speaker has arrived at a logical conclusion:

> I always see him leaving the station at 9 o'clock. He must come by train each day.

Have to has much the same meaning as *must*. But note the difference in form:

I must I have to	read the whole book.

2. Past tense forms

The auxiliaries discussed in this unit have special past tense forms. Look at the following table:

verb change	example
should → should have	I should have gone to football practice last night (but I went to the cinema instead).
ought to → ought to have (+ participle)	I ought to have finished the work last night.
must *have to → had to* (obligation)	I had to read the whole book.
must → must have (logical conclusion)	There's a lot of water around. It must have rained here yesterday.

3. Negative forms

Must not and *do not have to* express different meanings. Compare:

> You *must not* visit patients after 10 p. m. (It is against the rules of the hospital.)
> You *do not have to* visit patients after 10 p. m. (You are free to come earlier, if you wish.)
>
> It must not be produced in old-fashioned, conventional colours. (It is necessary to choose new colours.)
> The new model does not have to be cheaper than rackets already available. (It may be cheaper or dearer.)

Follow-up exercise: *Arbeitsbuch,* pp. 57–58.

4. Rewrite the sentences

Rewrite these guidelines, using the verbs indicated:

From: Management
To: Head of Publicity, Europe
Re: Stardrive Advertising Campaign in Britain

Not necessary to promote "Stardrive" as a cheap racket (a/ not have to). But it's important to make it appeal to the British teenage market (b/ have to). It's best to aim for 16-19 year olds (c/ ought to). Aim for lively colours in the adverts (d/ must). And avoid using pictures of older players (e/ must not). Therefore, I suggest you sign up a leading British tennis star to sponsor "Stardrive" as soon as possible (f/ should).

Our advertising methods were successful in Germany. So I think it isn't necessary to change these methods in Britain (g/ not have to). However, we did make a mistake in not advertising the "Sun" basketball on German TV (h/ should). It will be necessary to examine TV advertising possibilities in Britain (i/ must). Also, last year, because we overestimated demand in Germany, we were forced to sell the last 200 basketballs at half-price (j/ have to). If only we had been more careful (k/ ought to)! Let's be sure not to overestimate this time (l/ must not).

Finally, while planning the campaign, keep a close eye on new products from European rivals (m/ ought to).

E. Vocabulary

Study this structure diagram and complete the blanks in the text which follows it, using the list at the end.

Multinational Corporations

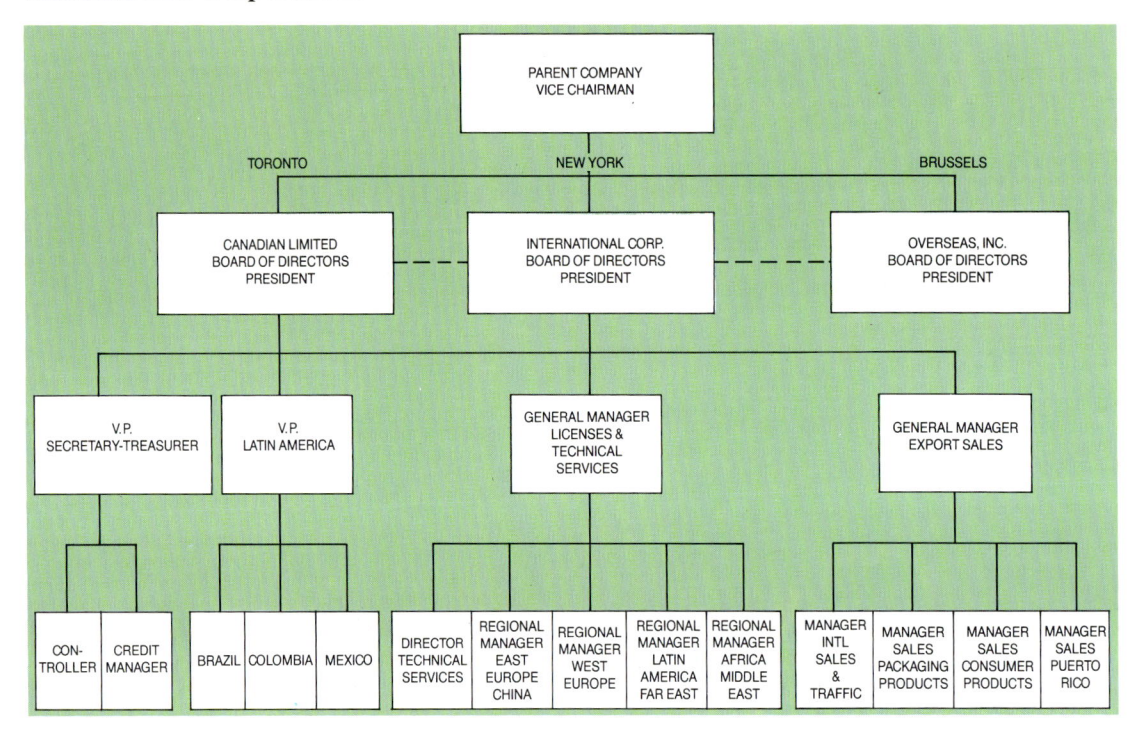

Sun Athletics is not an independent company, since 51% of it is owned by a Multinational Corporation (MNC), called Müller-Schmidt. An MNC is (a). Originally, Müller-Schmidt owned a few small engineering firms in Munich. But they expanded gradually into the U.S., Europe and South America, investing in sports goods, furniture, plastics and metal box producers. One of the chief strengths of an MNC is that it gets its income from (b), so it is able to spread the risk of a market collapse in a particular product or industry. MNCs are typically made up of foreign subsidiaries – in other words, (c). MNCs organize themselves, and reinvest their profits, so as to increase their access to world resources (such as (d)) and their market share. The subsidiaries have a lot of (e), but major decisions are made centrally, by (f) in Munich. They set the long-range goals, while the subsidiaries run local operations and even develop new products, like "Stardrive".

Müller-Schmidt were welcomed into other countries because they created (g). But they face difficulties too – strong trade unions in France; communication and cultural barriers in South America; unfavourable tax laws in the U.S. Also, Müller-Schmidt has to protect its (h) – a difficult thing when dealing in foreign currencies. And foreign governments may interfere with big MNCs in their countries, because of the unhealthy degree of (i) the MNCs can acquire.

– decision-making power
– diversified sources
– the parent company

– foreign assets
– new jobs, new products and new technology
– economic and political power
– raw materials, manpower and capital
– companies in which the parent company owns over 50%
– an organization controlling companies in several countries

F. Communication practice

1. Read and arrange

The following six communications are about the transportation of the first consignment of "Stardrive". Arrange them into the right order and summarize the course of events.

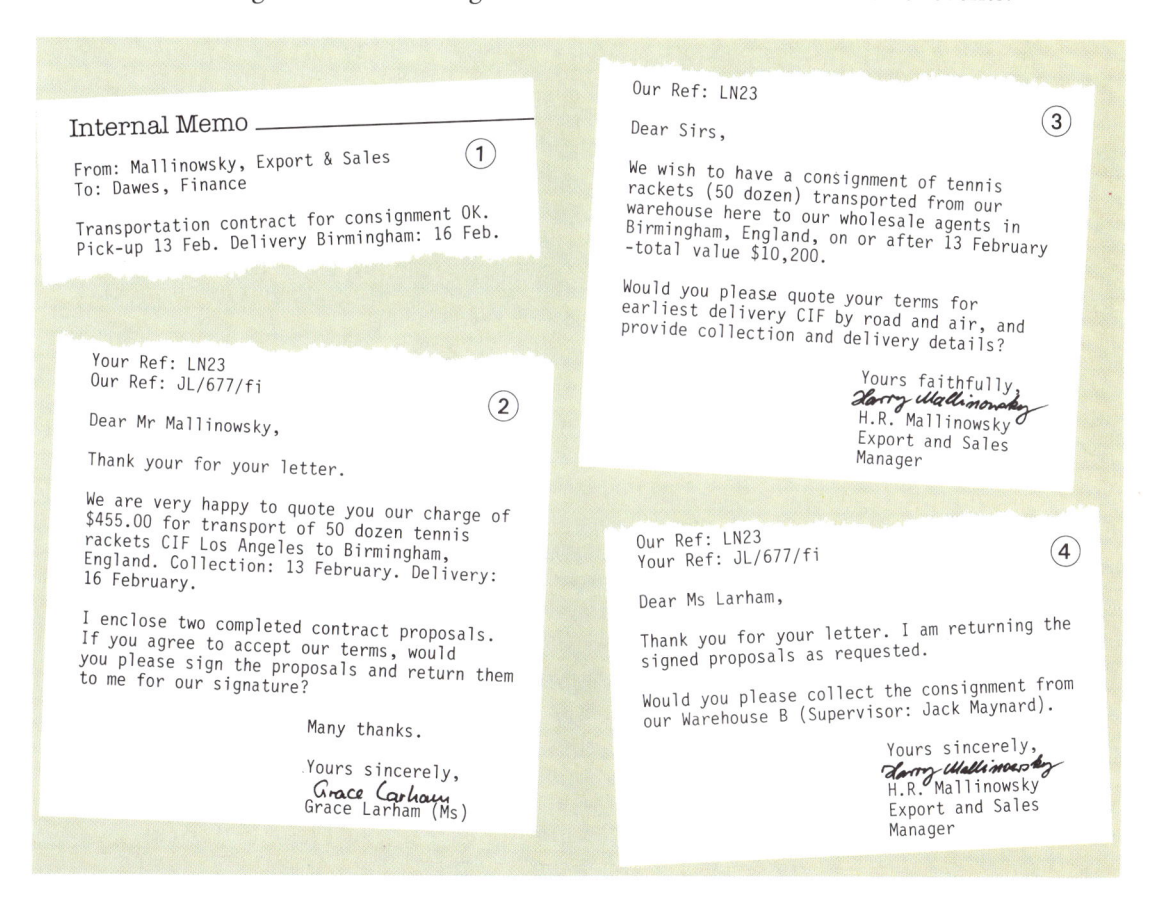

(1) Internal Memo

From: Mallinowsky, Export & Sales
To: Dawes, Finance

Transportation contract for consignment OK. Pick-up 13 Feb. Delivery Birmingham: 16 Feb.

(2)

Your Ref: LN23
Our Ref: JL/677/fi

Dear Mr Mallinowsky,

Thank your for your letter.

We are very happy to quote you our charge of $455.00 for transport of 50 dozen tennis rackets CIF Los Angeles to Birmingham, England. Collection: 13 February. Delivery: 16 February.

I enclose two completed contract proposals. If you agree to accept our terms, would you please sign the proposals and return them to me for our signature?

Many thanks.

Yours sincerely,
Grace Larham
Grace Larham (Ms)

(3)

Our Ref: LN23

Dear Sirs,

We wish to have a consignment of tennis rackets (50 dozen) transported from our warehouse here to our wholesale agents in Birmingham, England, on or after 13 February -total value $10,200.

Would you please quote your terms for earliest delivery CIF by road and air, and provide collection and delivery details?

Yours faithfully,
H.R. Mallinowsky
Export and Sales Manager

(4)

Our Ref: LN23
Your Ref: JL/677/fi

Dear Ms Larham,

Thank you for your letter. I am returning the signed proposals as requested.

Would you please collect the consignment from our Warehouse B (Supervisor: Jack Maynard).

Yours sincerely,
H.R. Mallinowsky
Export and Sales Manager

Unit 7 — Main Course

Internal Memo ⑤

From: Dawes, Finance
To: Mallinowsky, Export & Sales

Wd U contact our forwarding agent & arrange transport of consignment LN23: 50 dozen Stardrive to our wholesalers in Birmingham. 13 Feb earliest. Pls inform me of pick-up & delivery dates.

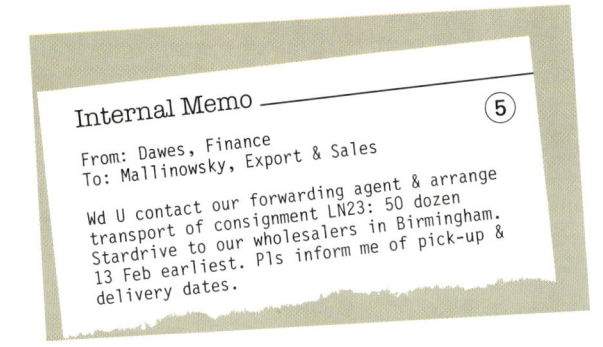

Your Ref: LN23
Our Ref: JL/677/fi ⑥

Dear Mr Mallinowsky,

I have received the signed contracts for the above consignment. Your copy is enclosed. I have arranged for pick-up at Warehouse B at 10.00a.m., 13 February.

We look forward to receiving further orders from you in the future.

Yours sincerely,
Grace Larham
Grace Larham (Ms)
Applications and Claims Dept

---

2. Now listen to the "mystery" phone conversation. As you listen, answer these questions:

   a. Who is making the call?
   b. Who is receiving the call?
   c. On which date?
   d. Who has sent a fax?

G. Further reading

Distribution of Goods

Manufacturers like Sun Athletics usually sell their products to wholesalers in bulk quantities. Each wholesaler then supplies the products to a number of retailers, who then sell them to the individual customers. In the case of "Stardrive" rackets, Sun Athletics' wholesaler in Britain delivered quantities of the new product to sports goods shops, where individual tennis players could see and buy it.

To export in this way, Sun Athletics needed forwarding agents – people who operate freight services around the world. Good cooperation between manufacturer, forwarding agent, wholesaler and retailer can greatly reduce the cost of moving products from factory to customer – and, as a result, reduce the price of the product itself.

But the question is often asked, "Why don't manufacturers ship their goods directly to retailers, so as to cut out the wholesaler and lower the price?" After all, the services of the wholesaler raise the selling price of the product by several per cent above the price he pays to the manufacturer. The basic answer is that the wholesaler is needed to make sure that goods find their way to the people who want them. But he also functions as a kind of valve, adjusting and regulating the flow of goods, and holding stocks of goods until they are required. Thanks to the wholesaler, manufacturers can keep up a steady production flow, regardless of short-term changes in supply and demand. And, conversely, the retailer does not need to maintain large stocks, because when consumer demand arises he can simply call on the wholesaler for supplies.

Answer the following questions:

a. Describe the function of a wholesaler in a single sentence.
b. What is the main benefit of a wholesaler, as far as the producer is concerned?
c. "Good co-operation between manufacturer, forwarding agent, wholesaler, and retailer can greatly reduce the cost." Can you think of ways in which this could happen?

Follow-up exercise: *Arbeitsbuch*, pp. 25–26.

Employment and Unemployment

A. Lead-in

Look at this advertisement and answer the questions which follow.

Now you can give young people a job and get paid for it.

There's a new scheme which allows you to take on young workers at realistic wages, and be paid £15 a week for each one.

It's as simple as that. No administrative problems. No complicated red tape.

In fact, no strings.

It's called the New Workers Scheme. Ideal for small and medium-sized businesses, but still attractive to large businesses.

The conditions are minimal.

The jobs must be full-time for one year. The wages must be no more than £55 (under 20), or £65 (aged 20).

You can take on as many workers as you like.

The people must be under 21, in their first year of employment and no longer eligible for YTS. Of course, they may have already completed YTS, perhaps even with you.

Jobcentres and Careers Offices will be glad to tell you about eligible young people.

And that's really all it is. Simple to set up and run. You'll be helping out young people, and helping yourself expand, without getting involved in unrealistic labour costs.

For more information dial 100 and ask for FREEFONE NEW WORKERS. (Lines are open from 9.00 am to 9.00 pm, seven days a week).

Or send in the coupon below.

ACTION FOR JOBS

To: New Workers Scheme, FREEPOST, Curzon House, 20-24 Lonsdale Road, London NW6 4YP Please send me details of the New Workers Scheme.
Name
Company
Position
Address

New Workers Scheme
Department of Employment DE

Unit 8 — Main Course

Notes

red tape: official paperwork (e. g. filling in forms)
no strings: (short form of) "no strings attached", i. e. no extra conditions
YTS: Youth Training Scheme, a government scheme for helping schoolleavers get work experience
Jobcentres and Careers Offices: government agencies which help people find work

a. Who is the advert aimed at?
b. How many advantages of the New Workers Scheme are mentioned in the advert? What are they?
c. Can you think of any *disadvantages*? Make a list of them.
d. Why do you think the Department of Employment are offering a scheme like this? Why do you think it is open only to people under 21?

B. Text

Newspaper Article

Government Predicts Unemployed Will Fall "below 3 million"

London, 16 April

A sharp drop in the number of unemployed has led the Government to predict that the total will fall below 3 million within a couple of months. Figures for March, just published, show that the total dropped by 30,100 to 3,042,900 – its lowest level for two-and-a-half years. There has been a downward trend since last August, and the March figure is 156,000 lower than a year ago. The total is falling steadily by 25,000 a month.

The Government's Minister of Employment welcomed the new figures. But according to an Opposition party representative, "Today's reduction reveals the Government's attempt to deceive the nation about the state of unemployment in the country. The figures show a shamefully distorted picture". He claimed that the reduction over the past 7 months was mostly due to special employment schemes. Schoolleavers, in particular, were being attracted to temporary training and "work experience" schemes.

"These measures mean that the Government can claim they have reduced the unemployment figures to 3 million by June," declared the Opposition spokesman, in reaction to the new figures. "The true level of unemployment is nearer 5,250,000," he insisted. The Minister of Employment pointed out that an international definition counts as unemployed "those without a job who are actively looking for work. For Great Britain, that definition puts unemployment below 3 million."

Despite the improved figures, there are still 1.4 million who have been out of work for more than a year. This compares with less than 0.5 million six years earlier.

C. Comprehension and analysis

1. Answer the following questions

a. Why did the Government expect the next unemployment figures to be less than 3 million?
b. Is the New Workers Scheme (see the advertisement above) an example of the kind of scheme the Opposition party spokesman referred to? Why or why not?
c. Why did he believe the true level of unemployment to be nearer 5,250,000?
d. Do you know of any similar government scheme? Do you think it is a success, a partial success or a failure? Give reasons.

2. True or false?

First, look at these unemployment statistics. They relate to a 10-month period: June to March. Are the following statements true or false? If false, correct them.

Regional Unemployment in Britain

(% of all employees)	June	March
South East	8.5	7.9
East Anglia	8.8	8.5
South West	9.7	9.2
East Midlands	11.1	10.6
Yorks & Humberside	13.6	12.7
West Midlands	13.8	12.8
Scotland	14.0	13.7
North	14.1	15.7
North West	14.3	13.4
Northern Ireland	18.6	18.6

a. Between June and March, the employment situation worsened in the North.
b. The employment situation remained unchanged in Northern Ireland.
c. Unemployment in the North West fell by more than 1%.
d. Unemployment in the South East worsened.
e. Employment figures improved in all but two of the regions.

D. Talking grammar: reporting verbs

For more help on this grammar point, refer to *Indirekte Rede* in **Basic Grammar,** pp. 208–09.

In Unit 2, we practised reporting speech. We shall now practise another way of doing this:

1. Look at the verbs in italics in these sentences.

> He *claimed* that the reduction over the past 7 months was mostly due to special employment schemes.
>
> "These measures mean that the Government can claim they have reduced the unemployment figures to 3 million by June", *declared* the Opposition spokesman.
>
> "The true level of unemployment is nearer 5,250,000," he *insisted*.
>
> The Minister of Employment *pointed out* that an international definition counts as unemployed "those without a job who are actively looking for work".

Claimed, declared, pointed out, etc. are reporting verbs. They are more expressive than *said.*

Note:
a. In writing, we often reverse the normal order of subject (i.e. speaker) and reporting verb:
declared the spokesman *or* the spokesman declared
b. In writing, we can put the reporting verb before *or* after the reported information:
"... to 3 million by June," declared the spokesman. *Or:* Declared the spokesman, "These measures mean ..."

2. Match these sentences with the reporting verbs which follow. Use each verb once.

– "Look, this is the way to do it," he (a).
– "I'll be here again tomorrow," she (b).
– "Why don't you visit them tomorrow?" he (c).
– "It was entirely my fault," she (d).
– "You must stay another night – you can't leave so soon," he (e).
– "You're always talking about football, and you know I'm not interested in it," she (f).
– "In this city, most shops are closed on Monday," he (g).
– "You tried to leave without paying," she (h).
– "Are you related to Mrs Danby, by any chance?" he (i).
– "We can now give you the official result of the election," she (j).

enquired	accused	complained
suggested	pointed out	insisted
admitted	explained	
promised	announced	

Follow-up exercise: *Arbeitsbuch*, pp. 58–59.

E. Vocabulary

1. NVQs means National Vocational Qualifications. They are British qualifications based on skills and work done in industry and commerce. You cannot get NVQs by attending classes.

2. The information below is about a programme to train people for NVQs in Administration. As you read it, find phrases in the text which fit these meanings:

a. (3 words): conditions to be satisfied before beginning the programme
b. (4 words): ability in reading, writing and mathematics
c. (2 words): receive credit
d. (2 words): at the business college
e. (2 words): simple manual uses of computers
f. (3 words): general skill and ability in the job
g. (2 words): sending messages by fax, e-mail, etc.
h. (4 words): independently, not under supervision
i. (2 words): independent judge, from outside the organization

Royal Society of Arts (RSA) – NVQs in Administration

Level 1 – Foundation
Level 2 – Intermediate
Level 3 – Advanced

This programme is ideally suited to those wishing to attain up-to-date office skills and experience on a flexible basis.

Entry Requirements

Levels 1 and 2 have no formal entry requirements other than basic literacy and numeracy skills. Level 3 requires competence at Level 2 either in the form of a certificate or evidence of past office experience.
The programme is designed for those attracted to work in an office environment or those already employed who would like to extend their skills or gain recognition for their previous experience.

Programme Content

Programmes are delivered on a flexible basis on campus or entirely in the workplace.
Level 1:
Contains nine units and is designed for complete newcomers to office work. It includes: basic keyboarding; filing; telephone work; reprographics; reception; mail; etc.
Level 2:
Contains nine units and is designed to develop existing skills and produce all-round professional competence. It includes: planning and organizing own work; using computer applications; electronic transmission; responding to correspondence; etc.
Level 3:
Contains ten units and is designed for those wishing to work on their own initiative and undertake more responsibility. Some experience or access to supervisory work is necessary. Guidance is provided, with assessment taking place on the job or on work experience.
If you have office experience/competence but have no qualification to show for it, you may be able to obtain accreditation without participating in the full programme.
All the above qualifications may be integrated with other skills subjects.

Assessment

Units are assessed in the workplace throughout the year and client evidence is sampled by an external verifier. There is no examination.

Follow-up exercise: *Arbeitsbuch*, pp. 71–72.

F. Communication practice

1. Training for Life

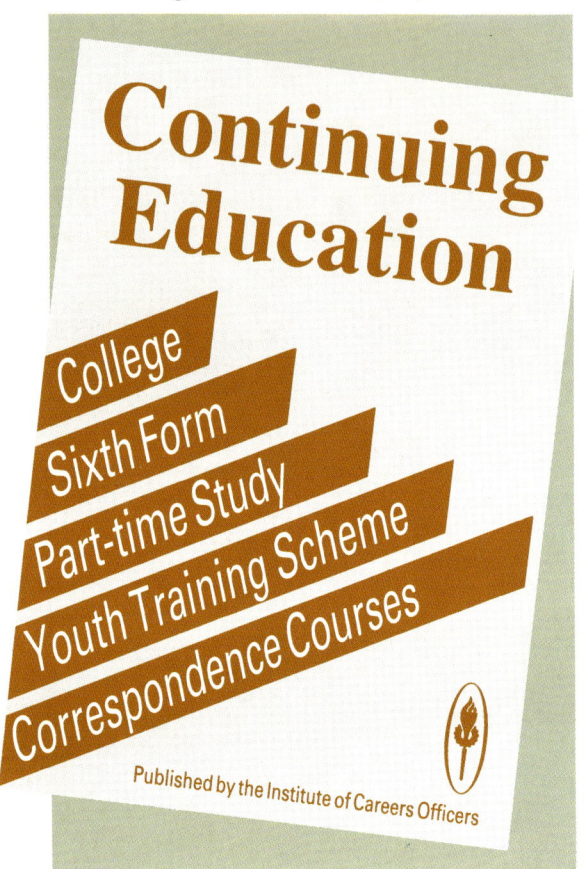

Continuing Education
College
Sixth Form
Part-time Study
Youth Training Scheme
Correspondence Courses

Published by the Institute of Careers Officers

The following recording presents part of a discussion between
- Lorraine, a schoolleaver
- Madeleine, a representative of a training scheme called Training for Life.

Listen and, in pairs, find 5 phrases in the interview which have the following meanings. Each phrase has 2 words.

a. the right kind of job
b. abilities in dealing with people
c. one day a week taken off work, in order to train or study
d. someone who helps young people choose a profession or job
e. a time in which someone is tested to see if he or she is suitable

Write down the 5 phrases in a list, then compare them with other pairs' lists. You should all have the same phrases on your lists.

2. Jobclub

Read the brochure on the following page advertising an organization which was founded to help people find work. Then try to match the labels with the blanks.

Jobfinder

The aim of Jobfinder is to help you find the best possible job in the shortest time. This means we don't just try to push you into any old job, but help you find the right one for you.

To help you do this, we spend some time in small groups discussing the different ways to go about looking for work. We look at

★ Where to find jobs
★ Preparation of your CV
★ How to make effective phone calls and applications
★ How to really "sell yourself" at interview

You will also be able to discuss your situation on an individual, one-to-one basis with the Jobfinder Leader.

Main Course — Unit 8

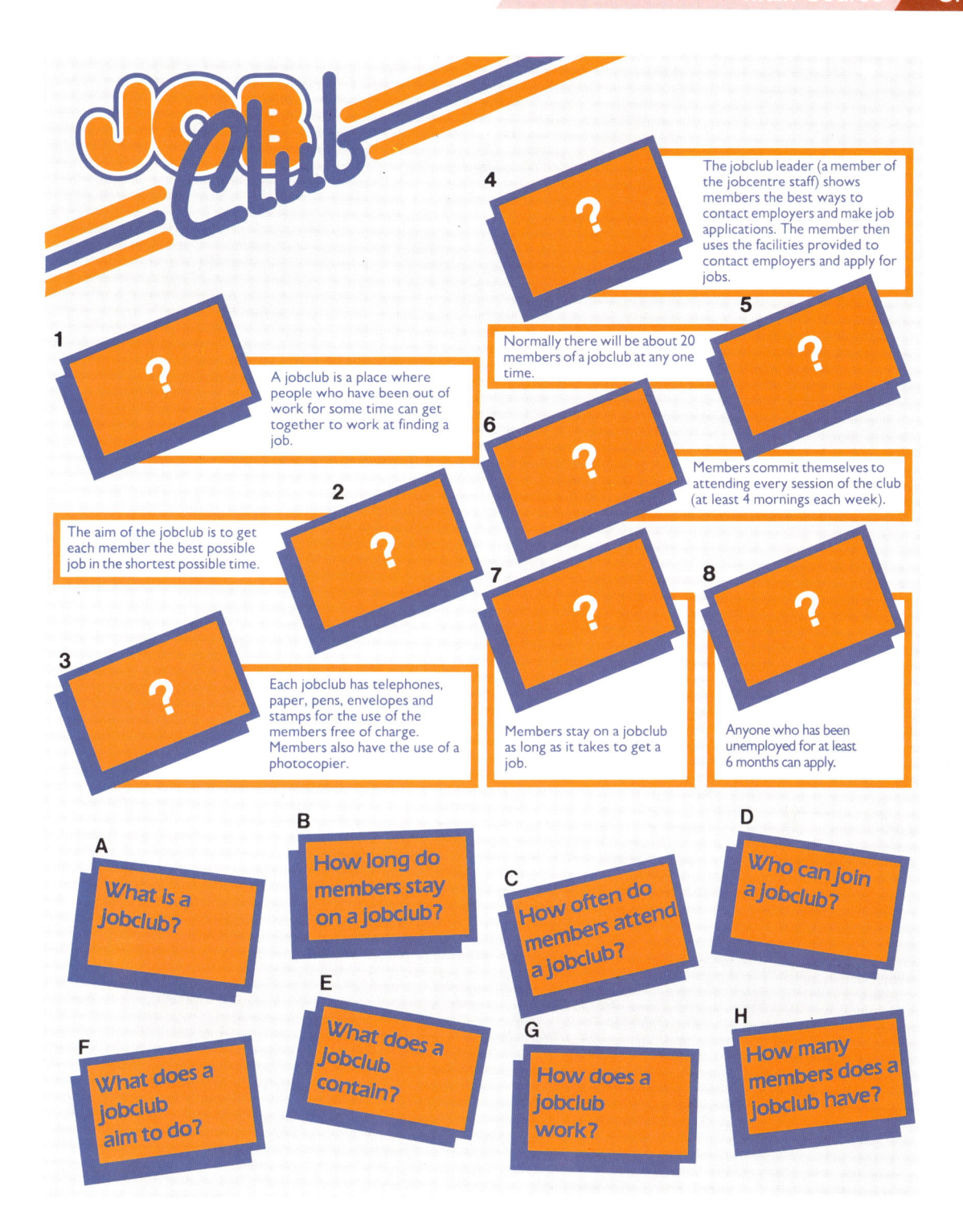

Job Club

1. ❓
A jobclub is a place where people who have been out of work for some time can get together to work at finding a job.

2. ❓
The aim of the jobclub is to get each member the best possible job in the shortest possible time.

3. ❓
Each jobclub has telephones, paper, pens, envelopes and stamps for the use of the members free of charge. Members also have the use of a photocopier.

4. ❓
The jobclub leader (a member of the jobcentre staff) shows members the best ways to contact employers and make job applications. The member then uses the facilities provided to contact employers and apply for jobs.

5. ❓
Normally there will be about 20 members of a jobclub at any one time.

6. ❓
Members commit themselves to attending every session of the club (at least 4 mornings each week).

7. ❓
Members stay on a jobclub as long as it takes to get a job.

8. ❓
Anyone who has been unemployed for at least 6 months can apply.

A. What is a jobclub?

B. How long do members stay on a jobclub?

C. How often do members attend a jobclub?

D. Who can join a jobclub?

E. What does a jobclub contain?

F. What does a jobclub aim to do?

G. How does a jobclub work?

H. How many members does a jobclub have?

G. Further reading

Text 1

New Industries for Old

Britain's traditional export industries can no longer find a world market. Consequently, the industrial economy of the country has had to change – a painful process which has led to unemployment (see article on page 96). It has been possible to create new jobs in Britain only with new industries and businesses.

The electronics industry has been one of the fastest developing industries in the British economy. It is largely situated in central Scotland, nicknamed Silicon Glen (after the larger and better-known Silicon Valley in California). Scottish factories produce computers, silicon chips and other electronic components. The fact that 250 companies employed 42,000 workers in the narrow area between Edinburgh and Glasgow seems to prove the point just mentioned – that new industries and businesses create new jobs.

In fact, while the computer industry is important to the British economy, it has not created many new jobs. Of course, it brought relief to a hard-working, well-educated Scottish labour force whose steel mills and shipyards had disappeared. But the computer industry was not able to absorb the 16% of Scotland's labour force who were unemployed. More important, the companies who buy the industry's computer products often require fewer workers as a result – and the ones who lose their jobs are usually unskilled and unable to find alternative employment.

Furthermore, a few large foreign (mostly U.S.) companies dominate the Scottish computer industry, having been attracted to Britain by government grants. Whenever these companies have to cut their production, they tend to decide that the jobs must be lost in their foreign branches (e. g. in Scotland), rather than in their own countries.

Answer the following questions:
1. Why has Britain tried to develop new industries?
2. How do the electronics companies seem to help solve the problems of Britain's industrial economy?
3. In what two ways is the effect of the computer industry on employment not very beneficial?
4. Can you think of any other difficulties associated with bringing new industries into an area whose old ones have run down?

Text 2

The Youth Training Scheme

1. Look at this cartoon. Describe the situation and the characters in it.
What do you think the cartoonist is suggesting?
What could be a main criticism of the Youth Training Scheme (YTS)?

2. Now read this newspaper extract about the Youth Training Scheme:

When Britain was faced with a rise in youth unemployment in the 1980s, the Government reformed vocational training by creating the Youth Training Scheme (YTS). This was intended to give schoolleavers a year's training and education. It was not planned as an answer to youth unemployment, but rather as a way of creating opportunities for young people, especially those who in the past had been left untrained, unskilled and unqualified.

But no other country had been able to construct a worthwhile 1-year programme of vocational training. So, many people asked, how could Britain expect to do so – especially when she trailed far behind other countries in her vocational training methods? As an illustration, when government inspectors visited 34 colleges offering vocational and pre-vocational courses, they found that "study skills" (e. g. student-centred learning, use of the library, private study activities) were seriously neglected. Furthermore, Britain was the only major industrial economy where the majority of young people expect to start work at 16 without further education and training.

The weaknesses of a 1-year scheme soon became apparent. Plans for a 2-year YTS were discussed, and the organizers looked at the relatively successful German system of vocational training and the *Berufsbildungsgesetz*. In Germany, British observers reported, young people had the chance to get a recognized vocational qualification at the end of the (2-year) course. These qualified trainees had little difficulty getting a job – either in the firm where they did their training or somewhere else. A company training school in Munich, for example, offered employment to all their qualified trainees (250 per year). As a result of all this, the British Youth Training Scheme was extended to two years, and formal qualifications were introduced.

3. Answer the following questions:
a. Why did a big change in vocational training become necessary?
b. Why did the 1-year YTS seem unlikely to succeed?
c. Why did German vocational training attract attention in Britain?
d. Do you think the German scheme has any advantages or disadvantages not mentioned in the text?

Follow-up exercises: *Arbeitsbuch*, pp. 27–28 and 74–75.

Resources and the Environment

A. Lead-in

1. Our natural resources can be divided into

- "depleting" resources: they will one day disappear if we keep using them, e. g. oil;
- "non-depleting" resources: they are not affected by human use, and will not disappear, e. g. the sun.

Divide these resources into depleting and non-depleting:

fresh water   coal
wind   nuclear power
timber   natural (underground) gas

2. Which of the following priorities do you see as (a) the most urgent, (b) least urgent? Give reasons for your choices:

- supplying food for everyone
- stopping depletion of energy resources
- preserving adequate living space
- keeping the world's population growth under control
- controlling the world's climate
- expanding research in space
- saving water
- giving all societies a share of basic resources
- developing alternative forms of energy

B. Text

Water, Water Everywhere

The human race is using up some of its natural resources very quickly. Rich and poor nations alike are coming to accept the need for a more planned and careful use of resources.
⁵ Take water, for example. All living things need it for survival, but many of us think of it as a free, unlimited resource. And, since about 70% of the earth's surface has been covered by water for around 600 million years, there is no real danger that we will run ¹⁰ short of it in the future.

The picture is not that simple, though. First, very little of this natural resource comes to us as fresh (that is, drinkable) water. Second, human population growth is making tremendous demands on water supply. The United Nations has estimated that by the year 2000, the world's population will be about 6,000 million, more than half of whom will be living in cities. This will mean a huge demand not only for drinking water. Due to economic progress, more and more water is also consumed by industry, as the following figures show:

In order to make	this much water is needed (in litres)
1 litre of petroleum	10
1 can of vegetables	40
1 kilogram of paper	100
1 ton of woolen cloth	600
1 ton of dry cement	4,500
1 ton of steel	20,500

In fact, our water needs are increasing several times more rapidly than the growth of the population. Clearly, we need to plan our water use more carefully.

But what does this mean in practice? Perhaps the first idea that you can think of is to purify seawater, as (for example) a big desalting plant does at Rosario Beach in California. It can freshen up to 7,500,000 gallons of seawater per day. Also, waste water could be treated in order to reuse it. Something else that you probably thought of is conserving water. For example, for their cooling processes, industries could use only low-quality water. Evaporation from reservoirs could be scientifically controlled so as to conserve the supply. And, particularly in developing countries, wasteful water supply systems could be modernized.

There is sufficient water to meet all needs if this resource is properly developed and managed. River control is an illustration of this. In the late 1980s, the River Rhine became so contaminated by industrial waste that it could no longer support any form of life. Water supply in continental land masses like Europe has been compared to the blood circulation of the human body. Just as a continent has its rivers, so the body has its arteries. But the body also has its veins, to transport away waste and impure products. We have to prevent impure water (our domestic and industrial waste) from entering the rivers – the "arteries" of the continent. As a direct result of the contamination of the Rhine, a number of European states, including Germany, introduced laws and a system of controls to guard against, and limit, future pollution of major rivers.

C. Comprehension and analysis

Answer the following questions:

a. In what two ways does increased population mean increased water consumption?
b. What is the point of the writer's reference to arteries and veins?
c. In your opinion, what methods of conserving water would be possible in your own environment?
d. Look at the following advertisement. What does the picture suggest? And what does the text point out?

Unit 9 — Main Course

[Amanda age 5]

Is this how you see a multi-billion pound industry?

If only supplying water was this simple.

But it takes an industry, and no pint-sized industry at that, to get water where you want it when you want it.

Not just supplying water to 74% of homes, but taking it away again.

Last year the 10 Water and Sewage Businesses of England and Wales had a turnover approaching £3 billion and re-invested over £1 billion.

But unlike other industrial giants most of our infrastructure is out of sight.

Much of it below ground.

You don't see much, but then that's one of our great strengths.

And goes some way towards making turning on the tap, child's play.

If you would like to know more about us, write to: The Water Authorities Association, P.O. Box 358, London SW1H 9YQ.

The 10 Water and Sewage Businesses of England and Wales.

ANGLIAN WATER · NORTHUMBRIAN WATER · NORTH WEST WATER · SEVERN TRENT WATER · SOUTHERN WATER · SOUTH WEST WATER · THAMES WATER · WELSH WATER · WESSEX WATER · YORKSHIRE WATER

D. Talking grammar: pronoun use

Notice how the pronouns in italics (below) refer back to something:

We need to plan our water use more carefully. But what does *this* mean in practice?

...as a big desalting plant does at Rosario Beach in California. *It* can freshen up to 7,500,000 gallons of seawater per day.

Pronouns – words like *this/these* and *it* – are useful: they *refer back* to something. Notice how pronouns

- avoid repetition
- keep key phrases alive in the reader's mind
- keep a text linked together

On a separate sheet, complete the following sentences in any suitable way. In each case, indicate what the pronoun refers back to:

a. He had always wanted to be a great musician. This ...
b. Solar energy cannot meet the needs of large-scale industry. But it ...
c. The Government has passed several laws limiting and controlling the use of pesticides. This ...
d. In Sweden, each person uses an average of 8,045 kilowatt hours of electricity per year, compared with 111 hours in India. This ...
e. He was well aware that being lazy was his main handicap in life. It ...

Follow-up exercise: *Arbeitsbuch*, pp. 59–60.

E. Vocabulary

Match these sources of energy with their correct definitions:

energy	definitions
a. coal	1. This fuel is very profitable to sell. So, even in very difficult conditions (e. g. the sea between Britain and Norway, or the ice-floes of Alaska), it is economically worth drilling for.
b. natural gas	2. This is always found wherever crude oil is found. But it is difficult to transport, so it could never meet any general world energy shortage.

energy	definitions
c. nuclear power	3. This source of energy is found wherever there are rivers and waterfalls. But these are needed for other purposes too – irrigation, navigation and fishing, for example. And it is difficult to carry on these activities and produce this kind of energy at the same time.
d. solar energy	4. This rock, which is formed from the remains of long-dead plants, can be burned. It is by far the most plentiful of underground fuels.
e. hydroelectric power	5. Atoms of uranium can be broken up to release this form of energy. This energy, which is far greater than any other, is used in many countries to provide electricity.
f. wind power	6. This kind of energy falls on the earth's surface from above. But, with our present technology, we don't know how to collect and use more than a tiny fraction of it.
g. wood	7. This source is extremely difficult to convert into useable energy. This is because ocean waves are not regular and constant in their flow.
h. tidal power	8. Many people think that the machines needed to produce this form of power are attractive, compared with oil wells and nuclear power stations. But a vast number of them would be needed to make any real difference to our energy needs.
i. oil	9. This represents about 15% of the world's fuel consumption, mostly in underdeveloped countries. But it is very limited and inefficient as an energy source. And, without proper control, it could be the first of the world's energy sources to run out.

F. Communication practice

1. Study and arrange

This diagram shows a "Trombe" wall – a method of using solar energy. First, study the diagram. Then, in pairs, arrange the sentences which follow into their correct order.

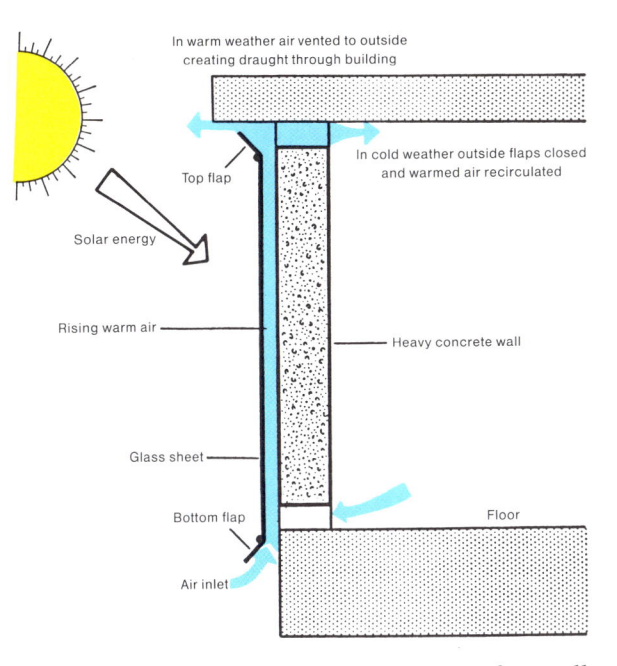

Diagram labels:
- In warm weather air vented to outside creating draught through building
- Top flap
- Solar energy
- In cold weather outside flaps closed and warmed air recirculated
- Rising warm air
- Heavy concrete wall
- Glass sheet
- Bottom flap
- Air inlet
- Floor

a. A glass sheet is fixed in front of a wall facing the heat of the sun.
b. This causes the air to rise.
c. To heat the building, the reverse is necessary; the top flap is closed and the bottom one left open.
d. To cool the building, the bottom flap in the glass sheet is kept shut and the top one opened.
e. The wall absorbs this heat and in turn heats the air in the gap between wall and glass.
f. The heated warm air flows upwards and draws cool air into the house from the shaded rear.

2. Discuss

Look at these cartoons. What do they have in common? What point does each make? Do you think the point (in each case) is a valid one?

In your discussion, use the following expressions for adding an idea:

Furthermore …
In addition …
Besides (this) …
What's more …
And another thing …

"*Personally, I prefer the old method of ringing.*"

109

G. Further reading

Green Belts

Organizations like the Council for the Protection of Rural England are fighting to prevent the English countryside from being invaded by "urban sprawl" – the tendency of
5 the residential areas of towns to spread outwards into the countryside. In particular, they are fighting to preserve the Green Belt areas – some 6,600 square miles of English countryside on which further building is pro-
10 hibited. But developers and building companies say that Green Belts are severely limiting their ability to provide housing for the workforce. There would, to be sure, be many eager and willing buyers for the homes they would
15 like to build. The developers promise new homes and new high-technology jobs. They say that Green Belts (which were conceived in the spacious 1930s) are luxuries Britain can no longer afford. Only 20% of available
20 derelict land is suitable for building, they say, and the existence of Green Belts limits their free enterprise. But local residents hold on tight to the Green Belt principle. What is at stake, they say, is the future of England's
25 countryside.

Especially in prosperous southeast England (a large portion of which is in a Green Belt area), the question of releasing new land for housing development has reached an *im-*
30 *passe*. On the one hand, everyone wants a house away from the unhealthy living conditions of the city. At the same time, everyone wants to put a stop to urban sprawl, recognizing that it may destroy forever the
35 countryside of England.

The controversy has led developers to be more careful about blending in their buildings with the landscape and even improving on nature. For example, they are planting underused agricultural land with new woods.
40 Wild meadows are being restored, providing a habitat for wild life. And tastefully-designed old-style houses are being built to blend in with the surrounding countryside and architecture. And, say the developers,
45 besides being made to look green and pleasant, their new towns can combine health, education and leisure facilities, together with workplaces. In the light of this kind of positive planning, housing development in pro-
50 tected areas is becoming more acceptable, provided it is kept within limits.

Developer's illustration of a new town plan in a Green Belt

Answer the following questions:

a. What is the reason for the Green Belt policy?
b. Why don't developers simply build all new homes outside the Green Belts?
c. How would you deal with the problem of "urban sprawl"? Do you think it is enough to prohibit building in specified rural areas?

Follow-up exercises: *Arbeitsbuch*, pp. 29–31 and 111.

Graphs, Charts and Tables

A. Lead-in

Study the *bar charts* comparing holidaymakers' travel habits in six European countries. Decide if each of the following ten statements is *true* or *false*.

%age of holidaymakers – who leave home for their holiday

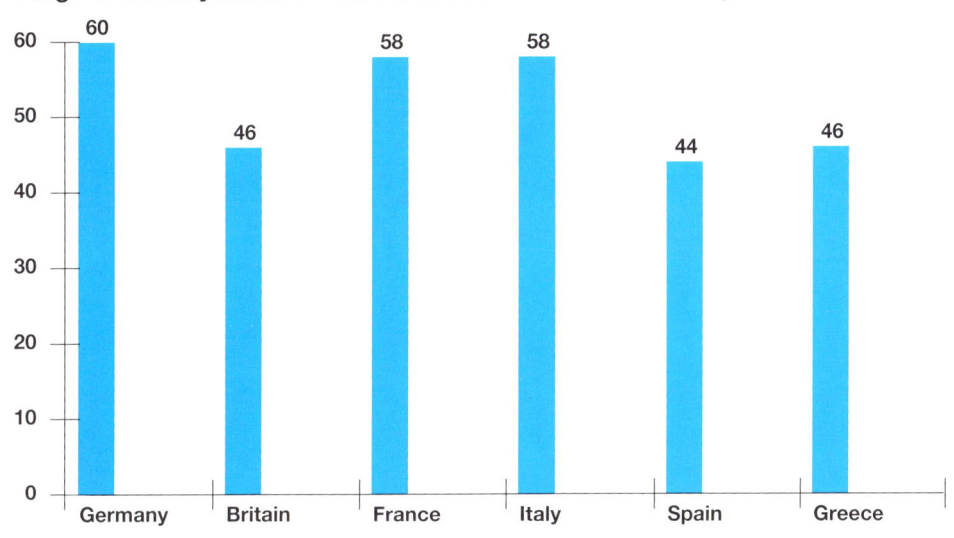

Germany	Britain	France	Italy	Spain	Greece
60	46	58	58	44	46

%age of holidaymakers – who travel abroad

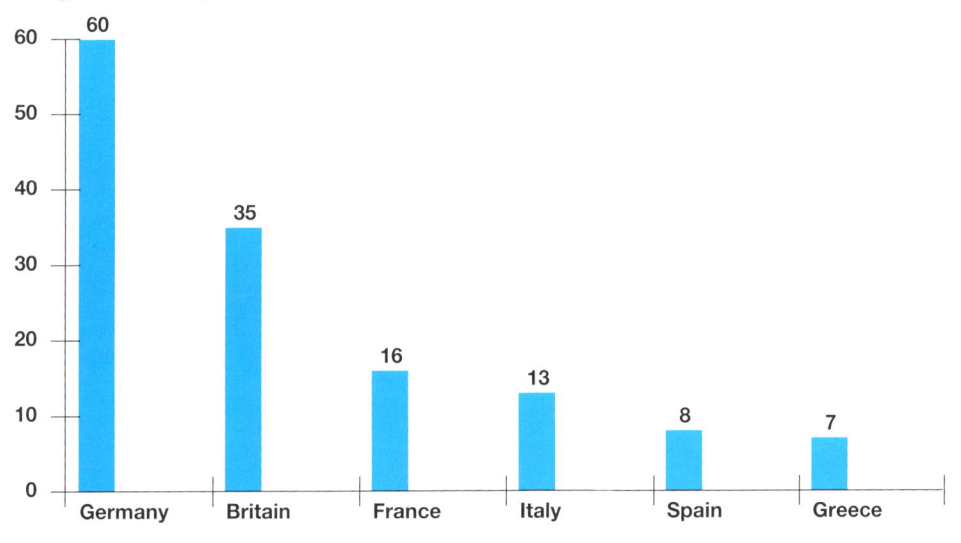

Germany	Britain	France	Italy	Spain	Greece
60	35	16	13	8	7

Unit 10 *Main Course*

1. Of the countries surveyed, Germany has the highest proportion of holidaymakers who go abroad.	*True or false?*
2. Although more than half of French holidaymakers leave home, less than a fifth of them leave France.	*True or false?*
3. In all the countries surveyed, more than 40% of holidaymakers leave home.	*True or false?*
4. Compared with Spain, France has twice as many holidaymakers who go abroad.	*True or false?*
5. Almost half of British holidaymakers leave home, and more than a third go abroad.	*True or false?*
6. Only 13% of Italian holidaymakers go abroad, but more than four times as many leave home.	*True or false?*
7. More than nine in every ten Greeks who go on holiday do so in their own country.	*True or false?*
8. In France and Italy, the same number of holidaymakers leave home.	*True or false?*
9. Greece has the lowest percentages of holidaymakers who leave home and holidaymakers who travel abroad.	*True or false?*
10. In only one of the countries surveyed do more than half of its holidaymakers travel abroad.	*True or false?*

B. Text

Remember Stardrive, in Unit 7? Look at this *graph* showing Stardrive's sales figures. Then read the report which follows.

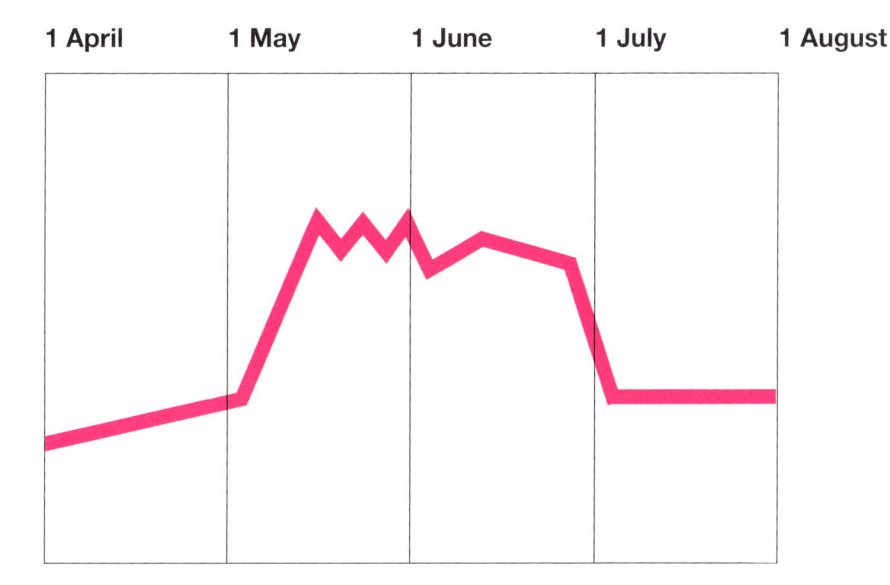

1 April   1 May   1 June   1 July   1 August

Stardrive: the first four months' sales

Stardrive: Current Sales Report

1. The graph records Stardrive's sales over the four months following the launch of the new product. We know that sales of tennis rackets remain low during the winter. Christmas normally brings only a slight increase in sales. So it is important to know what sales strategy we should follow next spring and summer. The graph shows us what buying pattern we can expect of our target group then.

2. Following our publicity campaign, sales rose steadily over the first four weeks. And, as the tennis season really got started, they climbed steeply, reaching a peak in mid-May. Then sales fluctuated for a couple of weeks, before falling slightly. There was a brief recovery, but during June the overall trend in sales was one of steady decline. And, around the beginning of July, they fell dramatically. But they soon levelled off and have remained constant since then.

3. Stardrive's most profitable period was before mid-May. This was partly the result of consumer demand for new rackets early in the tennis season. But it was probably due, too, to our strong publicity. The demand for Stardrive has dropped since the end of May, while the tennis season has been in full swing. Sales have remained at a low but steady level since July. We are still selling

Stardrives, even though the early-season peak is well past. So there is a continuing, though limited, market for the product.

4. In view of the successful sales in early May, we should start advertising earlier next year. As there was a significant decline after mid-May, we recommend spending less on advertising after May next year. But we suggest that the company produces enough reserve stocks of Stardrive rackets to meet the limited demand after June.

C. Comprehension and analysis

a. Each paragraph in the report requires a heading. To which paragraph does each of these headings belong?

Analysis   Recommendations
Conclusions   Reference

b. What was the main purpose of recording Stardrive's sales on a graph?
c. Why did Stardrive make most profits before the middle of May?
d. How many recommendations finally come out of the report?

D. Talking grammar

1. Look at how tenses are used to refer to graphs, charts and tables.

Tense	refers to a fact which	Example
Simple present	is always true	Sales of tennis rackets *remain* low during the winter.
Present continuous	is true at this moment	We are still *selling* Stardrives.
Simple past	was true in the past	Sales *rose* steadily over the first four weeks.
Present perfect	was true in the past and is still true now	Sales *have remained* at a low but steady level since July.

2. Complete four sentences by choosing the correct tense for the verb *increase*. Each sentence should begin *Prices*...

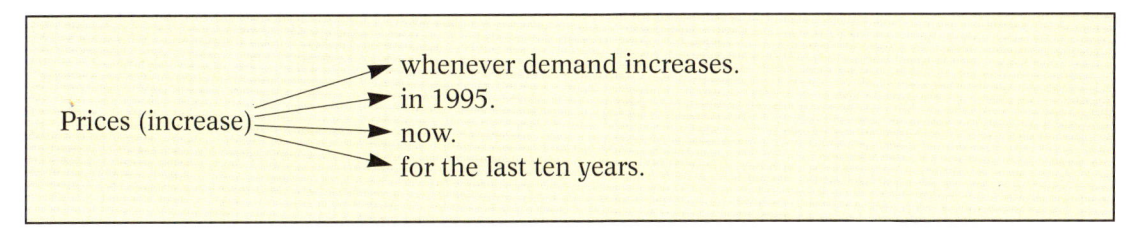

Prices (increase)
- whenever demand increases.
- in 1995.
- now.
- for the last ten years.

3. Choose the correct tenses for the verbs in brackets.

a. Early in the season, there (be) a sudden increase in sales.
b. Tennis rackets always sell well in the early in the season, but then sales (decline).
c. Sales (fall) since reaching a peak in May.
d. We (sell) about 200 Stardrives a week right now.

E. Vocabulary

1. Study this list of words and phrases:

Vocabulary for graphs, charts and tables

a. Adjectives and adverbs

to show short, quick or unexpected changes:	sudden/ly	sharp/ly
		abrupt/ly
to show small but important changes:	significant/ly	marked/ly
to show large, important changes:	substantial/ly	steep/ly
to show small changes:	noticeable/noticeably	barely
		slow/ly
to show slow, long changes:	gradual/ly	general/ly
		steady/steadily
to show short-lasting changes:	short-lived	brief/ly

115

Unit 10 — Main Course

b. Nouns and verbs

	noun	verb
to describe increase:	an increase an expansion a rise growth	to increase to expand to rise to grow
to describe decrease:	a decrease a drop a fall	to decrease to drop to fall
to describe a strong, unexpected increase:	a leap a surge	to leap to surge
to describe a strong, unexpected decrease:	a collapse a plunge	to collapse to (take a) plunge
to indicate "no change":	 no change	to remain constant/ stable/steady not to change
other useful expressions:	recovery a peak fluctuations overall/general/ main trend levelling-off	to recover to reach a peak to fluctuate to describe irregular changes to level off

2. Here are some more words taken from the Stardrive sales report on page 113–14:

dramatic/ally   slight/ly   a decline/to decline   a climb/to climb

Add these words to the appropriate lists in *Vocabulary for graphs, charts and tables*.

F. Communication practice

1. Look at the *pie chart* below. It shows the expenditure of an average British family.

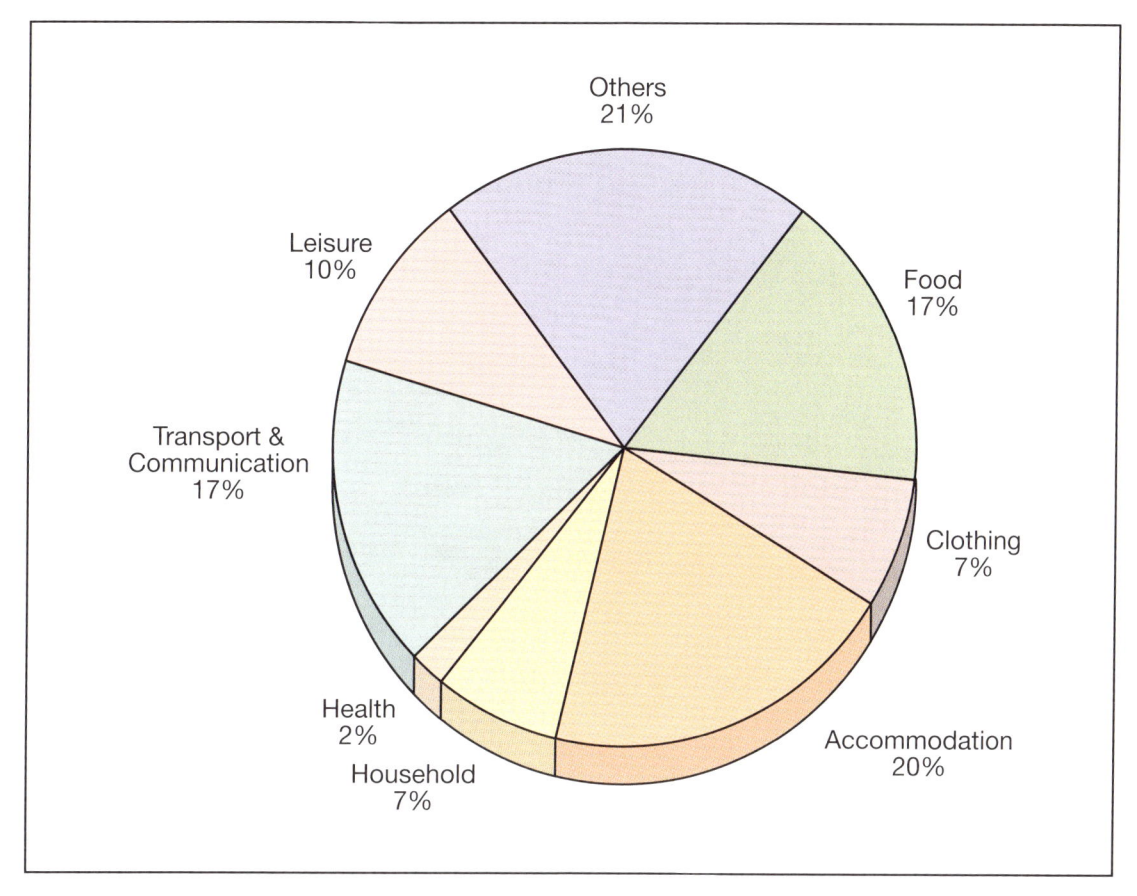

- Others 21%
- Food 17%
- Clothing 7%
- Accommodation 20%
- Household 7%
- Health 2%
- Transport & Communication 17%
- Leisure 10%

Accommodation (here): rent or mortgage payments
Household (here): furniture, appliances and other goods for the home

Give questions to these answers. Begin each question: "How much do the family spend on ...?"

a. The same amount as they spend on clothing.
b. Five times as much.
c. One fifth of their total expenditure.
d. 17% on each.
e. A tenth of their total expenditure.
f. Altogether, 30%.
g. Only one pound in every fifty.

2. Listen to the phone conversation. Cathy has lost her copy of the graph, and is calling Rob at the office to ask a few questions. As you listen, you will hear the speakers make three mistakes. Can you spot them?

3. Here is another kind of visual information. It is a *table of statistics* about newspaper readers in a region of Britain.

	Estimated number of readers (in thousands)		
	Burtown Weekly News	*Thurlow Free Press*	*Valley Advertiser*
Total adults (Age 15+)	46	40	43
Men	22	19	22
Women	24	21	21
Adults working at home	20	17	19
Men	4	8	3
Women	16	9	16
Income groups			
higher income	17	19	13
lower income	29	21	30
Age groups			
15–24	9	4	10
25–34	8	4	10
35–54	13	11	10
55+	16	21	13

Your company wishes to market the following *new* goods and services:

pizza delivery
local bus excursions
home keep-fit equipment
Mediterranean luxury cruise
video game: "War of the Giants"
orthopaedic armchair for the elderly
pop music magazine
nut-flavoured coffee

You are the Regional Manager responsible for marketing *any three* of these products/services. Decide which weekly local newspaper – *Burtown News*, *Thurlow Free Press* or *Valley Advertiser* – would reach the best audience for *each* of your three products/services.

Write a report on the reasons for your choices. To do this, you could use expressions like these (taken from **Lead-in**):

more/less than half/a fifth/40%
nine in every ten
twice/four times as many
the highest/lowest percentage/proportion

G. Further reading

The Growth of Part-time Working

In the period of recession up to 1994, there was a significant growth of part-time working in the European Union. Whereas the total numbers in employment fell, part-time jobs
5 increased. The growth of part-time working helped to prevent the employment of women declining significantly over the recession period. However, the number of men working part-time also increased, while in all
10 except three EU member states, the number of men in full-time work declined – in many cases substantially. Whether this is related to the depressed level of economic activity or whether it marks the beginning of a trend to-
15 wards part-time working will only become clear with time.

The growth of part-time working raises a number of issues to do not only with working time and work-sharing, but also with the
20 terms and conditions of employment attached to such jobs and the status of the people taking them up. From one perspective, part-time jobs are a means of allowing people to fit together family responsibilities with working careers.
25 At the same time, they allow employers to organize their businesses more flexibly and to make more effective use of fixed capital and equipment (business premises as well as plant and machinery). From another perspec-
30 tive, they represent inferior jobs with limited career prospects which are taken up only because those concerned have no alternative option.

Growth of full and part-time jobs, 1988–94

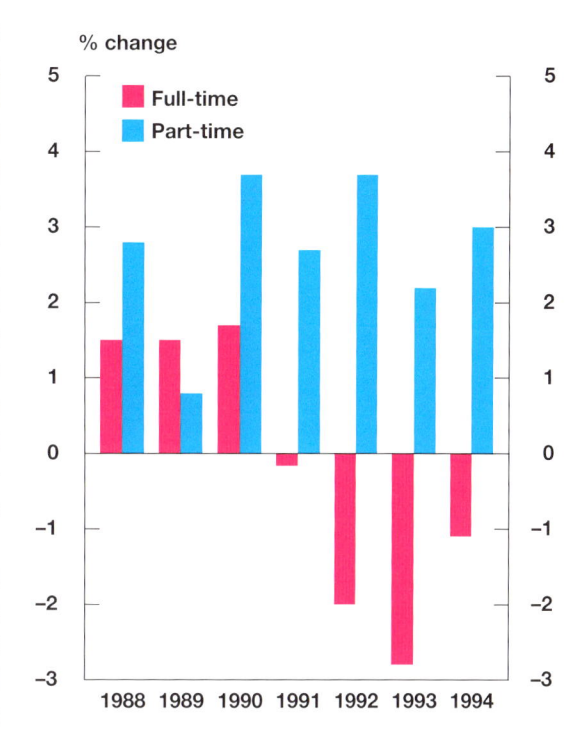

Answer the following questions:

a. When did the number of full-time jobs in the EU begin to fall?
b. In your opinion, how could part-time work enable "employers to organize their businesses more flexibly"?
c. In your own words, rephrase the point the writer makes in his last sentence.

R

Business Communication Course

Secretarial Activities
Commercial Correspondence

Telephoning in Business

A. Lead-in: useful expressions

Use this list of expressions to help you with the telephoning exercises on pages 125 to 135.

Starting the call

Can you put me through to (Extension 18/Mr ...), please?
Hullo, this is ... here.
I'm calling (to ask) about ...
May I speak to (Ms ...), please?
When will he be back?
Could you take a message, please?

Receiving a call

Good morning, ... speaking. What can I do for you?
Mrs ... isn't in./She's not available at the moment, I'm afraid.
May I help you/take a message?
Who's calling, please?

Getting to the point

The reason I'm calling is ...
I'd like to point out that ...
I've noticed that ... and I'm calling to ask whether ...
How can I help you, please?

Taking a message

Hold on a moment, please.
Just hold the line, will you? I'll get a pencil.
Now, where were we?
Let me run that through again.
May I have your name, please?

Can I take your number?
Do you want Mr ... to call you back?
Who shall I say called?

Interrupting/Asking for repetition

Excuse me, I didn't catch that.
Could you repeat that, please?
Hold on a second.

Dealing with acoustic problems

I'm afraid I can't hear you.
Could you speak up a bit?
It's a pretty bad line, isn't it?
Yes, I'm still with you. Go ahead.
Shall I call you back?

Ending a call

I think that takes care of everything.
Right you are.
I'll/You'll call again tomorrow, right?
Bye for now. Thanks for calling.
Thanks very much, and goodbye.

Leaving a message on an answerphone

This is ... of ...
I wonder if you would call me back, please.
My number is ...
You could call me between ... and ... tomorrow.
I'm looking forward to hearing from you.
Goodbye for now.

B. Tasks

1. Read this letter

Werner Appel Textile Supplies
60486 Frankfurt, Kurfürstenstraße 17

Telefon (069) 53 24 17
Telefax (069) 53 24 37

Antonio da Torre
Miguel Almeida Lda.
Rua de Santa Catarina 321
Porto
Portugal

21 January 19..

Re: Our Order No.: 665/12

Dear Senhor da Torre,

This is to confirm the order we made by phone yesterday. Please deliver the following goods by 30 March:

Items		Price
2000	tea towels ('Ocean Wave' printed)	esc. 400,000
2000	tea towels ('Mountain View' printed)	esc. 400,000
100	oven gloves (green & yellow)	esc. 60,000
100	aprons ('Highland Glen' printed)	esc. 40,000

As agreed, all goods to be shipped CIF to our Hamburg agent. Full payment to be made on delivery by banker's order.

In your last consignment, only the aprons had washing instruction labels attached. In your confirmation, please indicate that all goods in this order will have labels, which are necessary under local trading regulations here.

We are concerned that this order will arrive on time as we have to distribute the goods to our outlets before the holiday season begins. Would you please give us your assurance on this?

Yours sincerely,

B. Weber

Bodo Weber
Managing Director

Unit 1 — Secretarial Activities

2. List the errors

There are three errors in this confirmation of order. Make a list of them:

```
                        Miguel  Almeida  Lda.
                           Porto - Portugal



                          CONFIRMATION OF ORDER

Date                         29 January 19..

Order No. (Customer's ref.)  665/12

Date of Order                21 January 19..

Customer                     Werner Appel (Textile supplies)

Method of Dispatch           ship CIF Hamburg

Delivery by                  30 May 19..

Terms of Payment             Banker's order on delivery

Special Instructions         aprons to have washing instruction
                             labels attached
------------------------------------------------------------------
Quantity    Item            Type                      Price
------------------------------------------------------------------
2000        tea towels      "Ocean Wave" printed      esc. 400,000
2000        tea towels      "Mountain View" printed   esc. 400,000
 100        oven gloves     green                     esc.  60,000
 100        aprons          "Highland Glen" printed   esc.  40,000
------------------------------------------------------------------
Total price                                           esc. 900,000
------------------------------------------------------------------
Signed on behalf of Miguel Almeida Lda.


   ..Antonio..da..Torre......
   Antonio da Torre
```

3. Telephoning about the errors

Herr Weber is calling Senhor da Torre in order to sort out the mistakes. In pairs, take one role each and act out the phone conversation. Then change roles. First complete the sentences below. Some of the expressions you'll need are listed on page 122.

(*Secretary's voice*): Herr Weber? Sorry to keep you waiting. I've got hold of Senhor da Torre, and I'm putting you through now.

dT (a) here. Good morning, Herr Weber.
W Good morning, Senhor da Torre, I'm calling (b)
dT Ah really? (c) 665/12, did you say?
W Correct. (d) a number of important discrepancies between (e) and your (f)
dT (g) them, please?
W Certainly. First, (h)
dT Ah yes, you're right. Our office must have (i) mistake there.
W And the second (j)
dT Let me see. Yes, yes, you're absolutely (k) That's most unfortunate.
W And finally, (l)
dT Hm. Yes, indeed. Well, Herr Weber, I'm really very (m) What I suggest is (n) corrected confirmation immediately.
W I'd be very glad (o). And I'd like to point out that (p) especially important (q) delivered by (r)
dT Yes, as you said in your order, (s) distributed before (t) begins.
W Right. And as far as the (u) are concerned, it's very important that (v) the colour that we (w)
dT Certainly, Herr Weber. I'll see to that.
W And I hope you'll make sure (x) attached.
dT Indeed, I will. I can assure you that all these corrections (y) included in the new confirmation of order.
W Well, that seems to be all. Thank you very much, Senhor da Torre.
dT Thank you, Herr Weber, and goodbye.

"Problems with your conference call – Los Angeles is out to breakfast, New York's out to lunch and London's out to dinner."

4. Leaving a message on an answerphone

Your business phone calls will often be greeted by an answerphone message:

> "Hullo, you're through to Miguel Almeida of Porto. We're sorry we're not able to take your call right now. If you'd like to leave a message, we'll get back to you as soon as we can. Please speak after hearing the signal. *(beep)*"

Now practice giving the same information about the errors on the answerphone!

Follow-up exercises: *Arbeitsbuch*, pp. 34–35 and 76–77.

Appointments

A. Lead-in: useful expressions

1. On the telephone

Requesting an appointment

I'd like to meet (name)/one of your representatives.
Would it be possible to arrange an appointment with ...?
I'd like to discuss (the possibility of) ...

Getting necessary information

Who (in particular) would you like to make an appointment with?
When will you be in ... exactly?
How is that with you?

Suggesting arrangements

I think it would be best for you to meet ...
Anytime on the 2nd of May would be (very) convenient for me.
I'm/he's/we're free on the morning of the 2nd.
Shall we say 10 to 10.30?

Concluding arrangements

I'll write to you confirming that.
Could I have your name again, please?
We'll see you at 10 o'clock on the 2nd, then.

Arranging a follow-up meeting

When can we meet again?
I'll need about ... days.
Is the 12th all right for you?
Would Thursday morning/3 o'clock be convenient?

We'll need ... hours, at the very most.
We'd better meet at ... then.
I'll just check my appointments book.

Confirming follow-up arrangements

I can give you a provisional yes on that.
I'll confirm it with you tomorrow.
So you'll book the room and let me know.
Leave it to me.
See you on ...!
Could we just check what we agreed again?
So, our next appointment ... is on ...
On Monday the 3rd, to be exact.

2. In writing

Confirming arrangements

This to confirm the arrangement made during our phone conversation yesterday.
... will be very pleased to meet you here at ...

Offering help

I enclose a map of ... to help you ...
When you arrive, please ask at the reception desk for ...
I will be happy to ...
Please call me if you run into any difficulty.

Requesting/suggesting changes

Owing to ..., I am sorry to have to change the arrangement we made.
I would like to suggest an earlier meeting time. Would ... be all right?
I hope you will be able to manage this.

B. Tasks

1. Dialogue completion

Parts of the following telephone conversation are missing.
In pairs, act out the conversation. Use the telephone expressions above to help you complete the missing phrases.
Then change roles.

HE Good morning. Hain Electronics?
PR Good morning. Peter Routledge of East Anglian Transformers here. I'm calling from Cambridge. I'll be in Germany next month and I'd (a) one of your representatives (b) possibility of a supply contract.
HE I see. Is there (c) you've been dealing with, please?
PR No. This is the first time (d) your company.
HE I see. I think (e) best if I (f) meet our Herr Petersen. He's our Business Manager.
PR Yes. That would be fine.
HE When (g) in Paderborn exactly?
PR Well, anytime (h) 2nd of May (i) convenient for me. How (j) with you? I (k) about 30 minutes, if possible.
HE Let me see. I have Herr Petersen's appointments calendar here – yes, I see he's (l) the morning of the 2nd. (m) 10 to 10.30?
PR Yes, I'll be travelling by car from Dortmund that morning, so that should be quite all right.
HE Very well. I'll (n) confirming that, Mr – er, could I have your name again, please?
PR Routledge. R–O–U–T–L–E–D–G–E. Of East Anglian Transformers, Cambridge. Oh, and I wonder if (o) also (p) directions to help me to get there, please. I don't know Paderborn at all.
HE Yes, I'll certainly do that, Mr Routledge. So we'll see you at (q), then.
PR That's right. Well, thank you very much, and goodbye.
HE Goodbye.

2. Letter writing

Drawing from the writing phrases listed above, complete this letter in any suitable way:

Dear Mr Routledge,

Confirm arrangement – phone conversation yesterday. Our Business Manager Herr Petersen – meet you – 10.00 – 2nd May.

Map – Paderborn city centre – find your way here – ask at reception desk for me – take you to Petersen's office directly.

Call me – any difficulty.

Yours sincerely,

Unit 2 — Secretarial Activities

3. Matching

After you have sent the letter, Herr Petersen learns that he has to visit Frankfurt on important business on 2nd May, leaving Paderborn at 10 a.m. His appointment will have to be changed.

List A
Owing to unavoidable circumstances,
If I do not hear from you,
As Herr Petersen now has to leave Paderborn that morning,
I hope

On a separate sheet, match the expressions in List A and List B so as to form 4 complete sentences. Then arrange the sentences into a logical order, so as to complete a second letter to Mr Routledge.

List B
I will assume that the new time is convenient for you.
I would like to suggest an earlier meeting time of 9 o'clock.
I am sorry to have to change the arrangement we made for 2nd May.
you will be able to manage this.

4. Calling Mr Cull

Use some of the telephone expressions on pages 122 and 126, to help you.

Telephoning Role A: Gunter Schwarz of Rüppel & Schwarz (Software) in Mannheim. A customer has given you the name and phone number of software designer Brian Cull of Reading, England. You think he could be a possible supplier for you. You'll be in England on 25–29 June. Call him to arrange an appointment.

Telephoning Role B: Brian Cull, a self-employed software designer in Reading, England. You'll be on holiday in June, returning late on Friday, the 28th. You work at home, so you normally meet clients at the Railway Hotel in Reading. You will receive a phone call from Germany. Deal with it in a co-operative way.

5. A follow-up meeting

Telephoning Role A (Schwarz): You & Mr Cull made progress in your last meeting, but you think you should meet again. Call to ask when he would be free – is the 11th all right for him? At the Bull Inn this time, for lunch – convenient? You think you'll need about three hours, but this point can be left open.

Telephoning Role B (Cull): Having had a meeting with you, Herr Schwarz is calling again. You're free any afternoon, between the 10th and the 15th. Suggest 12.30 p.m. Give a provisional yes to the arrangements – confirm them tomorrow. You think you could finish in two hours next time. Before ending the call, check what you agreed on.

Follow-up exercise: *Arbeitsbuch*, pp. 36–37.

Secretarial Activities / Unit 3

Travelling Arrangements

A. Lead in: useful expressions

Asking about travel requirements

Would you like me to reserve a sleeping berth for you?
Do you wish to return directly after the conference, or to stay longer in Germany?
Will you require a smoking or non-smoking compartment?

Confirming travel arrangements

We have made a reservation for you on Flight LH 667, departing Frankfurt at 14.15 on Tuesday.

As requested, you will have a seat in the non-smoking compartment.
Please pick up the tickets at the check-in counter.

Giving additional information

This means you will be able to reach... with... hours to spare.
There is a connecting service to Darmstadt.
(Unfortunately,) there are no other flights available on that day.
There will be someone to meet you at...

B. Tasks

1. Find the correct expression

Use the above expressions for the blanks in the following letter:

```
Dear Mr and Mrs Johnson,

I'm looking forward to meeting you at Friday's conference here.

I (a) Flight BA124, departing Munich (b) 08.00 (c) Friday. As
requested, (d) two seats (e) non-smoking (f). Please pick up
(g) information desk at Munich airport.

You will arrive in Birmingham at 10.30. This means (h)
conference centre (i) four hours to spare. Unfortunately,
(j) no later flights (k) that day.

(l) you wish (m) return directly (n) or (o) Britain?

Yours sincerely,
```

Unit 3 — Secretarial Activities

2. Letter writing

Mr Burns, who lives in Manchester, is one of your customers. You have invited him to Hamburg to discuss further sales contracts. Using the following airline information, you have made the necessary flight reservations for Mr Burns. On arrival, he should take a taxi from the airport to Hotel Iris (about 20 minutes).

Write to Mr Burns, giving him relevant information regarding his travel arrangements and his schedule in Hamburg.

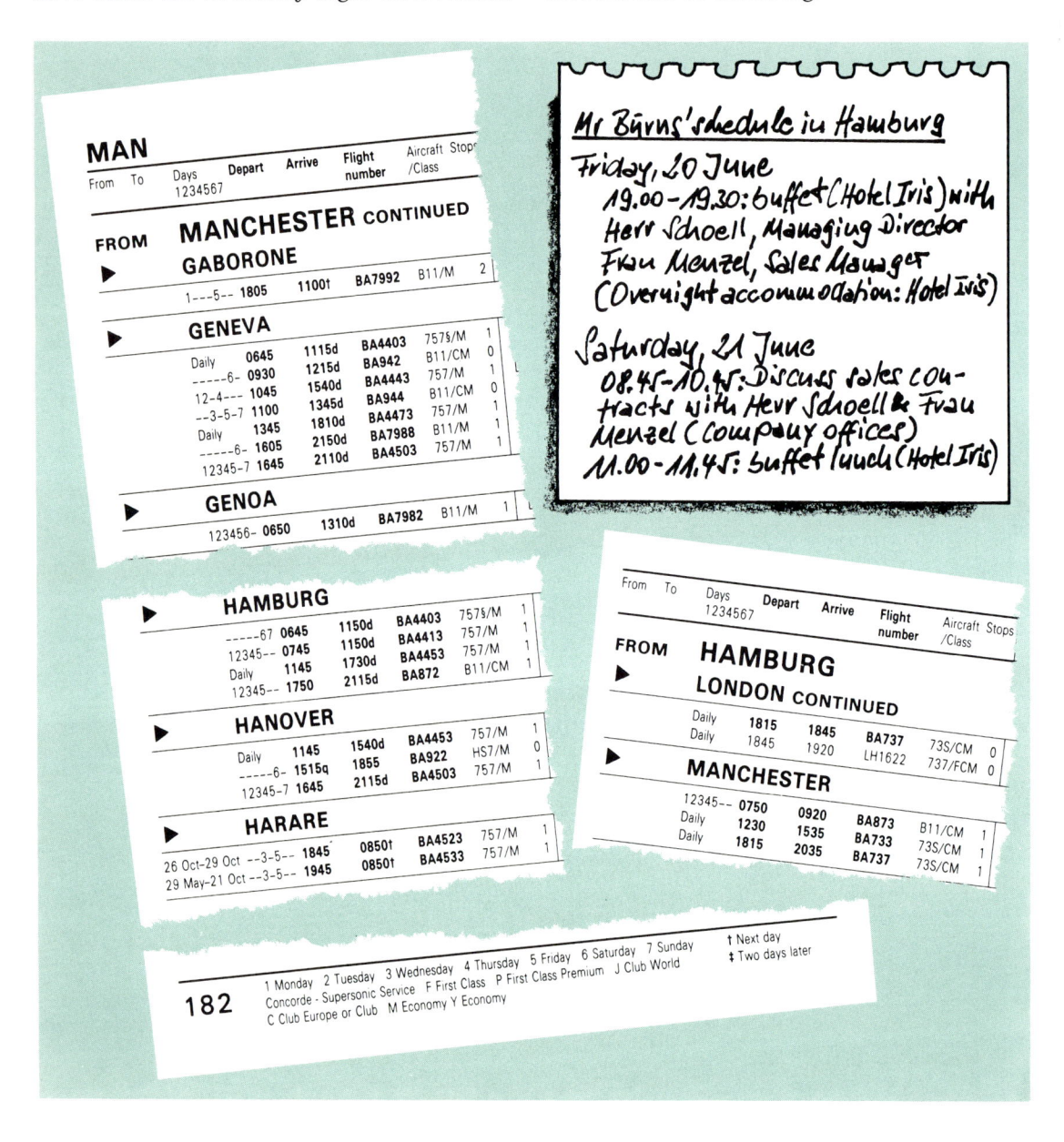

MAN

From	To	Days 1234567	Depart	Arrive	Flight number	Aircraft /Class	Stops
FROM	**MANCHESTER** CONTINUED						
▶	GABORONE						
		1---5--	1805	1100†	BA7992	B11/M	2
▶	GENEVA						
		Daily	0645	1115d	BA4403	757§/M	1
		-----6-	0930	1215d	BA942	B11/CM	0
		12-4---	1045	1540d	BA4443	757/M	1
		--3-5-7	1100	1345d	BA944	B11/CM	0
		Daily	1345	1810d	BA4473	757/M	1
		-----6-	1605	2150d	BA7988	B11/M	1
		12345-7	1645	2110d	BA4503	757/M	1
▶	GENOA						
		123456-	0650	1310d	BA7982	B11/M	1
▶	HAMBURG						
		-----67	0645	1150d	BA4403	757§/M	1
		12345--	0745	1150d	BA4413	757/M	1
		Daily	1145	1730d	BA4453	757/M	1
		12345--	1750	2115d	BA872	B11/CM	1
▶	HANOVER						
		Daily	1145	1540d	BA4453	757/M	1
		-----6-	1515q	1855	BA922	HS7/M	0
		12345-7	1645	2115d	BA4503	757/M	1
▶	HARARE						
		26 Oct-29 Oct --3-5--	1845	0850†	BA4523	757/M	1
		29 May-21 Oct --3-5--	1945	0850†	BA4533	757/M	1

From	To	Days 1234567	Depart	Arrive	Flight number	Aircraft /Class	Stops
FROM	**HAMBURG**						
▶	LONDON CONTINUED						
		Daily	1815	1845	BA737	73S/CM	0
		Daily	1845	1920	LH1622	737/FCM	0
▶	MANCHESTER						
		12345--	0750	0920	BA873	B11/CM	1
		Daily	1230	1535	BA733	73S/CM	1
		Daily	1815	2035	BA737	73S/CM	1

Mr Burns' schedule in Hamburg

Friday, 20 June
19.00–19.30: buffet (Hotel Iris) with Herr Schoell, Managing Director, Frau Menzel, Sales Manager
(Overnight accommodation: Hotel Iris)

Saturday, 21 June
08.45–10.45: Discuss sales contracts with Herr Schoell & Frau Menzel (Company offices)
11.00–11.45: buffet lunch (Hotel Iris)

† Next day   ‡ Two days later
1 Monday 2 Tuesday 3 Wednesday 4 Thursday 5 Friday 6 Saturday 7 Sunday
Concorde - Supersonic Service   F First Class   P First Class Premium   J Club World
C Club Europe or Club   M Economy   Y Economy

182

Unit 3

3. Telephoning about travel arrangements

Use some of the telephone expressions on p. 122 to help you.

Telephoning Role A (Lars Natus in Würzburg): You're to have talks with Ms Bickel tomorrow, at your office. She'll travel from Kassel-Wilhelmshöhe, but you don't know when. Call her and find out when she'll come.

The rail timetable (below) will help. Suggest you'll pick her up, drive directly to your office, then discuss the question of licences. Leave everything else till tomorrow. You've reserved a hotel room for her (1 night).

Kassel-Wilhelmshöhe → Würzburg Hbf
225 km

ab	Zug		an	Verkehrstage	ab	Zug		an	Verkehrstage
6.20	ICE 987	✕	7.20	Mo - Sa	14.22	ICE 789	✕	15.20	täglich
7.22	ICE 581	✕	8.20	täglich	15.22	ICE 589	✕	16.20	täglich
8.22	ICE 783	✕	9.20	täglich	16.22	ICE 881	✕	17.20	täglich
9.22	ICE 583	✕	10.20	täglich	17.22	ICE 681	✕	18.20	täglich
10.22	ICE 785	✕	11.20	täglich	18.22	ICE 883	✕	19.20	täglich
10.57	IC 781	⚲	12.05	Mo - Fr, So	19.22	ICE 683	✕	20.20	Mo - Fr, So
11.22	ICE 585	✕	12.20	täglich	20.22	ICE 885	✕	21.20	Mo - Fr, So 03
12.22	ICE 787	✕	13.20	täglich	21.22	ICE 887	✕	22.20	täglich
13.22	ICE 587	✕	14.20	täglich					

Telephoning Role B (Val Bickel in Kassel): As your diary (right) shows, you'll travel to Würzburg to meet Herr Natus tomorrow, but you have no train timetable.
He'll call you –
you have questions:
How/when to get
to Würzburg?
How to reach his office?
When to discuss the
French market?
Hotel reservation?

Diary entries:
8 MONTAG / MONDAY — APRIL 1996 — Ostermontag Woche 15
- Wagner, Kassel (2 hrs)
- Bremer Bank, Kassel (30-40 mins),
- Kassel → Würzburg (Natus)

9 DIENSTAG / TUESDAY
- Würzburg → Munich

10 MITTWOCH / WEDNESDAY

Follow-up exercise:
Arbeitsbuch, pp. 37–38.

Room Reservations

A. Lead-in: useful expressions

Reserving hotel accommodation

Your hotel has been recommended to us by...
Please reserve two single rooms with bath for the night of 23rd February.
The guests' names are...
They will be arriving at approximately...

Reserving a room for a meeting

Would you please arrange for us to have a conference/meeting room for 10 people from 9.00 a.m. to 5.00 p.m. on (date).
We would appreciate the use of a tape recorder/ a slide projector.
We will need...
Please make sure that...
Please reserve... places for lunch.
Will it be possible to have morning coffee/ afternoon tea served?

Concluding a letter of reservation

I look forward to receiving your confirmation.
If a deposit is required, would you please send me your invoice as soon as possible?

Informing people about reservations you have made

This is to let you know that we have booked a single/double room for you at... on (date).
We have made a provisional reservation for you at... Hotel.
Please let me know by (date) if you will be coming.

Checking in

I have a reservation.
My name is...
I reserved a single room with bath, for two nights.
I reserved by fax about two weeks ago.
Would it be possible to have some coffee, please?

B. Tasks

1. Letter writing: Guests in Leeds

Your managing director has gone to Leeds in England to meet some British customers there. They arrive 4th May and will need accommodation for one night.

Hotels

Kings Hotel: D, T; F, S; T/C; TV; CH; L
Bristol Hotel: D, T; S; TV; CH; E
The Royal: D, T; S; DI; TV; CH

Key
D, T; F, S – *double bed, twin bed; family room, single room*
DI – *suitable for the disabled*
T/C – *tea/coffee facilities in room*
TV – *television in room or lounge*
CH – *central heating*
L – *licensed bar*
E – *evening meal available*

THE GUESTS
Mr Lyle – uses walking sticks; has difficulty getting around
Mrs Sainsbury – arriving early, requires afternoon tea
Miss Churchill – requires a bar (meeting friends in evening)
Mr Hancock – arriving late, needs a meal at 7.30 pm
Mr Sanders – will bring his wife and 2-year-old son

2. Letter writing: The Leeds meeting

Now, using these notes, write to Leeds Conference Centre to reserve a room for the meeting.

```
Notes

Date of meeting: 5 May
No. of people: 6
Required:
- meeting room (10am-3pm) / slide projector
- morning coffee / lunch at 1.00pm
```

Write letters to the hotels mentioned above, reserving suitable accommodation for the people concerned (see guest-list on the right). How many letters will you have to write?

3. Checking in

> *Speaking Role A* (Herr Rohmann): About three weeks ago, you reserved (by fax) a room with bath, for two nights, commencing tonight. You're now checking in to the hotel, and speaking to the receptionist. You'd like some coffee, while making some phone calls from your room.

> *Speaking Role B* (Hotel receptionist): A guest is checking in. Questions: how to spell this guest's name? When did he reserve? Give him his key: Room 38, third floor. You'll have his luggage brought up directly. If he asks for coffee, he can have it in the lounge or brought up to his room.

Follow-up exercise: *Arbeitsbuch*, p. 39.

Invitations

A. Lead-in: useful expressions

1. In writing

Inviting

We would very much like to invite ...
We are willing to (pay expenses ...)
Would you be able to ...?

Explaining the purpose of the invitation

We will (certainly) need to discuss ...
I would welcome your views/opinions about ...
If you were agreeable, we might/should ...

Proposing an agenda

I enclose a provisional agenda.
We will probably need about 2 hours/the whole afternoon to discuss ...
Could we (also) (agree to) look at ...

Ending the invitation

Please let me know if you will be travelling alone. We should make hotel and flight reservations for you.
I hope you find these arrangements satisfactory.
I look forward to hearing from you on this.

2. On the telephone

Suggesting

Why don't you come and meet me for lunch tomorrow?
Would you like to join me for a drink a little later?
May I invite you to meet me over lunch?
Tomorrow maybe? Wednesday then?
Be my guest.

Making the arrangements

How about the ... (Steakhouse) at, say, ...?
I suggest we meet in the lounge at ...
Would 1.30 be convenient for you?
I'll reserve a table.

B. Tasks

1. Expanding notes

Look at the following notes. Expand them into a formal letter of invitation, using suitable expressions.

Suggest we meet – discuss contract proposal – invite you here – willing to pay hotel and travel expenses – am away for two weeks from the 4th – meet 19th? – please notify me or my assistant Brian Heffer – he is acquainted with your proposal – would welcome recommendation from you, concerning advertising policy – prefer an agency experienced in promoting your goods – look forward to your reply

2. Inviting a representative

You are a ladies' fashion design company in Heidelberg. Read the following letter, which you have received from a British manufacturer:

> Dear Manager,
>
> We have just received your "Nostalgia" designs, dispatched on 13 June. Many thanks. They will be included in our brochure next season. Our market reports show that 1950s designs are making a comeback, so yours might be successful.
>
> We'll know by Christmas how well they are likely to sell next year, so we can let you know in January about further orders. Meanwhile, I'll be in Germany next month and would be very interested in meeting you to discuss new designs, especially for lightweight cotton goods.
>
> Sincerely yours,
> Jill Cadorath

Write a suitable letter of invitation, suggesting a meeting at your Heidelberg office on the 12th of next month. Offer to pay travel expenses.

3. Inviting by phone

Use some of the telephone expressions on p. 134 to help you.

> *Telephoning Role A: Helga Walter* of Walter & Braun GmbH, a Düsseldorf tool production company. You met Doreen Prewer (of Hi-Tech Blades, UK) just once, at the Paris Trades Fair two years ago. You've heard that she's travelling in your area. Call her: invite her to meet you for dinner tomorrow (Tuesday). If not, then Wednesday. Invite her to be your guest. You'd like to discuss a distributorship proposal you have in mind. You have two favourite restaurants – the Berliner Steakhouse and Nudel Palace. You'll reserve a table. Suggest 7.30 p.m.

> *Telephoning Role B: Doreen Prewer* of Hi-Tech Blades UK, currently on business in Düsseldorf. You don't remember meeting Helga Walter. But you're delighted to get her phone call, and interested in her proposal. Accept her invitation. Where and when? You can't get away till 7.30 p.m., you're not free on Tuesday – and you're vegetarian.

Follow-up exercise: *Arbeitsbuch*, p. 40.

Unit 6 — Secretarial Activities

Visitors to the Company

A. Lead-in: useful expressions

Welcoming

Hello, I'm glad to see you got here safely/pleased to meet you.
How was your flight?
Would you like to rest for a while/have a wash (before we go to ...)?

Introducing people

This is Frau Schmitz, our Publicity Manager. She (also) takes care of ...
I'd like you to meet our Production Manager, Niels Obersheimer: he's responsible for ...
I believe you know Susanne Vogt.

Taking care of the visitor(s)

Is there anything else you need right now?
If you would like to make a call/send a fax, please let me know.
You'll find the cafeteria on the first floor.

Keeping to the schedule

Let's deal with ... first. Then, if we can agree, we can ...
We could talk about ... over coffee.
I think we should break for lunch now? Then, directly afterwards, we could ...
I suggest we (now) discuss/have a look at ...

Addressing guests at a conference/meeting

I think we can begin.
Thank you for coming.
On behalf of the company, I'd like to welcome you all.
Before we get started, there are a couple of points. First ...
You should all have a folder containing ... Do you all have one?
It's my great pleasure to welcome to you ...
On behalf of the company, I'd like to wish you a very pleasant stay.

B. Tasks

1. A speech of welcome

You are Andrea Barthel, Production Manager of Findling Bau AG. You are to open your company's Products Demonstration Day with a speech of welcome. Practice your speech, using these notes:

> **Findling Bau AG**
>
> Notes (speech of welcome: 9.30 a. m., Tuesday)
>
> – introduce myself
> – all hear me? pleasant journey? thanks for coming
> – welcome our guests: staff & friends of Laydon Hydraulics, Hull, UK
> – everything OK? if help needed, see Herr Bracht, reception desk.

- lunch: cafeteria, 12 o'clock onwards
- any questions?
- hand over to Ms June Brent, Manager, Laydon Hydraulics (she wants to say a few words)

2. Pairwork

Look again at the letter you wrote to Jill Cadorath in the previous unit.
By telephone, she has accepted your invitation. You propose the following schedule:

```
Schedule for the visit of          10.00: arrival at Design Centre
Jill Cadorath, Ladyline Fashions   10.15: look around Design Centre
                                   10.45: coffee – discuss Christmas orders
                                   12.30: lunch
                                   13.30: discuss orders for next year
                                   15.00: coffee
                                   15.30: discuss new design ideas
                                   17.00: depart for airport
```

Now, in pairs, take roles, and act out Jill Cadorath's arrival, using the following notes:

A: representative of the host company	B: Jill Cadorath
Welcome visitor.	Apologize – flight 30 minutes late.
Make sure she is all right/has all she needs.	Everything OK. Ready to start immediately.
Introduce Helga Schmitz (Publicity), Niels Obersheimer (Production), Susanne Vogt (Sales & Accounts).	Meet company staff (you met Susanne Vogt at London Textile Fair last year).
Summarize the schedule. Owing to lateness, suggest: (a) cancel visit to Design Centre, (b) have coffee now.	Agree to change in schedule.
Get discussions started. Explain: company needs Christmas orders by mid-October.	Christmas orders: explain difficulty of predicting fashion trends by mid-October. Suggest a compromise.
Respond to Cadorath's suggestion.	

Follow-up exercise: *Arbeitsbuch*, pp. 40–42.

Unit 7 — Secretarial Activities

Socializing

A. Lead-in: useful expressions

Sometimes, you'll want to socialize with clients and visitors – that is, make 'small talk' and chat with them to make them feel 'at home'. You can choose from many topics – but not to do with business! Examples:

Do you travel much in your job, Mr …?
It's a break from the daily grind, isn't it?

I hope German cuisine agrees with you.
I've been reading the news from Britain. I hear that …
You've brought good weather with you. How is it in …?

You will find more useful expressions during the following tasks.

B. Tasks

1. Talking about your guest's home area

Herr Wischer, a German businessman, is socializing with Mr Lloyd, his visitor from Britain.

But the parts of their conversation are shown in the wrong order here!

In pairs, rearrange the parts – then practice the conversation together, as a role play.

Herr Wischer (host):

1. No, we spent most of our holiday in the Yorkshire Dales. Are you from Yorkshire yourself?
2. You're based in Leeds, are you, Mr Lloyd?
3. Oh, from long ago. My wife and I had a driving tour of the north of England. Lovely part of the world.
4. It's in Yorkshire, isn't it?

Mr Lloyd (guest):

5. Oh, you know Yorkshire, do you?
6. No, I'm from the other end of the country – born and bred in London, actually.
7. Yes, that's where we have our main office.
8. Ha, not Leeds, I'm afraid. Have you actually been there?

2. Talking about your own home area

This time, Herr Wischer is socializing with a Danish visitor, Mr Andersen, before they get down to business. Here is a transcript of their conversation – but some of the expressions used by Herr Wischer, the host, are incomplete.
On a separate sheet, try to write them down in their completed form.

1. Have a g--- t---?
   Yes, pretty good. The touchdown at Munich was right on time.
2. Is this y--- f---- t--- i- Munich, Mr Andersen?
   Oh, I've been here several times – but always on short trips.
3. So you've never h-- a c----- to really s-- the p----?
   I'm afraid not.
4. That's a pity. It's w--- w---- s------ the extra day or two, if you c---- manage it.
   So I've heard. Supposing I had the chance – what would you recommend me to see or do here?
5. Go out and d------- Munich the w-- you'd d------- any city. Just walk the streets.
   I'd love to. But, tomorrow, I've got to be on that 8.15 flight – unfortunately!
6. Mr Andersen, p------- your p----- in Newcastle to let you s--- on l----- next t---. Be our guest!
7. I'd really like that. But, somehow, I don't think they'd like the idea of slaving away in the office while I'm having a good time in Bavaria!

3. Role play

In pairs, role play a first meeting between
(a) a business host in *your* town or local area,
(b) a foreign English-speaking visitor.
Invent the identities yourselves – but don't discuss business!

"... but then my psychiatrist cured me of those social inhibitions."

Unit 1 — *Commercial Correspondence*

English – the Language of Business Communication

A. Lead-in

1. Have a look at the following chart

IMPORT	of the the leading nations	EXPORT
USA	809 973 / 566 396	USA
Germany	439 800 / 567 720	Germany
France	304 339 / 294 624	France
Great Britain and Northern Ireland	333 109 / 234 911	Great Britain and Northern Ireland
Japan	329 683 / 465 907	Japan
Italy	243 302 / 225 984	Italy
Russia	181 699 / 187 497	Russia
Canada	188 116 / 196 902	Canada
The Netherlands	174 810 / 181 340	The Netherlands
Belgium – Luxemburg	165 440 / 163 680	Belgium – Luxemburg

(in Million DM)

Being among the leading importing and exporting nations in the world, Germany essentially depends on international contacts and cooperation to maintain her role in the world market. As this is equally true of other nations, a common language is of great help in making international business possible. This role has mainly been taken over by the English language. The reasons for this can be found in the long-standing trading and commercial power of both Great Britain and the USA.

Working for a German company will necessarily mean that you have to "internationalize" your qualifications because you will have to contact foreign companies to buy from or sell goods to them or you may even need to go abroad for business. You may have to answer phone calls from abroad or welcome foreign visitors to your company. You may also be expected to translate texts in English into German for further use in your company.

All this requires some background knowledge not only about the countries involved, but also about basic rules of business.

Communication is based on four skills: speaking, listening, reading and writing. This also applies to business communication and telecommunications (e.g. telephone, fax, e-mail). The advantages of telecommunications are plain to see: even over long distances they provide an instant exchange of information which, in general, is not limited to office hours.

Although the world-wide telecommunications network keeps growing rapidly and new means are being developed, the business letter still plays an important role. It provides a written record of agreements made orally and may provide evidence in the case of conflict. Moreover, it is often easier to write a letter if you have something upsetting or embarrassing to say.

2. Understanding and making notes

With the help of an English-German dictionary, make sure you understand the text above. Then prepare for an oral report on the text by making notes (these should be key words rather than complete sentences). Your report should at least answer the following questions:

a. Which are the leading importing/exporting nations?
b. What role does English play in international business?
c. What qualifications may be expected of you in a German company?
d. Which skills are required for the means of (tele-)communications mentioned in the text?
e. What are the advantages and disadvantages of the different forms of communication?

Unit 2 — Commercial Correspondence

Layout of the Business Letter

A. Lead-in

Form	block form (most commonly used)	semi-block form (see specimen letter, page 146)	indented form (see specimen letter, page 179)
Letterhead 1	name type of business address including postcode	**M & C** ___Advanced Computer Technology___ 76 Browning Terrace Birmingham B13 9SQ	Telephone: (021) 245 7012 Fax: (021) 343 4987
Date 2	🇬🇧 10. 11. 19..	🇬🇧 🇺🇸 10th November 19.. 10 November 19.. November 10, 19.. 10 Nov 19..	🇺🇸 11.10.19.. 11/10/19..
		day/month/year	⚠ month/day/year
Addressee 3	Messrs Amerson & Sons Mmes Smith & Wexter Mr Brown Ms Simpson Mrs Simpson	Opus Supplies Password Electronics Ltd.	
	firms trading under personal name	firms trading under impersonal name	
Salutation 4	🇬🇧 Dear Sirs and Mesdames,	🇬🇧 🇺🇸 Dear Sir(s), Dear Madam, Dear Mesdames, *addressed to an individual:* Dear Mr Owen, Dear Ms Hopper, Dear John,	🇺🇸 Gentlemen: Ladies and Gentlemen:
Complimentary close 6	🇬🇧 Yours faithfully, Faithfully yours,	🇬🇧 🇺🇸 *addressed to an individual:* Yours sincerely, Sincerely yours, With best wishes,	🇺🇸 Yours (very) truly, Very truly yours, Truly yours,

(5) Body of the letter
It carries the information intended for the addressee. *Note:* the text of the body always starts with a capital letter.

(7) Signature
The letter is signed by the person who is responsible for it. It is advisable to type the name of the person signing the letter and his/her job title.

(a) Reference
This may consist of the initials of the person dictating the letter and the typist or refer to a particular department or file number.

(b) Attention line
When a letter is intended to be seen by a particular person, it is common practice to insert *For the attention of Mr/Ms ....*

(c) Subject heading
This is to inform the addressee briefly about the contents of the letter.

(d) Enclosures
When additional material is sent with a letter, attention should be drawn to it by typing *Enclosure(s)/Enc(s)*. When there are several enclosures, the number should be indicated.

B. Tasks

1. Reorganizing a letter

Below you will find mixed-up parts of a letter. Put them into their correct order. The result should be a block-form letter with the letterhead *AdlerCom, 44289 Dortmund*.
Jürgen Schmidt – We refer to your letter of 5 March in which you asked for information about our RX-50 computer – JS/KK – USA – RX-50 COMPUTER – Gentlemen: – 14 March 19.. – 66 Heneage Street – Enclosed please find our catalogue together with the export price list – Encs. 2 – Birmingham, AL 35204 – Sales Manager – Cash & Carry Computers – Yours very truly, – We should be glad to hear from you again soon

2. Considering formal aspects

Have a look at the following addresses (with additional details given in *italics*) and decide on the following points:

a. Is it necessary to add Messrs/Mmes/Mrs(Ms)/Mr? If so, which is correct?
b. What is the correct salutation?
c. What is the correct complimentary close?
d. Decide whether or not an attention line is necessary.

1. Computers Limited
   Invincible Road
   Farnborough
   Hampshire GU14 7QU
   (Made up of men only, no previous business.)

2. HEXAGON Inc.
   707 Fairmount Ave.
   Saginaw, MI 48710
   (You want your letter to be directed to Mr Roebuck, no previous business.)

3. Svenson & Webster
   220 Blegborough Road
   London NW16 6DL
   (Made up of women only, no previous business.)

4. Smith & Co.
   87 Normandy Street
   Alton
   Hants GU34 1BR
   (You want your letter to be directed to Sam Smith, an old business friend of yours.)

3. Specimen letter (block form)

M & C
———— Advanced Computer Technology ————

76 Browning Terrace
Birmingham B13 9SQ

Telephone: (021) 245 7012
Fax: (021) 343 4987

15 March 19..

SC/SL

Ingrid Bilker KG
Alpenring 12-14
D-81377 München
Germany

For the attention of Herr Hagen

Dear Herr Hagen,

SPECIFICATIONS PC 70/3

As requested at your recent meeting with Ms Mace, I am sending you a leaflet containing the technical data on our PC 70/3. In order to discuss the specific requirements of German users, I propose another meeting in Munich on 19 May. Please inform me if this date suits you.
I look forward to your early reply.

Yours sincerely,

Stephen Clark
Stephen Clark
Technical Director

Enc.

Enquiry

A. Lead-in

1. Before opening a business relationship, a company will very often want to obtain information in order to make careful decisions. A request for information is called an *enquiry*.
If the company asks for price lists, catalogues, visits from representatives, they will send a *general enquiry*. If, however, specific details, e. g., certain kinds of products, quotations of prices, terms of delivery and payment, samples or drawings, are required, a *special enquiry* will be written. Both types are without any legal obligation for the enquirer. Nevertheless, it is an important step towards a business contract.

2. Understanding and making notes

a. What is the function of an enquiry?
b. What are the different types of enquiries?
c. What are their respective purposes?
d. Why is an enquiry important for a potential business relationship?

3. Specimen letter

M & C
———— Advanced Computer Technology ————

76 Browning Terrace
Birmingham B13 9SQ

Telephone: (021) 245 7012
Fax: (021) 343 4987

Our Ref. JM/SL   14 May 19..

D.D. Lee & Sons
Office Equipment International
5 Camac Street
P.O. Box 812
Singapore 20

Dear Sir or Madam,

           COMPUTER EQUIPMENT FURNITURE

We have learned from Mr Singh, your representative at the recent trade fair in London, that you produce furniture designed for computer equipment.

Many of our customers are interested not only in hardware/software supplies, but also in suitable furniture. So that we can meet our customers' requirements in every respect, we would like you to send us detailed descriptions and illustrations of your products, together with your latest price lists.

In addition, please let us know if you would perhaps be prepared to make furniture to specification to meet our individual range of products.

If your products and terms of sale, especially your export prices, are satisfactory, we will be very happy to place a trial order with you.

We hope to hear from you soon.

                              Yours faithfully,

                              Jean Mace
                              Sales Manager

Registered in England No. 601417

B. Tasks

1. Finding phrases to express intention

The following list contains intentions expressed in the letter above. Find out which phrases are used for each. Think of corresponding German phrases.
- making requests
- expressing positive expectations
- getting in touch
- showing interest
- expressing willingness

2. English-German translation

Translate the body of the letter into German. Make the text look like a German one (e. g. by using the German forms of the intentional phrases you have found).

C. Letter writing practice

1. Schreiben Sie im Auftrag der Firma Bilker in München an die Firma Office Electronics, Wilshire Blvd., Beverly Hills, CA USA. Datum des Schreibens ist der 17. 11. des laufenden Jahres. Sie haben die Anschrift der amerikanischen Firma von gemeinsamen Geschäftsfreunden, der Fa. Müller und Söhne in Frankfurt, erhalten. Sie sind sehr an der neuen Fotokopiererserie COPY-SWIFT interessiert und bitten um Unterlagen, damit Sie sich über die technischen Daten der Kopierer informieren können. Weisen Sie außerdem darauf hin, dass Sie wegen Ihrer führenden Position auf dem deutschen Markt größere Mengen des Kopierers bestellen würden, wenn das Gerät Ihren Anforderungen genügt. Erbitten Sie ebenfalls die Angabe des günstigsten Preises bei einer Bestellung von 500 Stück wie auch der Zahlungs- und Lieferbedingungen. Geben Sie Ihrer Erwartung in Bezug auf eine baldige Antwort Ausdruck.

Intention	
getting in touch	we have been given your name by [n]
	we have received your address from [n]
	your firm was recommended to us by [n]
showing interest	we are very (much) interested in [n] / [vb+-ing]
making requests	please [vb]
	we would like (you) [to+vb]
pointing out	we should like to point out [that-clause]
expressing positive expectations	we hope [to+vb] / [that-clause]
	we look forward to [n] / [vb+-ing]
	we would be (very) happy [to+vb]

Unit 3 — Commercial Correspondence

Structure

daher / deshalb / deswegen	therefore
damit / so dass	so that
um ... zu	(in order) to
außerdem / darüber hinaus	besides / in addition
wenn (falls)	if / provided
wegen / aufgrund	owing to / due to
ebenfalls / auch	also / ... too / ... as well
wie auch	as well as

Contents

gemeinsame Geschäftsfreunde	mutual business friends
Fotokopierer	photocopier
Serie	series
Unterlagen (über)	here: literature (on)
technische Daten	technical data
sich über etw. informieren	inform oneself about s. th.
führende Position	leading position
größere Mengen	substantial quantities
jmnds Anforderungen genügen	meet s. o.'s requirements
günstigster Preis	most favourable price
(einen Preis etc.) angeben	quote (a price, etc.)
Bestellung / Auftrag (über)	order (for)
Lieferbedingungen	terms of delivery
Stück (Plural)	units
Zahlung	payment
baldige Antwort (erhalten)	(receive) s. o.'s early reply

2. Wenden Sie sich am 23. 4. des laufenden Jahres im Auftrag der Firma Ossmann & Co. in Dortmund an die englische Firma OFF-TEC Ltd., 38 Churchfield Road, Tickhill, Doncaster DN11 9LA, die Bürobedarf herstellt. Beziehen Sie sich auf Ihr Gespräch mit dem Vertreter der Firma, Mr Soreham, anlässlich der letzten LONDON OFFICE FAIR. Dabei hatte dieser Ihnen zugesagt Unterlagen über die neue Heftmaschine STAPLEWONDER zuzusenden, die aber bisher nicht eingetroffen sind. Weisen Sie auf Ihr nach wie vor großes Interesse an dieser Maschine hin und bitten Sie um Zusendung eines Angebotes über 200 Stück mit vollständigen Angaben über Exportpreise, Zahlungsbedingungen und Rabatte für regelmäßige Käufe. Da Mr Soreham Lieferung innerhalb von zwei Monaten zugesagt hatte, soll Ihnen die englische Firma auch mitteilen, ob sie diese Lieferfrist bestätigen kann. Bitten Sie um umgehende Antwort.

Intention

referring to s. th. / s. o.	we refer to [n]
	referring to [n]
pointing out (cont.)	we wish to point out [that-clause]
making requests (cont.)	we should appreciate it if you would [vb]
	we should be grateful if you would [vb]
	it would be appreciated if you could [vb]
	[n] would be appreciated

Structure

da (im Sinne von *weil*)	as
wir bitten um Zusendung von X	*wir bitten Sie, uns X zuzusenden*
ob	if / whether
bisher	so far / up to now
nach wie vor / immer noch	still

Contents

Gespräch	discussion
Vertreter	representative
letzte	recent
*da*bei (bei der Gelegenheit)	on that occasion
jmdm etw zusagen / versprechen	promise s. o. (to do) s. th.
Heftmaschine	stapling machine
bei jmdm eintreffen	reach s. o.
Angebot (über)	quotation (for)
vollständige Angaben	full information (about)
	detailed information (about)
Rabatt	discount (for)
regelmäßig	regular
Kauf	purchase
innerhalb von	within
jmdm etw mitteilen	let s. o. know s. th.
etw bestätigen	confirm s. th.
Lieferfrist	delivery period
(Antwort) erhalten	receive a reply
umgehend / baldmöglichst	as soon as possible

3. Der Softwarespezialist Hausmann & Söhne in Hamburg hat von seinem Vertreter in England erfahren, dass die Firma COM-SOFT PLC, 10 Lawrence Road, Hounslow

HS3 7JH, Middx. ein neues Datenbankprogramm entwickelt hat. Am 3. 9. des laufenden Jahres wenden Sie sich im Auftrag von Hausmann & Söhne an die o. a. Firma. Sie haben Interesse das neue Datenbankprogramm auf dem deutschen Markt anzubieten. Weisen Sie jedoch darauf hin, dass dieses Programm Ihrer Meinung nach nur mit deutschen Anweisungen verkäuflich ist. Darüber hinaus sollte das Handbuch in die deutsche Sprache übersetzt werden, da sonst der potenzielle Kundenkreis zu klein wäre. Bitten Sie um Informationen, ob die Firma das Programm entsprechend ändern kann und wie lange dies dauern wird. Schlagen Sie vor die Übersetzung des Handbuches durch einen Mitarbeiter Ihrer Firma vornehmen zu lassen um Zeit zu sparen. Bitten Sie darum, dass sich die englische Firma umgehend mit Ihrem Vertreter in England in Verbindung setzt um Einzelheiten zu besprechen. Verweisen Sie auf den mit getrennter Post versandten Katalog, der der englischen Firma einen Eindruck von Ihrer Angebotspalette vermitteln soll. Beenden Sie Ihr Schreiben mit einer Verabschiedungsformel.

Intention

making suggestions	(may) we suggest [vb+-ing]
drawing attention to enclosure(s)	please find enclosed [n]
	we are also sending you [n]
drawing attention to accompanying mail	under separate cover we are sending you [n]

Structure

sonst / ansonsten / andernfalls	otherwise
(dem-)entsprechend	accordingly

Contents

Datenbankprogramm	database program
jmnds Meinung nach	in s. o.'s opinion
Anweisungen	instructions
verkäuflich (marktfähig)	marketable
Handbuch	manual
potenziell	prospective
Kundenkreis	range of customers
ändern	modify
dauern	take
lassen / veranlassen	arrange for
Mitarbeiter	member of staff
sich mit jmdm in Verbindung setzen	contact s. o.
Eindruck vermitteln	give an impression (of)
Angebotspalette	range of products

4. Sie sind Mitarbeiter der Firma Sölker & Söhne in Darmstadt und wenden sich am 27. 9. des laufenden Jahres an die Firma Master Bros., 16 Wayside, High Wycombe, Bucks. HP13 5PG. Diese Firma hat in einer Anzeige in der Zeitschrift *Office World* eine neuartige ölfreie Stempelfarbe angeboten. Beziehen Sie sich auf diese Anzeige und erbitten Sie den neuesten Katalog der Firma wie auch die Exportpreisliste. Weisen Sie darüber hinaus darauf hin, dass Sie ständig an Produkten interessiert sind, die auf dem deutschen Markt noch nicht vertreten sind. Deshalb würden Sie es begrüßen, wenn Ihnen die englische Firma in Zukunft regelmäßig Informationen über neu entwickelte Artikel zukommen ließe. Bitten Sie um baldige Beantwortung Ihres Schreibens.

Contents

(Zeitungs-)Anzeige	advertisement
neuartig	a new kind of
ölfreie Stempelfarbe	stamp pad ink without oil
neuester Katalog	latest catalogue
Preisliste	price list
vertreten (erhältlich) sein	be available
in Zukunft	in future
neu entwickelt	newly-developed
Artikel	article

5. Ihr Vorgesetzter reicht ihnen die Fotokopie einer Anzeige aus der Zeitschrift *Com-com* herein und bittet Sie, unter Berücksichtigung der handschriftlichen Anmerkungen, eine Anfrage zu schreiben. Datum des Schreibens ist der 25. Juni des laufenden Jahres.

DataLogic

✗ DM 2 Word Processor £ 29.50
DM 3 Spread Sheet Calculator £ 29.50
✗ DM 9 RAM Database £ 29.50
User Definable Graphics £ 17.50
Home Budget £ 17.35

Dealers! For information write to:
DataLogic Ltd., Tipton Trading Estate, Bloomfield Road, Tipton, West Midlands DY4 9AH. Overseas enquiries welcome.

– weitere Einzelheiten über die angekreuzten Programme
– Zahlungsbedingungen
– Einführungsrabatt?
– Lieferbedingungen
– Lieferung innerhalb von 2 Wochen möglich?
– rege Nachfrage, weitere Aufträge in Aussicht stellen!
– machen Sie es eilig!

Unit 3 Commercial Correspondence

D. Listening comprehension & note-taking

Introduction

Herr Schumann of Bilker's is going to be in charge of all matters concerning the co-operation between Bilker KG and M & C. He is sent to Birmingham for a month in order to learn about M & C's business activities. He accompanies Jean Mace through her daily routine, first observing, but then getting involved in the day-to-day business of the company.
The listening texts in this and the following units are based on the above-mentioned background.
Concerning the tasks following the listening texts, you are expected to put yourself into Herr Schumann's place.
You will hear each conversation several times.

Note-taking

Take notes on the essential points of the listening text (these should be key words rather than complete sentences). With the help of these notes you should be able to

– give an oral or written report on what has been said and/or

– respond to what has been said (e.g. by writing a letter, making a phone call, etc.).

The following list mentions points which might be of interest:

– *who* (is talking to whom)?

– *where/when* (does the conversation take place)?

– *reasons* (for the conversation)?

– *topics* (discussed)?

– *details* (discussed with each topic)?

– *decisions* (made)?

1. Listen to the telephone conversation. Herr Schumann needs help and is phoning a friend for advice.

2. Imagine that you are Herr Schumann and write a suitable letter of enquiry to Care Transit, 15 George St., Cardiff CF2 4HJ.

E. Contiletter

Task	Note
Separate words, sentences and paragraphs. Decide which words to start with a capital letter. Decide where to punctuate.	In Enquiry 1, the sentence structure remains unchanged. In Enquiry 2, the sentence structure has been jumbled, i. e. the letter has to be reorganized.

Enquiry 1

dearsirormadamwehavelearnedfromourmutualbusinessfriendsmessrsSmith&Browntha tyouhavedevelopedanewkindofphotocopieraswewouldliketoinformourselvesaboutthet echnicaldataofthisphotocopierpleasesendusyourlatestcataloguetogetherwithyourpriceli stduetoourleadingpositiononthegermanmarketwewouldordersubstantialquantitiesofthe copierifyourpricesarefavourablebesidesthiswewouldliketopointoutthatwearealwaysinte restedinproductsthatmeetourcustomersrequirementsthereforewewouldbegratefulifyouc ouldkeepusinformedaboutnewlydevelopedarticlesifyourproductsandtermsofsalearesatis factorywewillbeveryhappytoplaceanorderwithyouwelookforwardtoreceivingyourearlyre plyyoursfaithfully

Enquiry 2

tosavetimewesuggesthavingthemanualtranslatedbyastaffmemberofourcompanyasaleadi ngsoftwarecompanyingermanyweareverymuchinterestedinofferingyournewdatabasesyst emDABASonthegermanmarketgentlementhereforeweshouldappreciateitifyoucouldinfo rmusassoonaspossiblewhetheryouagreetoourproposalandhowlongitwilltakeyoutoprovi dethegermanversionwehopetohearfromyousoonunderseparatecoverwearesendingyouo urcataloguetogiveyouanimpressionofourrangeofproductsaswehavereceivedmanyenquir iesfordatabasesystemswhichareeasytohandlewewouldlikeyoutosendusasampleofyourpr ogramfortrialtogetherwiththemanualtrulyyoursyourfirmwasrecommendedtousbymessrs Jackson&Smithontheoccasionoftherecenthanoverfairiftheprogrammeetsourrequiremen tswewouldordersubstantialquantitiesonconditionhoweverthatyouprovidegermanversio nsofboththeprogramandthemanual.

Follow-up exercises: *Arbeitsbuch,* pp. 82–85.

Offer

A. Lead-in

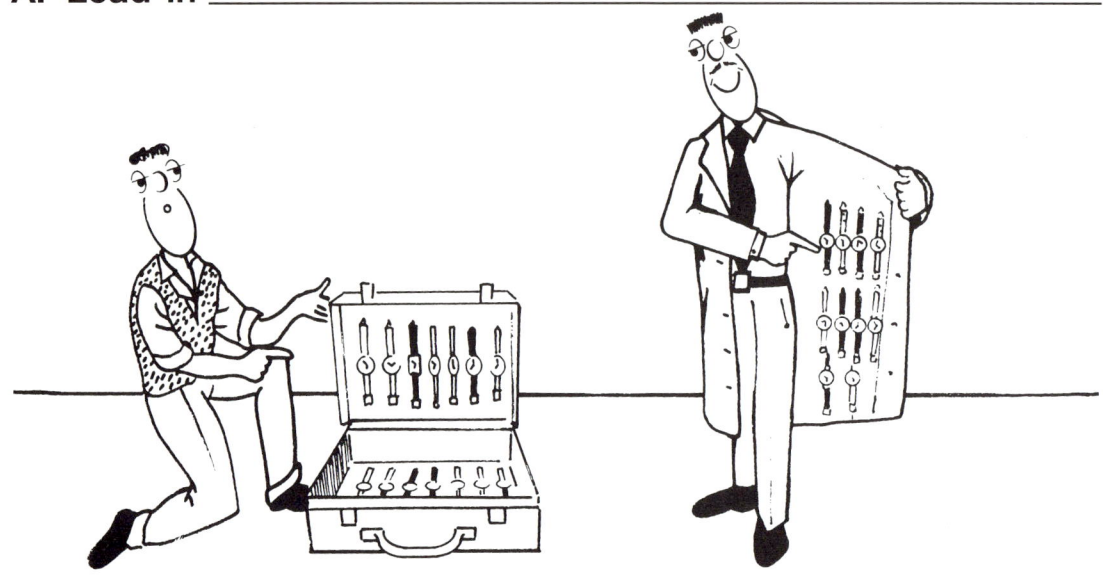

1. A supplier expresses his readiness to enter into business relations with a customer by means of an *offer*. Offers can be made in oral or written form. There are two kinds of offers. First, the *solicited offer* which is the supplier's answer to a customer's enquiry. With it, the supplier will send all details he has been asked for. Second, the *unsolicited* or *voluntary offer* which the supplier will send without having been asked. This can serve different purposes. The supplier might have the intention of reminding the customer of his firm, announcing special offers, advertising new services or products.

A detailed offer should consist of information about the kind and quality of the service or product offered, quantities, prices, terms of delivery and payment, and delivery periods.

A supplier is bound by his offer unless the customer does not react within a reasonable period of time, or the offer has been declared as one *without engagement* or contains the clause *subject to prior sale*. If an offer, already mailed, should be withdrawn, the withdrawal has to reach the customer not later than the offer.

2. Understanding and making notes

a. What are the different types of offers?
b. What formal requirements must be met?
c. What are the important elements of an offer?
d. What are the legal consequences of a supplier sending an offer?

3. Specimen letter

D.D. Lee & Sons
Office Equipment International

5 Camac Street
P.O. Box 812
Singapore 20

Tel. 378 4983
Fax 378 4990

21 May 19..

Ms Jean Mace
M & C
76 Browning Terrace
Birmingham B13 9SQ
England

Dear Ms Mace,

We wish to confirm receipt of your letter dated 14 May and are sending you our latest office furniture catalogue. The export price list is enclosed. On condition that sufficient quantities are ordered, we are quite prepared to meet individual requirements.

Our terms of payment for initial orders are: opening of an irrevocable and confirmed documentary letter of credit in our favour, payable at the First Singapore Bank. In the case of regular business we would deliver on the basis cash against documents, if desired.

Normally, the delivery period is about four weeks for our standard programme, but subject to change for individual specifications.

We think that you will find our conditions satisfactory, and therefore we hope to hear from you soon.

Sincerely yours,

Samuel Wong
Samuel Wong
Sales Department

Encs.

B. Tasks

1. Finding phrases to express intention

The following list contains intentions expressed in the letter above. Find out which phrases are used for each. Think of corresponding German phrases.

– drawing attention to enclosures
– acknowledging receipt
– expressing positive expectations
– expressing willingness

2. English-German translation

Translate the body of the letter into German. Make the text look like a German one (e. g. by using the German forms of the intentional phrases you have found).

C. Letter writing practice

1. Bestätigen Sie am 17. 1. des laufenden Jahres im Auftrag der Firma Kaiser & Söhne in Hannover die Anfrage der Firma M & C über 800 SUPERSHOT-Joysticks. Bieten Sie diese Menge zu einem Exportpreis von DM 12,50 pro Stück an, erklären Sie sich jedoch bereit einen Einführungsrabatt von 10% zu gewähren, so dass sich der Gesamtpreis auf DM 9 000,– FOB Hamburg belaufen würde. Ihre Zahlungsbedingungen bei Erstaufträgen sind Vorauskasse bzw. Dokumentenakkreditiv, zahlbar bei der Dresdner Bank in Hannover. Die Lieferung wird spätestens zwei Wochen nach Auftragseingang erfolgen. Geben Sie Ihrer Hoffnung auf die baldige Aufnahme einer Geschäftsverbindung Ausdruck.

Intention

acknowledging receipt	we have received [n]
	we are in receipt of [n]
	we were (very) pleased to receive [n]
offering something	we have the pleasure of [vb+-ing]
	we are happy [to+vb]
	we are glad [to+vb]
expressing willingness	we will be glad [to+vb]
	we will be pleased [to+vb]
	we will be happy [to+vb]

Structure

jedoch / allerdings	however
die Lieferung (erfolgt)	delivery (will be made/effected)
bei (im Falle von)	for

Contents

oben genannt	above-mentioned
zu einem Preis von	at a price of
pro Stück	per unit / each
Einführungsrabatt (von)	introductory discount (of)
einen Rabatt gewähren (auf)	grant a discount (on)
Gesamt-	total
sich belaufen auf	come to / amount to
Erstauftrag	first order / initial order
Vorauskasse	payment in advance
Dokumentenakkreditiv	documentary letter of credit
zu jmnds Gunsten	in s. o.'s favour / in s. o.'s name
zahlbar (bei)	payable (at)
spätestens (Datum/Frist)	not later than (date/period)
(Zeitraum) nach Auftragseingang	(period) from receipt of order
eine Geschäftsverbindung aufnehmen / haben (mit)	do business (with)

2. Bedanken Sie sich am 21. 2. des laufenden Jahres im Auftrag der Firma Prontodruck in München für die Anfrage vom 17. 2. bezüglich 10 000 selbsthaftender Diskettenaufkleber. Die Anfrage kam von der Firma MPI Ltd., 16 The Square, Kenilworth, Warwickshire CV8 1EB. Ihr Preis für die Aufkleber ist DM 995,50 bei Abnahme von mindestens 10 000 Stück. Erklären Sie sich jedoch bereit einen Rabatt von 5% bei einer Abnahme von mindestens 20 000 Stück zu gewähren. Weisen Sie auf das beiliegende Muster hin. Fügen Sie eine Proformarechnung über die oben genannte Menge bei mit der Bitte, bei einer Auftragserteilung die Zahlung per Wechsel durch die Bank des Kunden zu veranlassen und Ihnen die Bestätigung zuzusenden. Bei Nachbestellungen und Angabe von Referenzen könnte auf der Basis Kasse gegen Dokumente geliefert werden. Der Versand erfolgt FOB München Flughafen. Aufgrund größerer Lagerbestände können Sie die Lieferung innerhalb von fünf Tagen nach Auftragseingang fest zusagen. Geben Sie Ihrer Erwartung auf baldigen Auftragseingang Ausdruck und sichern Sie umgehende Ausführung zu.

Intention

expressing thanks	(we) thank you (very much) for [n] / [vb+-ing]
drawing attention to enclosure(s) (cont.)	enclosed (with this letter) we are sending you [n]
	at the same time we enclose [n]
expressing commitment	we assure you [that-clause]
	you may be sure [that-clause]

Structure

bei Abnahme von XYZ	*wenn Sie XYZ abnehmen*
D: bei [n]	GB: if [vb]
bezüglich (dieses Wort kann häufig Präpositionen ersetzen)	concerning / regarding

Contents

selbsthaftend	self-adhesive
Diskettenaufkleber	disk label
Abnahme	*Kauf*
mindestens	at least / not less than
Muster	sample
gleichzeitig	at the same time
Proformarechnung	pro forma invoice
durch (die Bank)	through (the bank)
per Wechsel	by draft
Bestätigung	confirmation
Nachbestellung	further order
Referenzen angeben	give references
auf der Basis	on the basis (of)
Versand	shipment
größere Lagerbestände	a good stock (of)
fest zusagen / garantieren	guarantee
umgehend / baldmöglichst / unverzüglich	immediate(ly) / as soon as possible

3. Bestätigen Sie am 22. 10. des laufenden Jahres als Sachbearbeiter der Firma Meyer & Co. in Gießen den Erhalt der Anfrage der dänischen Firma Dansk Micro, 32 Krogvej, Blåvand, DK6857, bezüglich des von Ihnen vertriebenen Laser-Druckers LASERSTAR. Teilen Sie der anfragenden Firma mit, dass der in Ihrem Katalog aufgeführte Preis von DM 720,– nicht mehr aktuell ist, da die Produktion des Druckers inzwischen eingestellt wurde. Erklären Sie deshalb Ihre Bereitschaft den Drucker zu einem um 10% reduzierten Preis anzubieten, allerdings unter der Voraussetzung, dass die dänische Firma den gesamten Restbestand von 200 Stück abnimmt. Der Gesamtpreis würde sich demnach auf DM 129 600,– frachtfrei Grenze, einschließlich Verpackung belaufen. Die Lieferung könnte innerhalb von zehn Tagen nach Auftragseingang durchgeführt werden. Zahlung soll durch unwiderrufliches Dokumentenakkreditiv erfolgen. Bitten Sie um Mitteilung, ob die anfragende Firma mit den oben genannten Bedingungen einverstanden ist.

Commercial Correspondence — Unit 4

Intention

acknowledging receipt (cont.)	it was a pleasure to receive [n]
	we wish to confirm receipt of [n]
expressing willingness (cont.)	we are prepared [to+vb]

Structure

der von Ihnen vertriebene Drucker	*der Drucker, den Sie vertreiben*
nicht mehr	no longer / not ... any longer
inzwischen	in the meantime / meanwhile
unter der Voraussetzung, dass	on condition that
demnach / demzufolge	consequently

Contents

vertreiben	distribute
Laserdrucker	laser printer
aufführen	mention / state
aktuell (gültig)	valid
einstellen	be discontinued
reduzieren (um)	reduce (by)
zu einem Preis von	at a price of
gesamt	entire
Restbestand	remaining stock
(Ware) abnehmen	take delivery (of)
einschließlich	including [n] / [n] included
oben genannt	above-mentioned [n]
	[n] mentioned above
mit etw einverstanden sein	agree to

4. Die Firma Office Specialists Inc., 16 Wayside, Hamburg, NY 10922 hat Ihnen eine Anfrage gesandt, die Sie am 12. 9. des laufenden Jahres im Auftrag der Firma Hammer & Schmidt in Karlsruhe beantworten. Gegenstand der Anfrage war der von Ihnen hergestellte ergonomisch geformte neue Drehstuhl Typ 2A. Bieten Sie den Drehstuhl zu einem Stückpreis von DM 230,– an und erklären Sie Ihre Bereitschaft bei einer Bestellung von 50 Stück einen Rabatt von 5% auf den Listenpreis zu gewähren. Weisen Sie darauf hin, dass bei einer größeren Bestellung Lieferung erst zwei bis drei Monate nach Auftragseingang möglich ist, da Sie nur eine geringe Anzahl auf Lager haben. Kleinere Stückzahlen können allerdings innerhalb von drei Wochen geliefert werden. Die angegebenen Preise verstehen sich netto, FAS Hamburg, ausschließlich Verpackung. Ihre Zahlungsbedingungen sind Kasse gegen Dokumente oder 3% Rabatt bei Zahlung durch Akkreditiv, zahlbar bei der Handelsbank in Karlsruhe. Weisen Sie auf den mit getrennter Post versandten Katalog hin, der dem Kunden einen Eindruck vom Umfang Ihres Angebots vermitteln soll. Geben Sie Ihrer Zuversicht bezüglich der baldigen Aufnahme von Geschäftsbeziehungen Ausdruck.

Contents

ergonomisch geformt	ergonomically shaped
Drehstuhl	swivel seat
Anzahl	number of items
auf Lager haben	stock (vb)
Stückzahlen	*Mengen*
ausschließlich A	A extra

Peanuts

Dear Gramma,

Thank you for the very nice Christmas present.

It was just what I wanted.

What was it?

5. In Ihrer Firma ist eine Anfrage eingegangen, die von Ihrem Vorgesetzten mit handschriftlichen Anmerkungen versehen und Ihnen zur weiteren Bearbeitung übergeben wurde. Erstellen Sie am 20. November des laufenden Jahres ein unterschriftsfertiges Antwortschreiben.

Commercial Correspondence — Unit 4

MailSoft PLC
797 King St
London W6 9LZ

MailSoft PLC

Tel.: 01-748 5351
Fax: 01-555 2561

9 November 19..

Messrs Abraham & Schmidt
Semerteichstr. 28
44141 Dortmund
Germany

Dear Sirs,

COMPUTER GAMES

You have been recommended to us by our mutual business friends, Messrs Banks & Sons in Leicester.

As a leading mail-order house dealing in software, we are always looking for novelties which have not yet been introduced onto the British market. We are especially interested in action games, and therefore we would like you to send us your latest special catalogue, as well as your export price list. Please also let us know if there are English versions of your games, since German ones would be of no use to us. *haben wir!*

[Erstauftrag: Vorauszahlung / Nachbestellung: Kasse gegen Dokumente]
Detailed information concerning terms of payment and earliest delivery date would also be appreciated. *← 10 Tage nach Auftragseingang*

Please let us have your reply as soon as possible, as we will have our new mail-order catalogue printed in December - hopefully containing some of your articles.

Yours faithfully,

G. Gray

Geoffrey Gray
Director

GG/JK

— Einführungsrabatt 10%
— zur Probe senden:
1x Spiders
1x Sabotage
1x Devil Riders

EILT 88

Unit 4 — Commercial Correspondence

D. Listening comprehension & note-taking

1. Listen to the telephone conversation. Herr Schuhmann has received a call from Denmark. He is talking to Ms Eva Jensen who runs a travel agency in Haubring/Denmark.

2. Imagine that you are Herr Schuhmann and write a suitable letter of offer to Ms Eva Jensen of Jensen Travel, Elleveg 3, 9600 Haubring, Denmark.

E. Contiletter

For instructions see page 153.

Offer 1

dearsirsormesdameswerefertoyourenquiryofmarch2019..forourinkjetprinterINKYwewouldbegladtoofferthisprinterataunitpriceofdm360fororderexceeding100unitshoweverwearepreparedtograntadiscountof10%onthelistpricewewishtopointoutthatthereisadeliveryperiodof3–4weeksifyouordermorethan100unitsotherwisewecouldsupplywithinoneweekfromreceiptofyourorderpricesarenetfobBremerhavenpackingextraourtermsofpaymentforfirstordersarecashinadvanceordocumentaryletterofcreditinournameswelookforwardtoreceivingyourordersoonfaithfullyyours

Offer 2

shouldyouplacefurtherorderswecouldsupplyonthebasiscashagainstdocumentswewouldnormallyofferthisseatatapriceofdm1,200eachbutwehavethepleasureofgrantingyouanintroductorydiscountofl5%sothatthetotalpricewouldamounttodm204000fobRostockpackingincludedwehopetoreceiveyourordersoonandpromisethatitwillbeexecutedpromptlyandcarefullyenclosedwiththisletterwearesendingyouaproformainvoicefortheabovementionedquantitygentlementhankyouverymuchforyourenquirydatedmarch14for200unitsofournewswivelseatCOM4verytrulyyoursifyouplaceyourorderpleasearrangeforpaymentbydraftthroughyourbank

Follow-up exercises: *Arbeitsbuch*, pp. 85–88.

Commercial Correspondence | Unit 5

Order

A. Lead-in

1. Before deciding where to buy necessary goods, a customer should examine and compare offers of different possible suppliers. After this, the customer will react to the most favourable offer by placing an *order*.

The order can be made orally, in writing or in any kind of modern telecommunications. Orders which have not been made in writing should be confirmed by written orders to provide evidence.

The order should list all the details contained in an offer (see Unit 4). Very often, letters to suppliers contain printed order sheets or order forms which standardize the process of ordering within a company.

A customer can place different kinds of orders:

initial (or first) order:

the customer orders goods from a particular supplier for the very first time

repeat (or re-) order:

the customer orders the same goods from the same supplier again

trial order:

the customer places an order to test the quality of the supplier's goods and/or his reliability

standing order:

the customer asks the supplier to deliver goods at certain intervals according to the customer's specifications

A sales contract is established if an order follows a firm offer. In the case of an offer without engagement, a customer's order must be acknowledged by the supplier (see Unit 6)

"Bad? I'll say things are bad – even the companies who don't intend to pay aren't placing orders!"

to establish a sales contract. This is also necessary if the customer has changed the conditions of the preceding offer substantially.

2. Understanding and making notes

a. How does a customer find out about the most favourable offer?
b. What types of orders are there?
c. Under what circumstances does an order establish a sales contract?
d. What is the advantage of placing an order in writing?

163

Unit 5 — Commercial Correspondence

3. Specimen letter

M & C
_____ Advanced Computer Technology _____

76 Browning Terrace
Birmingham B13 9SQ

Telephone: (021) 245 7012
Fax: (021) 343 4987

7 June 19..

JM/SL

Mr S. Wong
D.D. Lee & Sons
Office Equipment International
5 Camac Street
P.O. Box 812
Singapore 20

Dear Mr Wong,

Thank you very much for your letter of 21 May 19.. which we received last week together with your catalogue and the export price list. In accordance with your offer we are happy to place the following order with you:

Type	Quantity	Unit Price	Amount
PROTECTO security drawer	125	$ 45.25	$ 5,656.25
SPS Standard printer stand	250	$ 24.70	$ 6,175.00
SMS Standard monitor stand	250	$ 26.50	$ 6,625.00
		TOTAL	$ 18,456.25

Delivery: not later than 15 July
Packing: seaworthy packing included

Meanwhile, we have instructed Lords Bank, Birmingham, to open an irrevocable and confirmed letter of credit, payable at the First Singapore Bank.

We should like to point out that the delivery period mentioned by you must be met, as our customers expect punctual delivery.

We should appreciate it if you would acknowledge our order by return and inform us about the date of dispatch.

As we are planning to offer our new computer system together with a tailor-made workstation, we are in need of suitable desking. The desks which you offer, however, do not fit our purposes. Enclosed we are sending you data about all the components that belong to the system. Please state whether you can supply us with a specially-built desk that will fit it. If so, we should be glad if you would submit your offer as soon as possible.

Yours sincerely,

Jean Mace

Jean Mace
Sales Manager

Registered in England No. 601417

B. Tasks

1. Finding phrases to express intention

The following list contains intentions expressed in the letter above. Find out which phrases are used for each. Think of corresponding German phrases.
– making requests
– expressing thanks
– expressing willingness
– pointing out
– drawing attention to enclosures

2. English-German translation

Translate the body of the letter into German. Make the text look like a German one (e. g. by using the German forms of the intentional phrases you have found).

C. Letter writing practice

1. Bestätigen Sie am 15. 2. des laufenden Jahres im Auftrag der Firma Micropoint in Delmenhorst das am 14. Februar bei Ihnen eingegangene Angebot über 200 CD-ROM-Laufwerke. Absender war die Firma Opto Supplies, 310 Streatham High Rd, London W1. Stellen Sie noch einmal ausdrücklich fest, dass der Gesamtpreis für die o. a. 200 Stück £9,000 CIF Bremen beträgt. Sie sind mit dem Preis einverstanden und bitten die englische Firma dieses Schreiben als förmlichen Auftrag zu akzeptieren. Bitten Sie ausdrücklich um unverzüglichen Versand der Ware, da Sie bereits zahlreiche Anfragen von Kunden erhalten haben. Die Zahlung wird noch heute per Bankscheck erfolgen. Geben Sie Ihrer Erwartung Ausdruck in Zukunft weitere Aufträge erteilen zu können, da eine steigende Nachfrage nach Computerkomponenten zu verzeichnen ist.

Intention	
reconfirming statements	we note [that-clause]
	we understand [that-clause]
expressing ability	we are in a position [to+vb]

Structure	
bereits / schon	already

Contents	
bei jmdm eingehen	reach s. o.
CD-ROM-Laufwerk	CD-ROM drive
mit etw einverstanden sein	agree to s. th. / s. th. is/are agreed
akzeptieren	accept

Unit 5 — Commercial Correspondence

Contents

förmlicher Auftrag	official order
versenden	dispatch / ship
Waren(sendung)	consignment / shipment (of)
unverzüglich	without (further) delay / at the first opportunity
zahlreich	a great number (of)
Kunde	customer
Bankscheck	banker's draft
in Zukunft	in the future
weitere	further
einen Auftrag erteilen	place an order (with)
steigende Nachfrage (nach)	increasing demand (for)
Komponente (Bauteil)	component

2. Schreiben Sie am 12. 5. des laufenden Jahres als Sachbearbeiter der Firma Bilker/München an die Firma Offtech Ltd., 18 Cuttings Avenue, Sutton-in-Ashfield, Notts SA3 4LT, England. Beziehen Sie sich in Ihrem Schreiben auf das Angebot der Firma vom 17. 4. Drücken Sie Ihr Bedauern darüber aus, dass die englische Firma den von Ihnen erbetenen Einführungsrabatt von 5% für das neue Produkt DESKCOPIER nicht gewähren konnte. Signalisieren Sie Ihre Bereitschaft die Bestellung auf 200 Stück zu erhöhen, bestehen Sie aber unter diesen Umständen auf dem oben genannten Rabatt. Weisen Sie auf den beiliegenden Auftrag über die übrigen Angebotsposten hin und drängen Sie auf Einhaltung des angegebenen Liefertermins. Wie vereinbart, erfolgt die Zahlung innerhalb von zehn Tagen nach Eingang der Rechnung. Geben Sie Ihrer Erwartung Ausdruck weitere Aufträge erteilen zu können, wenn die englische Firma den obigen Vorschlag akzeptiert.

Intention

expressing regret	we note with regret [that-clause] / we (very much) regret [that-clause]
expressing inability	it is impossible for us [to+vb] / we are unable [to+vb] / we are not in a position [to+vb]
expressing urgency	we must ask you [to+vb]

Structure

unter diesen Umständen	under these circumstances

Contents

etw erbitten	request s. th.
erhöhen (auf)	raise (to)
bestehen (auf)	insist (on)
übrige Angebotsposten	remaining (number of) units
Termin	date
wie vereinbart	as agreed
Vorschlag	proposal

3. Bestellen Sie am 2. 10. des laufenden Jahres im Auftrage der Firma Garthmann & Söhne in Hannover bei der Firma Comsystems, 2111 Packard Rd., Ann Arbor, MI 48108 300 Festplattenlaufwerke vom Typ QM 2.1 GB. Sie benötigen die Laufwerke kurzfristig, da Sie beabsichtigen für das bevorstehende Weihnachtsgeschäft eine entsprechend aufgerüstete Version Ihres PC 33 anzubieten. Bitten Sie daher um vorrangige Behandlung Ihres Auftrags, da die Laufwerke spätestens am 15. November benötigt werden. Bestätigen Sie den Ihnen in Ihrer telefonischen Anfrage genannten Gesamtpreis von $54,900 CIF Hamburg, einschließlich Verpackung. Drängen Sie auf besonders sorgfältige Verpackung um jegliches Rutschen in den Kisten zu unterbinden. Weisen Sie darauf hin, dass dies bei früheren Lieferungen der amerikanischen Firma Gegenstand von Beanstandungen war. Bitten Sie um Mitteilung per Fax, sobald Einzelheiten der Verschiffung bekannt sind. Sie werden dann die Überweisung des Rechnungsbetrages gemäß Ihren früheren Vereinbarungen veranlassen.

Structure

entsprechend	accordingly
besonders	especially / particularly

Contents

Festplattenlaufwerk	hard disk drive
bevorstehend	coming
aufgerüstete Version	upgraded version
etw vorrangig behandeln	give priority to s. th.
rechtzeitig	punctual
Auslieferung	*Lieferung*
etw sicherstellen	ensure s. th.
telefonisch	by phone
auf etw sorgfältig achten	exercise care in [vb+-ing]
Rutschen	movement

Unit 5 — Commercial Correspondence

Contents

Kiste	case
unterbinden	avoid
frühere / vorhergehende	previous
Gegenstand sein von etw = Grund sein für etw	give cause (for)
Beanstandung	complaint
sobald	as soon as
per Fax	by fax
Überweisung (Zahlung)	remittance
gemäß	according to
Vereinbarung	agreement

4. Schreiben Sie am 5. 10. des laufenden Jahres als Mitarbeiter der Versandfirma ProCom in Essen einen Auftrag an die Firma Computer Warehouse, 10 East 53rd St, New York, NY 10022. Beziehen Sie sich dabei auf das Angebot vom 28. 9. und bedanken Sie sich in diesem Zusammenhang auch für den Ihnen gleichzeitig zugesandten Spezialkatalog. Ihr Auftrag umfasst folgende Posten: 1) 130 17" Farbmonitore vom Typ CM 17, Stückpreis $312.50; 2) 150 Diskettenlaufwerke 3,5" vom Typ HD 1.44MB, Stückpreis $38.50; 3) 60 Festplattenlaufwerke vom Typ QM 2.1 GB, Stückpreis $183 und 4) 500 verschließbare Diskettenboxen FB 5", Stückpreis $18.98. Weisen Sie darauf hin, dass Sie diesen Auftrag unter der Bedingung erteilen, dass die Lieferung bis spätestens Ende November erfolgt. Behalten Sie sich deshalb vor, die Lieferung auf Kosten und Gefahr der amerikanischen Firma zurückzusenden, wenn der o. a. Termin nicht eingehalten wird. Sie haben Ihre Bank angewiesen ein bis zum 30. November befristetes Akkreditiv zu Gunsten der amerikanischen Firma zu eröffnen. Bitten Sie um Bescheid per Fax, sobald die Waren verschifft sind.

Hinweis: Orientieren Sie sich bei der formalen Gestaltung dieses Schreibens an dem Musterbrief auf S. 164.

Contents

verschließbar	lockable
unter der Bedingung (vorbehaltlich)	subject to [n]
sich etw vorbehalten	reserve the right [to+vb]
auf jmnds Kosten	at s. o.'s expense
Gefahr (Risiko)	risk
zurücksenden	return
jmndn anweisen	instruct s. o. [to+vb]
befristet bis (gültig bis)	valid until
verschiffen	ship

5. Sie haben im Auftrage der Firma Södermann & Co. in Delmenhorst ein Angebot von der Firma Printstar Systems Ltd. in 22 Downham Rd, Wolverhampton, W. Midlands, WV11 LY7 eingeholt, das am 22. März des laufenden Jahres bei Ihnen eingegangen ist. Da Ihre Firma die Ware äußerst dringend benötigt, hat Ihre Kollegin am 23. telefonisch bestellt und Ihnen folgende Notiz hinterlassen:

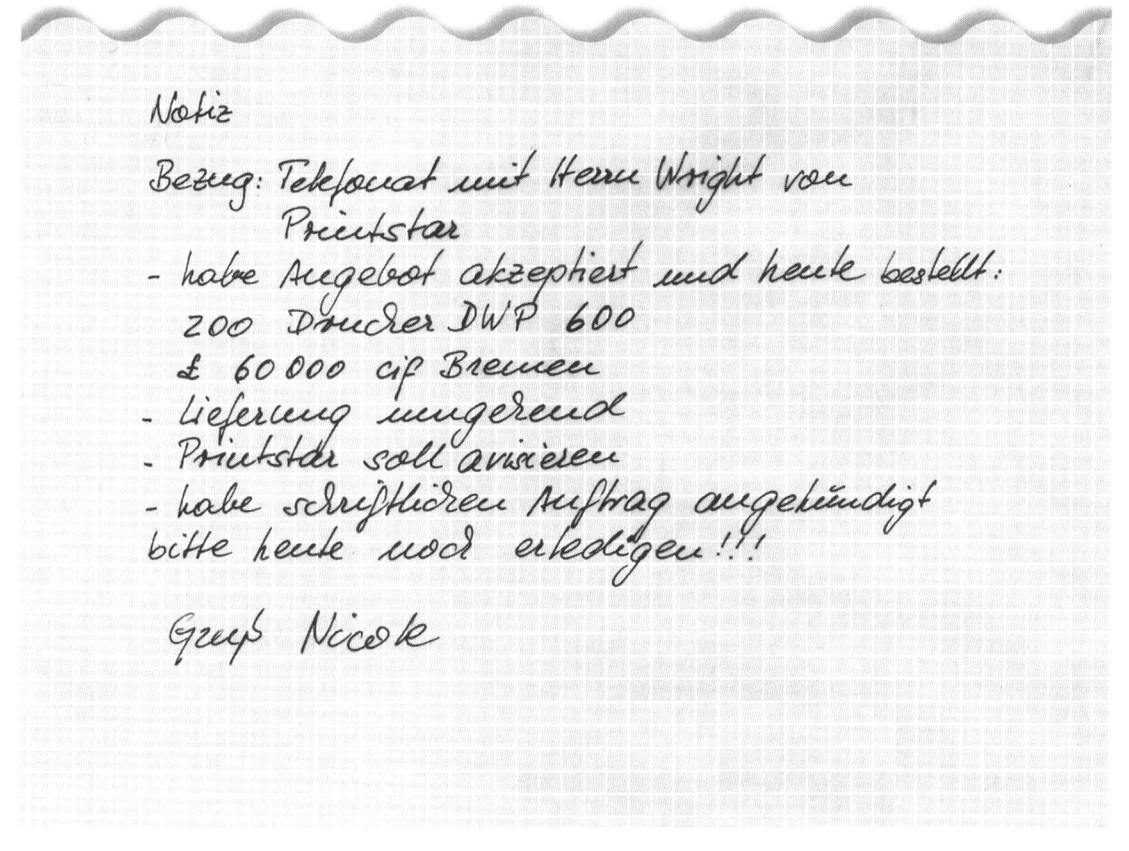

Notiz

Bezug: Telefonat mit Herrn Wright von Printstar

- habe Angebot akzeptiert und heute bestellt:
  200 Drucker DWP 600
  £ 60 000 cif Bremen
- Lieferung umgehend
- Printstar soll avisieren
- habe schriftlichen Auftrag angekündigt
  bitte heute noch erledigen!!!

Gruß Nicole

Erstellen Sie noch am gleichen Tag den offiziellen Auftrag und beziehen Sie sich dabei auf das o. a. Telefonat.

D. Listening comprehension & note-taking

1. Listen to the telephone conversation. Herr Schumann is calling about some printed instructions which M & C need for their products.

2. Imagine that you are Herr Schumann and write a suitable order to Standard Printers, 31 Raynham Rd., Lee, London SE12 2KL.

Unit 5 Commercial Correspondence

E. Contiletter

For instructions see page 153.

Order 1

dearsirsormesdamesthankyouverymuchforyourofferwhichwereceivedonoctober12wear egladtoplaceanorderfor160ofyourcolourmonitorstypeSMARTLINEat£295.50eachtheco nsignmentmusthavereachedusnotlaterthannovember15asthemonitorsareneededforthec omingchristmasbusinessthereforewereservetherighttoreturntheshipmentatyourexpensei ftheabovementioneddateisnotmetpleaseinformusbyfaxassoonasthemonitorshavebeensh ippedwewillthenarrangeforthesettlementoftheinvoiceamountwelookforwardtohearingfr omyousoonfaithfullyyours

Order 2

onlythencanweguaranteethedeliverydatementionedinyourorderhoweverifyouraiseyour ordertoatleast500unitswewouldbehappytograntthediscountmentionedabovesincerelyyo ursweshouldbegladtodobusinesswithyouofcoursethetermsofpaymentanddeliveryasstate dinourofferwillremainunchangeddearmrBrownshouldyouaccepttheaboveproposalpleas eletusknowimmediatelyaswehavealreadyreceivedagreatnumberoforderswithreferenceto yourorderofmay5weregrettoreportthatitisimpossibleforustograntanintroductorydiscoun tofl0%onthequantitywhichyouordered

Follow-up exercises: *Arbeitsbuch,* pp. 89–91.

Acknowledgement of Order

A. Lead-in

1. A letter of *acknowledgement* will not only be written to confirm a customer's order which has been placed on the basis of a preceding offer without engagement (see Unit 5). The supplier may also send an acknowledgement in the form of a letter or a fax to

- express his thanks for the customer's order
- express his willingness to accept an order which has not been preceded by an offer
- repeat the important details of an order which has been placed in a form other than writing
- ask for additional instructions concerning details not mentioned in the order
- answer a customer's counter-offer (either he accepts the conditions desired by the customer or he submits a counter-offer of his own)
- refuse acceptance of an order if he is not able or willing to supply.

In the case of acceptance of an order, the acknowledgement should contain all details stipulated in the order. If possible, it should prepare the customer for the arrival of the goods by informing him about delivery dates, mode of dispatch, etc.

2. Understanding and making notes

a. Under what circumstances does an acknowledgement constitute a sales contract between buyer and seller?
b. Which of the above-mentioned functions of the acknowledgement serve the following purposes:

The seller wants to
1. – request more information
2. – be polite
3. – avoid misunderstandings
4. – continue sales negotiations
5. – show that he cannot or does not want to do business

c. What should the customer be informed about in addition?

Unit 6 Commercial Correspondence

3. **Specimen letter**

D.D. Lee & Sons
Office Equipment International

5 Camac Street
P.O. Box 812
Singapore 20

Tel. 378 4983
Fax 378 4990

15 June 19..

Ms Jean Mace
M & C
76 Browning Terrace
Birmingham B13 9SQ
England

Dear Ms Mace,

Thank you very much for your order of 7 June 19.. which we were glad to receive yesterday and which we acknowledge as follows:

Type	Quantity	Unit Price	Amount
PROTECTO security drawer	125	$ 45.25	$ 5,656.25
SPS Standard printer stand	250	$ 24.70	$ 6,175.00
SMS Standard monitor stand	250	$ 26.50	$ 6,625.00
		TOTAL	$ 18,456.25

The goods will be dispatched with the S.S. "Asian Star" which will leave Singapore on 22nd June and is due to arrive in Portsmouth on 1st July. Please let us know as soon as you have received the goods.

With regard to your request for special desking, we are happy to inform you that we are in a position to develop a sketch to specification. We assure you that we will closely follow your instructions concerning design and measurements. However, it will be about four weeks before we can send you our blueprints and calculations.

Due to their excellent quality, we are convinced that our products will find a ready market in Great Britain and we hope to do regular business with your company.

Yours sincerely,

Samuel Wong

Samuel Wong
Sales Department

B. Tasks

1. Finding phrases to express intention

The following list contains intentions expressed in the letter above. Find out which phrases are used for each. Think of corresponding German phrases.

- expressing willingness
- expressing commitment
- expressing thanks
- making requests
- expressing ability

2. English-German translation

Translate the body of the letter into German. Make the text look like a German one (e. g. by using the German forms of the intentional phrases you have found).

C. Letter writing practice

1. Bedanken Sie sich am 15. 10. des laufenden Jahres im Auftrag der Firma Mann & Söhne, Frankfurt für den vom 5. 10. datierten Auftrag der Firma Micro Power, 1994 Ave. of the Americas, New York, NY 10020, USA. Drücken Sie Ihre Erwartung aus, dass die 300 bestellten Tastaturen in ca. vier Wochen versandbereit sein werden. Sie werden der amerikanischen Firma dann unverzüglich eine Versandanzeige zugehen lassen. Weisen Sie auf die beiliegende Proformarechnung hin und bitten Sie um Mitteilung, sobald das Dokumentenakkreditiv eröffnet worden ist.

Intention

acknowledging receipt (cont.)	we acknowledge with thanks [n]
expressing expectation	we trust [that-clause]
	we would hope [that-clause]
drawing attention to enclosure(s) (cont.)	we are enclosing [n]
	enclosed you will find [n]

Contents

Tastatur	keyboard
ca. / ungefähr	approximately / approx.
in x Wochen	in x weeks (' time)
versandbereit	ready for dispatch / shipment
Versandanzeige	dispatch advice
mitteilen (benachrichtigen)	notify / inform

2. Bestätigen Sie am 8. 10. des laufenden Jahres als Mitarbeiter der Firma Gebr. Sauer in Pforzheim den Eingang der Bestellung der Firma McBridle Inc., 309 Sunshine Blvd., Gainesville, FL 32601 über 4 000 Einheiten Ihres Diskettenreinigungsgerätes DIS-CLEAN. Drücken Sie Ihr Bedauern darüber aus, dass Sie diesen Auftrag so nicht bearbeiten können, da Sie zum ersten Mal mit der amerikanischen Firma Geschäfte machen. Außerdem hat die Firma darum gebeten bei Ihnen ein Konto zu eröffnen. Weisen Sie darauf hin, dass es zu Ihren Gepflogenheiten gehört alle neuen Kunden um Handels- und Bankreferenzen zu bitten. Erklären Sie Ihre Bereitschaft zukünftige Geschäfte auf Kreditbasis abzuwickeln.

Bitten Sie die amerikanische Firma um sofortige Mitteilung, ob dieser Erstauftrag auf der Basis eines Dokumentenakkreditivs erledigt werden sollte. Beenden Sie Ihr Schreiben mit einer entsprechenden Verabschiedungsformulierung.

Intentions

expressing regret (cont.)	we (very much) regret [vb+-ing]
	we are sorry [that-clause]
	much to our regret we [vb]

Contents

Diskettenreinigungsgerät	disk cleaning device
einen Auftrag bearbeiten	process an order
Konto (bei)	account (with)
Gepflogenheit	practice
Handelsreferenz	trade reference
ein Geschäft abwickeln	do business
auf Kreditbasis	on a credit basis
auf der Basis	on the basis (of)
einen Auftrag erledigen (ausführen) . . .	execute / carry out an order

3. Die Firma Gartsworth Computers Ltd, 87 Normandy Street, Alton, Hants GU34 1BR hat Ihnen am 25. 4. einen Auftrag über 100 tragbare Computer des Modells LT 20 zukommen lassen mit der Bitte um Lieferung bis spätestens 15. Mai. Beziehen Sie sich am 26. 4. des laufenden Jahres im Auftrag der Firma Sohrmann & Co in Berlin auf den o. a. Auftrag und geben Sie Ihrem Bedauern Ausdruck, dass das bestellte Modell wegen einer unvorhersehbaren Betriebsstörung in Ihrer Montagehalle erst wieder Ende Juni lieferbar ist. Bieten Sie stattdessen das Modell LT 30 an. Erklären Sie sich bereit dem Kunden dieses Modell zum gleichen Preis wie das bestellte zu überlassen, obwohl der Listenpreis 15% höher liegt. Weisen Sie darauf hin, dass Sie nur aufgrund Ihrer langjährigen Geschäftsverbindung zu diesem Entgegenkommen bereit sind. Bitten Sie um unverzügliche Mitteilung, ob die englische Firma mit Ihrem Vorschlag einverstanden ist.

Structure

erst	not ... until/before
stattdessen	instead
obwohl	although / though

Contents

tragbarer Computer	portable computer, laptop
unvorhersehbar	unforeseeable
Betriebsstörung	breakdown
Montagehalle	assembly shop
lieferbar / vorrätig	available
jmndm etw überlassen	let s. o. have s. th.
Listenpreis	list price
um 15% höher liegen	be 15% higher
langjährig	long-standing
Entgegenkommen	(make a) concession
unverzüglich	by return of post

4. Cancellation of an order

Sie haben als Mitarbeiter der Firma Sielmann & Walter, Konstanz am 19. 10. des laufenden Jahres bei der Firma Europaper B. V., Helderstraat 27, 1066 AZ Amsterdam 200 000 Blatt Endlospapier 11 × 9" bestellt. Inzwischen ist der Kunde, für den diese Ware gedacht war, zahlungsunfähig geworden, so dass Sie für das Papier keine Verwendung mehr haben.

Informieren Sie die niederländische Firma am 5. 11. über diesen Sachverhalt und äußern Sie Ihr Bedauern, dass Sie gezwungen sind, den Auftrag zu stornieren. Geben Sie der Hoffnung Ausdruck, dass die Herstellerfirma Ihrer Bitte entsprechen wird. Begründen Sie Ihre Erwartung mit Ihrer langjährigen Geschäftsbeziehung und stellen Sie für die Zukunft weitere Aufträge in Aussicht.

Contents

Endlospapier	continuous paper
für jmndn gedacht sein	be intended for s. o.
Konkurs anmelden	declare bankruptcy
keine Verwendung haben	have no use (for)
gezwungen sein	be forced / compelled (to+vb)
stornieren / annullieren	cancel / annul
einer Bitte entsprechen	comply with a request

5. In Ihrer Firma geht am 26. Mai des laufenden Jahres folgendes Schreiben ein, das Ihnen am gleichen Tag zur Bearbeitung übergeben wird:

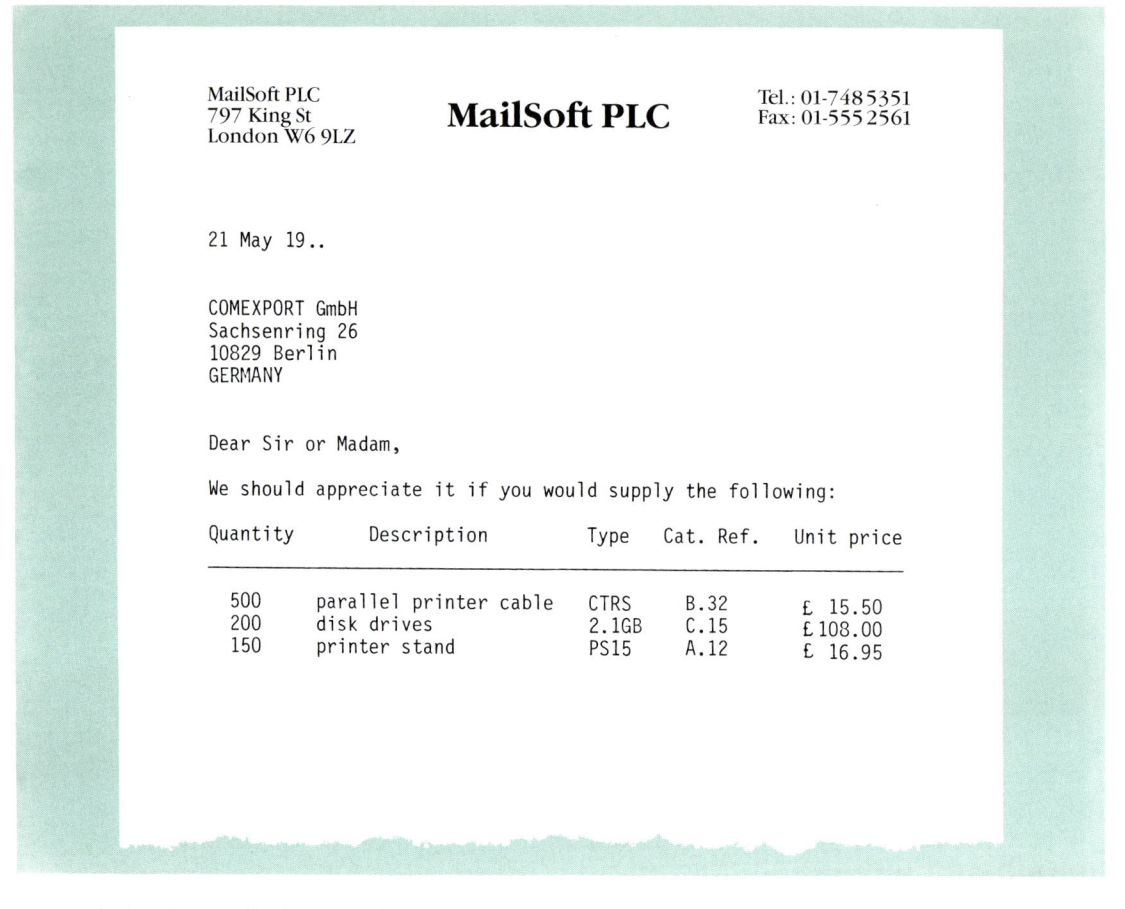

```
MailSoft PLC
797 King St                MailSoft PLC         Tel.: 01-748 5351
London W6 9LZ                                   Fax: 01-555 2561


21 May 19..


COMEXPORT GmbH
Sachsenring 26
10829 Berlin
GERMANY


Dear Sir or Madam,

We should appreciate it if you would supply the following:

Quantity      Description           Type    Cat. Ref.   Unit price
_____

  500      parallel printer cable   CTRS     B.32       £  15.50
  200      disk drives              2.1GB    C.15       £ 108.00
  150      printer stand            PS15     A.12       £  16.95
```

Zur Zeit ist der Artikel PS15 nicht lieferbar. Bieten Sie stattdessen den (etwas größeren) Druckerständer PS20 an und erklären Sie Ihre Bereitschaft dieses Modell zum gleichen Preis wie den Artikel PS15 zu liefern. Da der Auftrag eilig ist, weisen Sie darauf hin, dass Sie den umgehenden Versand der übrigen Angebotsposten veranlasst haben. Bitten Sie um umgehende Mitteilung, ob der Kunde mit Ihrem Vorschlag einverstanden ist.

D. Listening comprehension & note-taking

1. Listen to the telephone conversation. Herr Schumann has received a call from Senhor T. Rodrigues, one of M & C's customers in Portugal.

2. Imagine that you are Herr Schumann and write a suitable acknowledgement of order to Senhor T. Rodrigues, Ramos Wines, 4600 Vila Nova da Gaia, Portugal.

E. Contiletter

For instructions see page 153.

Acknowledgement of order 1

dearsirswehavepleasureinreceivingyourorderofmarch6for300unitsofyourSWIFTFAX120itiswithgreatregretthatwemustinformyouthatthismodelwillnotbeavailablebeforetheendofaprilthereforewewouldsuggestthatyouorderinsteadourmodelSWIFTFAX140whichwewouldbepreparedtoletyouhaveatthesamepriceasthemodelwhichyouorderedalthoughitslistpriceis12%higherpleaseinformuswhetheryouacceptourproposalorifyoupreferttowaituntiltheendofaprilinwhichcasewewouldgrantadiscountof5%yourearlyreplywouldbeappreciatedfaithfullyyours

Acknowledgement of order 2

weassureyouthatwewilldoourutmosttoexecuteyourordertoyourcompletesatisfactioninyourletteryouaskedtoopenanaccountwithusweacknowledgewiththanksyourorderof8junefor1000unitsofourkeyboardEASYCLICKsincewearedoingbusinesswithyouforthefirsttimeweregretthatweareunabletocomplywithyourrequestithasalwaysbeenourpracticetoaskallnewcustomersfortradeandbankreferencesgentlemenpleaseinformusbyreturnofpostwhetherthisfirstordershouldbeprocessedonthebasisofadocumentarycredityourstrulyifthesereferencesaregivenwewillbepreparedtodofuturebusinessonacreditbasis

Follow-up exercises: *Arbeitsbuch*, pp. 92–94.

Unit 7 — Commercial Correspondence

Delay in Delivery

A. Lead-in

1. As a result of a carefully developed sales contract, a customer will be able to expect punctual delivery in accordance with the agreed delivery date or period. If, however, the goods are not delivered on time, the customer should send a reminder in which he expresses his reaction. If he is depending heavily on the goods ordered, the customer will indicate a new delivery date or period. But if it is part of the contract, the customer might make use of his right to withdraw from the contract.

In cases of delays in delivery which are due to acts of God, the supplier is not responsible. But he should treat any delay very carefully, as his behaviour might be very important for the continuation of the business relationship. The supplier should inform his customer as soon as a delay in delivery seems to be likely. The customer is entitled to receive an explanation of the reasons and, if possible, information about the new date/period of delivery. The supplier can consider price reductions, partial shipments and/or paying extra costs incurred in this connection, in order to accommodate the customer.

2. Understanding and making notes

a. What is the purpose of fixing a date/period of delivery in a contract?
b. What should a customer do if his goods do not arrive on time?
c. What kind of delays can the supplier not be made responsible for?
d. What should a supplier's letter informing of a delay in delivery contain?

"I checked, but Mr Fogarty is not in any of his usual hiding places."

3. Specimen letter

M & C
Advanced Computer Technology

76 Browning Terrace
Birmingham B13 9SQ

Telephone: (021) 245 7012
Fax: (021) 343 4987

5 October 19..

JM/SL

D.D. Lee & Sons
Office Equipment International
5 Camac Street
P.O. Box 812
Singapore 20

For the attention of Mr Wong

Dear Mr Wong,

Our Order No. 1142/CL

Referring to our order of 25 July 19.., we are sorry to have to inform you that the consignment has not yet reached us. We wish to point out that your representative, Mr Singh, during his recent visit to our company, gave us an unqualified assurance of delivery within 9 weeks of receipt of order. Accordingly, the goods should have arrived in Birmingham not later than the beginning of this month.

As there is a great demand for our computer systems, this delay in delivery has placed us in a difficult situation, which might cause serious losses in business. Due to the excellent quality of your products, we are nevertheless prepared to accept the shipment if it is delivered within two weeks.

Although delays in the delivery of your goods have occurred repeatedly in recent months, we are still interested in doing business with your company. We trust that you will look into this matter without delay and inform us as soon as your investigations are successful. If, however, you are unable to keep to your delivery dates in future, we will be forced to turn to other suppliers.

Under the circumstances, we are sure that you will do your utmost to restore our confidence in you.

Yours sincerely,

Jean Mace

Jean Mace
Sales Manager

Registered in England No. 601417

Unit 7 — Commercial Correspondence

B. Tasks

1. Finding phrases to express intention

The following list contains intentions expressed in the letter above. Find out which phrases are used for each. Think of corresponding German phrases.

- expressing positive expectations
- pointing out
- expressing resolution
- referring to s. th.

2. English-German translation

Translate the body of the letter into German. Make the text look like a German one (e. g. by using the German forms of the intentional phrases you have found).

C. Letter writing practice

1. Verfassen Sie im Auftrag der Firma Borgmann & Schulze in Gütersloh am 15. 1. des laufenden Jahres ein Schreiben an die Firma Norsk Papir A/S, Dronningsgate 8, Oslo, Norwegen. Sie hatten der norwegischen Firma am 15. 11. des vergangenen Jahres einen Auftrag über 600 000 Blatt Endlospapier erteilt. Ihnen war in dem Angebot der o. a. Firma eine Lieferzeit von sechs Wochen zugesagt worden, so dass Sie mit Lieferung Anfang Januar rechneten. Bei der Auftragserteilung haben Sie außerdem ausdrücklich darauf hingewiesen, dass die Lieferzeit eine wesentliche Vertragsbedingung sei. Bis heute haben Sie jedoch noch immer keine Versandanzeige erhalten. Bitten Sie um unverzügliche Mitteilung, wann Sie mit der Lieferung rechnen können.

Structure

immer noch nicht / noch immer nicht	still not [vb] be still without [n]
bei Auftragserteilung	*als wir den Auftrag erteilten* *falls / wenn wir den Auftrag erteilen*

Contents

mit etw rechnen	expect [n] / [n+to+vb]
ausdrücklich	clearly
eine wesentliche Voraussetzung sein	be essential
Vertragsbedingung	condition of the contract
Versandanzeige	dispatch advice
unverzüglich	without further delay (adv.)

2. Sie haben im Auftrag der Firma Comimport in Kassel am 15. 9. des laufenden Jahres der Firma Hexagon Inc., 707 Fairmount Ave., Saginaw, MI 48601 einen Auftrag über 2000 Textverarbeitungsprogramme FASTEXT erteilt. Ihnen war Lieferung bis Ende Oktober verbindlich zugesagt worden. Bis zum heutigen Tag (5. 11.) ist jedoch die Lieferung trotz Ihrer wiederholten Anfragen nicht avisiert worden. Wenden Sie sich deshalb an die amerikanische Firma unter Bezugnahme auf den o. a. Sachverhalt. Drängen Sie darauf, dass die Lieferfirma den Sachverhalt überprüft und für umgehenden Versand der Ware sorgt. Machen Sie eindringlich klar, dass Sie bei weiterem Verzug entschlossen sind den Verlust zurückzufordern, den Sie durch diesen Lieferverzug eventuell erleiden. Da die Sache sehr eilig ist, bitten Sie nachdrücklich um Mitteilung per Fax, was die amerikanische Firma in dieser Angelegenheit zu unternehmen gedenke.

Intention

expressing emphasis	you will (certainly) understand [that-clause]
	you must realize [that-clause]
expressing urgency (cont.)	we must insist on [vb+-ing]
	we must insist [that-clause]

Structure

trotz	in spite of / despite

Contents

Textverarbeitungsprogramm	word processing system
verbindlich zusagen	guarantee
wiederholt	repeated
bis zum heutigen Tag	to this day
Sachverhalt (Angelegenheit)	matter
überprüfen	look into
für etw sorgen	arrange for
umgehend	immediate
Versand	dispatch
Verlust	loss
erleiden	suffer
etw von jmdm zurückfordern	claim s. th. from s. o.
eilig	urgent
unternehmen	*tun*
gedenken	hier: *beabsichtigen*

3. Wenden Sie sich am 8. 11. des laufenden Jahres als Mitarbeiter der Firma Lautenschläger & Rohrmann in Aachen an die Firma Torstved A/B, Riksväg 111, Göteborg, Schweden. Weisen Sie in Ihrem Schreiben darauf hin, dass Ihr Lagerbestand an Netzteilen Typ PSU 200 W zu Ende geht, da die für Anfang November zugesagte Sendung von 2000 Stück bisher nicht eingetroffen ist. Machen Sie dem Lieferanten eindringlich klar, dass jeder weitere Lieferverzug Ihnen beträchtliche Unannehmlichkeiten verursachen wird, da die Netzteile für einen Posten Computer bestimmt sind, der noch vor Ende des Jahres ausgeliefert werden muss. Drängen Sie auf Lieferung bis Ende November. Geben Sie Ihrer Entschlossenheit Ausdruck den Auftrag zu stornieren und die Netzteile bei einem anderen Lieferanten zu kaufen, falls die Lieferung nicht bis zu dem o. a. Termin eintrifft. Bitten Sie um umgehende Beantwortung Ihres Schreibens.

Intention

expressing resolution	we shall have to [vb]
	we shall have no alternative other than [to+vb]
	we shall be compelled [to+vb]

Structure

falls / wenn nicht	
es sei denn, dass	unless
bisher / bis heute	so far / up to now
noch vor [+ Zeitpunkt]	as late as [+ point of time]

Contents

Netzteil	power supply unit
ein Lagerbestand geht zu Ende	a stock is running low
Lieferverzug	delay in delivery
jmdm etw verursachen	cause s.o. s.th.
beträchtlich	considerable
Unannehmlichkeiten	inconvenience
bestimmt sein für	*benötigt werden für*

4. Ihre Firma, Westmann & Söhne, Kronenstr. 15, 65203 Wiesbaden kann den der Firma Corotec (UK), Little End Road, Doncaster DN 4 OBE zugesagten Liefertermin (Auftragsnr. 12433 vom 19. März) nicht einhalten, da eine beträchtliche Nachfrage nach den bestellten Artikeln dazu geführt hat, dass Ihre Zulieferer die benötigten Mengen nicht rechtzeitig liefern können. Wenden Sie sich am 2. April an den Kunden und geben Sie Ihrem Bedauern über diese Situation Ausdruck, die Sie zwingt um eine Verlängerung der Lieferzeit zu bitten. Weisen Sie jedoch darauf hin, dass Ihre Zulieferer verbindlich zugesagt haben bis Ende nächster Woche zu liefern, so dass *Sie* wiederum bis Ende April liefern könnten. Entschuldigen Sie sich für den Verzug und geben Sie Ihrer Hoffnung Ausdruck, dass er dem Kunden keine allzu großen Unannehmlichkeiten verursacht.

Contents

Zulieferer	subcontractor
rechtzeitig	on time
Verlängerung (Aufschub) der Lieferzeit	extension of time for the execution of an order
wiederum	in turn
sich für etwas entschuldigen	to apologize for s. th.
allzu große Unannehmlichkeiten	serious inconvenience

5. Wenden Sie sich im Auftrag der Firma Mannschmidt & Söhne, Rauendahl 12, 58452 Witten/Ruhr an die englische Firma Sam Brown Systems Ltd., 27 Belleville Road, London SW11 6QS, deren Sachbearbeiterin, Frau Roberts, Sie gestern (2. November des laufenden Jahres) angerufen hat und darauf hinwies, dass die zugesagte Lieferung (Auftrag Nr. 915/90) noch nicht eingetroffen ist. Sie haben kurz telefonisch die Gründe dargelegt, Frau Roberts hat jedoch auf einer ergänzenden schriftlichen Darlegung des Sachverhalts bestanden. Beziehen Sie sich auf dieses Telefonat und machen Sie folgende Gründe für den Lieferverzug geltend:

– Der Lieferverzug eines Zulieferers hat Ihnen beträchtliche Unannehmlichkeiten verursacht.

– Die Lieferung der Teile ist Ihnen jedoch bis zum 8. November verbindlich zugesagt worden.

– Da Sie ca. 5 Tage benötigen um die Teile zu montieren, wird die Lieferung bis spätestens 13. November erfolgen.

– Geben Sie Ihrem Bedauern Ausdruck und weisen Sie darauf hin, dass Sie die Teile in Zukunft von einem anderen Lieferanten beziehen werden.

D. Listening comprehension & note-taking

1. Listen to the telephone conversation. Herr Schumann is speaking to Jean Mace about the order he sent to Standard Printers – see page 169.

2. Imagine that you are Herr Schumann and write a suitable letter concerning delay in delivery to Standard Printers, 31 Raynham Rd., Lee, London SE 12 2KL.

E. Contiletter

For instructions see page 153.

Delay in delivery 1

dearmesdameswithreferencetoourorderofaugust12for6000unitsofyourdiskettestoragebox STORESAFEwewishtopointoutthatwearestillwithoutyourdispatchadvicethestoragebo xesareurgentlyneededaswehavealreadypromiseddeliverytoanimportantcustomerwemus ttherefoerinsistondeliverybytheendofnextweekunlesswehavereceivedtheconsignmentby thisdateweshallhavenoalternativeotherthantocancelourorderandhavetheboxesdelivered byanothersupplieryoumustofcourserealizethatwewillhavetoclaimfromyouanylosswhich wemaysufferasthisismosturgentpleaseinformusbyfaxwhatyouintendtodointhismatterfait hfullyyours

Delay in delivery 2

wemustapologizeforthisdelayandhopethatitwillnotcauseyouanyseriousinconveniencela diesandgentlemenmuchtoourregretwehavetoaskyouforanextensionoftimeintheexecutio nofyourorderpleaseinformuswithoutdelayifyouwishtotakedeliveryofthepartconsignmen thoweverweareinapositiontomakeimmediatedeliveryof2000unitswhichhavebeenreturn edbyacustomertrulyyourswetrustthattheremainingnumberof18000unitswillbereadyfordi spatchbytheendofmarchwerefertoyourorderNo55/3offebruary10duetoanunforeseeable breakdowninourassemblyshopthequantityof20000unitswhichyouorderedcannotbesupp liedbythedatewhichweguaranteed

Follow-up exercises: *Arbeitsbuch*, pp. 95–97.

Commercial Correspondence Unit 8

Complaints and their Adjustments

A. Lead-in

1. Not only can a delay in delivery (see Unit 7) cause serious problems in the execution of a sales contract. In view of the rights and responsibilities resulting from the contract, both business partners can place each other in difficult situations.

The seller may fail in his responsibilities by sending goods which are not up to the quality or quantity ordered; or the goods might have been damaged during packing or transport. The customer will have to complain about this, as he expects a faultless delivery. On the other hand, the seller might be forced to complain because the customer refuses acceptance of a delivery although it is in perfect condition, or because the customer does not pay according to the terms of the contract.

If a complaint is justified, the business partner who is responsible should do his best to solve the problems involved. This includes not only explanations and apologies, but also replacements and, if requested or advisable, compensation.

Complaints and their replies must be made with care in order to both substantiate one's position and maintain the business relationship if this is desirable.

2. Understanding and making notes

a. How can a delivery of goods lead to a customer's complaint?
b. Why might it be necessary for a seller to complain?
c. When is a trading partner forced to react to a complaint?
d. What can a trading partner do in order to settle a complaint?

"May I tell him who's furious?"

3. Specimen letters

M & C
Advanced Computer Technology

76 Browning Terrace
Birmingham B13 9SQ

Telephone: (021) 245 7012
Fax: (021) 343 4987

9 October 19..

JM/SL

D.D. Lee & Sons
Office Equipment International
5 Camac Street
P.O. Box 812
Singapore 20

For the attention of Mr Wong

Dear Mr Wong,

Further to our fax of today concerning your shipment of 30 September, it is with great regret that we have to complain about its execution.

27 of the PROTECTO security drawers have arrived in damaged condition. 15 of them are completely unfit for use and the rest are slightly damaged. This was obviously due to inadequate seaworthy packing. We are prepared to keep the 12 slightly damaged drawers if a price reduction could be granted, since we will not be able to sell them at the regular price. As for the other 15 drawers, we must insist on immediate replacements for them.

In addition, two of the special TOPSTAR desking units do not meet our specifications as regards measurements. As a result, we definitely cannot use them and therefore cannot accept them. Please inform us immediately about the delivery date of the replacements, and what we should do with the two desking units.

Yours sincerely,

Jean Mace

Jean Mace
Sales Manager

Registered in England No. 601417

Commercial Correspondence — Unit 8

D.D. Lee & Sons
Office Equipment International

5 Camac Street
P.O. Box 812
Singapore 20

Tel. 378 4983
Fax 378 4990

16 October 19..

Ms Jean Mace
M & C
76 Browning Terrace
Birmingham B13 9SQ
England

Dear Ms Mace,

We have received your letter complaining of our latest consignment and apologize for the inconvenience you have suffered.

We should like to inform you that we will dispatch replacements for the damaged goods by air next Monday. Of course we are quite prepared to grant you a price reduction of 45% for the 12 drawers which have only been partly damaged. Unfortunately, the packing material we have been receiving for several weeks has been insufficient. However, this will not happen again, as we have changed our supplier.

Please return by ship at our expense the goods which cannot be used or sold. We especially need the two desking units in order to examine them. In the meantime, we have intensified our quality control so as to avoid similar mistakes.

We hope that these steps will meet with your approval and assure you that there will be no further cause for complaint in future.

Sincerely yours,

Samuel Wong

Samuel Wong
Sales Department

B. Tasks

1. Finding phrases to express intention

The following list contains intentions expressed in the letters above. Find out which phrases are used for each. Think of corresponding German phrases.
- expressing willingness
- expressing regret
- acknowledging receipt
- making requests
- apologizing
- expressing urgency
- expressing positive expectations

2. English-German translation

Translate the body of the second letter into German. Make the text look like a German one (e. g. by using the German forms of the intentional phrases you have found).

C. Letter writing practice

1. Als Mitarbeiter der Firma Brockmann & Söhne in 60599 Frankfurt/Main, Hirschgraben 12 bedanken Sie sich am 27. Dezember des laufenden Jahres bei der Firma Percom PLC, 220 Blegborough Road, London NW 16 6DL für die prompte Lieferung der von Ihnen am 29. November bestellten Bausätze COM-DESK. Machen Sie allerdings die englische Firma darauf aufmerksam, dass die Rechnung Nr. C 9335 offensichtlich unrichtig ist. Statt des Sonderrabattes von 5%, den Ihnen die Lieferfirma in ihrem Angebot vom 2. November zugesagt hatte, wurden Ihnen nur 3% gewährt. Weisen Sie deshalb darauf hin, dass Sie £60 vom Rechnungsbetrag abgezogen und Ihre Bank angewiesen haben, den Betrag von £2,850 zum vollen Ausgleich der Rechnung der Lieferfirma zu überweisen.

Intention

directing attention to s. th. . . . . we wish to draw your attention to [n]

Structure

statt . . . . instead of [n] / [vb+-ing]

Contents

Bausatz . . . . kit
offensichtlich . . . . obvious(ly)
unrichtig . . . . incorrect
Sonderrabatt . . . . special discount
abziehen von . . . . deduct from
jmndn anweisen . . . . instruct s. o. [to+vb]

Contents

zum vollen Ausgleich (Sie betrachten die Rechnung als voll beglichen)	in full settlement (of)
etw überweisen	remit s. th.

2. Sie haben am 17. März des laufenden Jahres im Auftrag der Firma Geiger & Söhne, Ackerweg 32, 82319 Starnberg eine Sendung Farbmonitore bestellt. Lieferfirma war die Fortex Inc., 108 Rochester Row, Albany, New York 12208. Am 12. Mai wenden Sie sich an die o. a. Firma und drücken Ihr Bedauern über die Tatsache aus, dass Sie inzwischen zahlreiche Reklamationen erhalten haben. Bereits 15 Monitore wurden von Kunden zurückgegeben. Aus diesem Grund sehen Sie sich gezwungen die amerikanische Firma zu bitten, die Farbmonitore durch solche der bestellten Qualität zu ersetzen. Geben Sie Ihrer Erwartung Ausdruck, dass die Lieferfirma alle notwendigen Schritte unternehmen wird um die sofortige Zusendung der Ersatzlieferung zu gewährleisten. Bitten Sie um fernmündliche Mitteilung, wann Sie mit der Lieferung rechnen können. Gleichzeitig soll Ihnen die Lieferfirma mitteilen, wie Sie mit den fehlerhaften Geräten verfahren sollen.

Intention

expressing compulsion	we have no other choice but [to+vb]
	we have no alternative but [to+vb]

Contents

zahlreich	a great number of [n] / numerous
Reklamation	complaint
etw zurückgeben (zurücksenden)	return s. th.
etw durch etw ersetzen	replace s. th. with/by s. th.
Schritte unternehmen (Maßnahmen ergreifen)	take steps [to+vb]
gewährleisten / sicherstellen	ensure [that-clause]
Ersatz(lieferung)	replacement(s)
fernmündlich mitteilen	inform by phone
mit etw verfahren	deal with s. th.
fehlerhaft	faulty

3. Bestätigen Sie für die Firma Sollmann KG, Friedrichstr. 22, 65201 Wiesbaden den Empfang der 100 am 16. 6. des laufenden Jahres von Ihnen bestellten Tintenstrahldrucker SPARKJET. Die Ware ist am Vormittag des 12. 7. in äußerst schlechtem Zustand bei Ihnen eingetroffen. Wenden Sie sich deshalb noch am gleichen Tage an die

Lieferfirma, Jessop & Sons, 19 Bridge Street, Cincinnati, OH 45202. Geben Sie Ihrer Verärgerung über den Zustand der Ware Ausdruck, der auf unzulängliche Verpackung zurückzuführen ist, wie auch über die Tatsache, dass Ihre Packanweisungen offensichtlich nicht beachtet wurden, so dass 15 Drucker durch Seewasser unbrauchbar wurden. Zeigen Sie sich über die nachlässige Ausführung Ihres Auftrags verärgert. Da es Ihnen unmöglich ist, die Drucker unrepariert zu verkaufen, schlagen Sie dem Lieferanten vor, ihn mit den ungefähren Kosten von $ 100 pro Gerät zu belasten. Für den Fall, dass der amerikanischen Firma dieser Vorschlag nicht zusagt, werden Sie die Drucker zu ihren Lasten zurückschicken und sich den Kaufbetrag zurückerstatten lassen. Geben Sie der Hoffnung Ausdruck, dass die Lieferfirma dieser Angelegenheit nachgehen und Ihnen unverzüglich Mitteilung machen wird.

Intention

[politely] expressing annoyance	we regret [to+vb] / [that-clause]
	we are sorry [that-clause]
	we are greatly surprised at [n]
	we are greatly surprised [that-clause]

Structure

äußerst	most [+adj/adv]

Contents

in schlechtem Zustand	in an unsatisfactory condition
Packanweisungen	packing instructions
(eine Anweisung) befolgen	follow
auf etw zurückzuführen sein	*aufgrund/wegen*
unzulängliche Verpackung	inadequate packing
etw unbrauchbar machen	ruin s. th.
nachlässig	careless(ly)
jmdm unmöglich sein	be impossible for s. o. [to+vb]
unrepariert	*ohne Reparatur*
jmndn mit etw belasten	charge s. o. for s. th.
ungefähr (annähernd/geschätzt)	approximate
jmdm zusagen (gefallen)	suit s. o.
zu jmnds Lasten	at s. o.'s expense
Kaufbetrag	money
zurückerstatten	refund
einer Angelegenheit nachgehen	look into a matter

4. Wenden Sie sich am 12. 4. des laufenden Jahres als Mitarbeiter der Firma Blechschmitt & Huber in 70192 Stuttgart, Ehrmannstr. 90 an die Firma Digicom, 64 Welsh Row, Nantwich, Cheshire CW5 5ES. Drücken Sie Ihr Bedauern darüber aus, dass der Kunde mit der Sendung unzufrieden ist, die Ihre Firma am 5. 4. geliefert hat. Teilen Sie dem Kunden mit, dass Sie unverzüglich Nachforschungen in Ihrer Versandabteilung angestellt und erfahren haben, dass die Ware unglücklicherweise nicht sorgfältig genug geprüft wurde, so dass 20 von einem anderen Kunden bestellte Einzelposten in die Kiste verpackt wurden, die für die englische Firma bestimmt war. Um die Angelegenheit in Ordnung zu bringen haben Sie veranlasst, dass dem Kunden die richtige Ware unverzüglich zugesandt wird. In Anbetracht der Dringlichkeit wird die Ware per Luftfracht versandt. Bitten Sie den Kunden, Ihnen die irrtümlich zugesandten Diskettenlaufwerke zu Ihren Lasten zurückzusenden und bedanken Sie sich dafür, dass er Sie auf diesen Irrtum aufmerksam gemacht hat. Versprechen Sie, dass Sie Ihr Bestes tun werden, um künftige Aufträge mit größter Sorgfalt auszuführen.

Contents

mit etw unzufrieden sein	be dissatisfied with s. th.
Nachforschungen anstellen	make enquiries
Versandabteilung	dispatch department
unglücklicherweise	unfortunately
prüfen	check
Einzelposten	item
Kiste	case
bestimmt sein für	be intended for
eine Angelegenheit in Ordnung bringen	put a matter right
jmndm etw zusenden	dispatch s. th. to s. o.
in Anbetracht	in view (of)
Dringlichkeit	urgency
per Luftfracht	by airfreight
irrtümlich	in error
auf etw aufmerksam machen	call s. th. to s. o.'s attention
Irrtum	error
sein Bestes tun	do o's best [to+vb]
mit größter Sorgfalt	with greatest care

5. In der Versandabteilung Ihrer Firma, Rossmann & Co., Böckmannstr. 32, 30177 Hannover wurde unmittelbar nach dem Versand einer Warensendung festgestellt, dass die Ware nicht entsprechend den Anweisungen des Kunden verpackt wurde. Wenden Sie sich deshalb als Mitarbeiter der oben genannten Firma an den Kunden, Cobra Technology Ltd., 70 Shrotton St, London W1 und teilen Sie ihm die Sachlage mit. Bitten Sie ihn die Ware nach Eingang sofort zu überprüfen und Ihnen fernmündlich Mitteilung

Unit 8 — Commercial Correspondence

zu machen, ob die Sendung in gutem Zustand eingetroffen ist. Falls es Gründe zur Beanstandung geben sollte, werden Sie sofort eine Ersatzlieferung per Luftfracht zum Versand bringen. Teilen Sie dem Kunden Ihr Bedauern über diesen Irrtum mit und sagen Sie ihm sorgfältige Ausführung seiner zukünftigen Aufträge zu.

D. Listening comprehension & note-taking

1. Listen to the telephone conversation. Herr Schumann is speaking to Stephen Clark of M & C. They are talking about the managing director of Walkers Transport (Ipswich), a customer of M & C's.

2. Imagine that you are Herr Schumann and write a suitable letter concerning complaint and adjustment to Mr G. Marshall, Managing Director, Walkers Transport, Ash Way, Ipswich, IP4 3BN.

E. Contiletter

For instructions see page 153.

Complaints and their adjustments 1

dearsirsonmay26weorderedaconsignmentof300PROTECTOsecuritydrawersfromyoumuchtoourregretwehavetoinformyouthat59ofthedrawersarrivedinanunsatisfactoryconditionobviouslyourpackinginstructionshadnotbeenfollowedcarefullyenoughwehopethatyouwillarrangeforreplacementstobedispatchedtousstraightawayinviewoftheurgencywemustinsistondeliverybyairfreightpleaseinformusbyphonewhenwecanexpectdeliverythedamageddrawerswillofcoursebereturnedtoyouatyourexpensewehopethatyouwilldoyourbesttoexecutefurtherorderswithgreatestcarefaithfullyyours

Complaints and their adjustments 2

wemustapologizeforthiserrorandhopethatitwillnotcauseyouanyseriousinconvenienceto savetimewehaveaskedthefrenchcustomertosendthegoodstoyourcompanyattheearliestpossibledatewehavereceivedyourphonecallthismorningandaresorrytolearnthattheshipmentwhichwedeliveredonseptember3doesnotcomplywiththeorderwhichyouplacedwithusonaugust15accordinglywewouldliketoaskyoutosendtheconsignmentwhichyoureceivedtoourfrenchcustomerwhoseaddressyoufindenclosedallchargesatourexpenseverytrulyyoursoncheckinginourdispatchdepartmentwefoundoutthattheconsignmentwhichyoureceivedwasintendedforacustomerinfrancewhointurntookdeliveryoftheconsignmentwhichwasintendedforyouladiesandgentlemen

Follow-up exercises: *Arbeitsbuch*, pp. 98–100.

Translation Exercises German–English

Nicht selten wird man Sie im Geschäftsleben bitten Texte aus dem Englischen ins Deutsche zu übertragen. Diese Fertigkeit ist an zahlreichen Stellen dieses Buches trainiert worden. Es kann sich aber auch die Notwendigkeit ergeben deutsche Texte unterschiedlicher Art ins Englische zu übersetzen.
Für diesen Arbeitsbereich finden Sie im Folgenden Übungsmaterial. Die ausgewählten, völlig unterschiedlichen Texte sind Beispiel für Übersetzungsaufgaben, wie sie im Wirtschaftsleben häufig auf Sie zukommen werden. Die Angabe in Klammern informiert darüber, welchen Units von *Trademark* die Texte jeweils thematisch zugeordnet sind.
Ziehen Sie ein Wörterbuch für unbekannte Wörter/Ausdrücke heran.

1. Übersetzen Sie den folgenden Abschnitt aus einer Informationsbroschüre für Verbraucher ins Englische (*Main Course*, Units 3, 4):

DIE ZWEI SEITEN DER WERBUNG

Werbung ist aus unserer Wirtschaft nicht mehr wegzudenken. Ihre vielfältigen Erscheinungsformen sind uns allen bekannt: Anzeigen in Tageszeitungen und Zeitschriften, Werbespots im Rundfunk und im Fernsehen, Kataloge, Prospekte und Plakate. Werbung ist sicherlich eine Orientierungshilfe. Aber ihr Sinn und Zweck, das Ausmaß sowie die verwendeten Mittel sind umstritten.

Als vorteilhaft wird genannt:

- Werbung macht neue Produkte einer breiten Öffentlichkeit bekannt.
- Werbung bietet dem Verbraucher notwendige Informationen über das Angebot an Waren und Dienstleistungen.
- Werbung hilft dem Verbraucher bei der Befriedigung seiner Bedürfnisse.

Als nachteilig wird angeführt:

- Werbung informiert nicht exakt, da negative Aspekte der Waren nicht genannt werden.
- Werbung manipuliert, d.h. sie weckt Wünsche beim Verbraucher, verhindert rationale Verhaltensweisen.
- Werbung verleitet Verbraucher dazu, mehr zu kaufen, als sie bezahlen können.
- Werbung verursacht Kosten, die den Warenpreis steigen lassen.

> Sinnvoll genutzte Werbung bietet dem Verbraucher die Möglichkeit, das vorhandene Angebot zu überblicken, um im Vergleich eine rationale Kaufentscheidung zu treffen.

2. Übersetzen Sie die folgende Stellenausschreibung ins Englische (*Main Course, Units 1, 6, 8*):

Als expandierende Bank sind wir europaweit in der Baufinanzierung tätig. Dynamisches und kundenorientiertes Arbeiten hat uns zu dem gemacht, was wir sind: kompetente Finanzierungsexperten.

Für den Ausbau unserer britischen Tochtergesellschaft beabsichtigen wir zum Beginn des nächsten Jahres mehrere qualifizierte

Operator

einzustellen.

Wir arbeiten mit weltbekannten Computersystemen. Kenntnisse in unterschiedlichen Systemen wären von Vorteil.

Neben der Bereitschaft zu flexiblen Arbeitszeiten zu arbeiten, erwarten wir die Fähigkeit sich einem jungen Team anzupassen.

Das Gehalt entspricht den Anforderungen. Interne und externe Weiterbildungsmöglichkeiten sind für unser Unternehmen selbstverständlich.

Bitte richten Sie Ihre Bewerbung mit allen üblichen Unterlagen an unsere Personalabteilung.

Eurobank AG · Ihr direkter Partner für solide Finanzierungen

EUROBANK AG
Kleiststraße 12–17
60381 Frankfurt a. M.
Telefon (069) 5 42 33 10

3. Übersetzen Sie den folgenden Anzeigentext ins Englische (*Main Course*, Units 4, 7):

Rückruf von Elektronic-Toastern

Wir haben aufgrund von umfangreichen Untersuchungen festgestellt, dass bei einem Teil der von uns produzierten Electronic-Toaster die elektrische Sicherheit nicht unbedingt gewährleistet ist, wenn verschiedene ungünstige Umstände zusammentreffen.

Als verantwortungsbewusster Hersteller rufen wir deshalb alle von uns hergestellten Electronic-Toaster zurück, um jedes Risiko für die Benutzer auszuschließen.

Es handelt sich um alle Geräte mit der Typenbezeichnung »Toaststar« und »Toaststar deluxe« mit der Nummer XT-4366-77841 LM.

Falls Sie ein solches Gerät besitzen, bringen Sie es bitte sofort zu dem Händler, bei dem Sie es erworben haben, zurück oder zu jedem anderen Händler, der Produkte der Firma »InterElectron« führt.

Die Überprüfung und eventuelle Fehlerbeseitigung erfolgt umgehend und für Sie völlig kostenlos.

Bitte betrachten Sie diese Rückrufaktion als Beweis des hohen Verantwortungsbewusstseins gegenüber unseren Kunden.

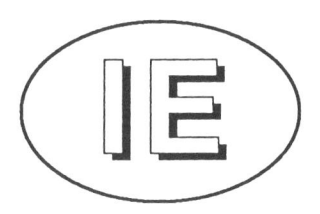

InterElectron
Wuppertaler Str. 207 · 40219 Düsseldorf

4. Übersetzen Sie die folgenden Lexikoneinträge ins Englische (*Main Course*, Unit 6):

Hardware

Alle technischen Bestandteile einer Datenverarbeitungsanlage. Im Mittelpunkt steht die sogenannte Zentraleinheit des Computers, der eigentliche Rechner, hauptsächlich bestehend aus Chips mit verschiedenen Funktionen und Verbindungen. Die Aufgaben der sogenannten Peripherie-Geräte – Bildschirm, Tastatur, Drucker – bestehen im Erfassen, Aufbereiten, Ein- und Ausgeben, Speichern und Weitervermitteln von Daten.

Heimcomputer

Elektronischer Kleinrechner, der nach individuellen Bedürfnissen programmiert werden kann. Heimcomputer werden vor allem in Privathaushalten eingesetzt. Je nach Speicherkapazität können Heimcomputer zur Unterhaltung, für Lernprogramme oder zur Buchhaltung benutzt werden. Die nächste Computerklasse ist der Personalcomputer.

Software

Alle nichttechnischen Programmbestandteile einer Datenverarbeitungsanlage. Man unterscheidet „System-Software" (Grundlagenprogramme) und „Anwender-Software", die zur Lösung individueller Benutzerprobleme dient.

5. Übersetzen Sie den folgenden Auszug aus einem Zeitschriftenartikel ins Englische (*Main Course*, Units 1, 4, 6):

Die Superchip-Karte

Die Entwicklung neuer Zahlungsformen wird dahin führen, dass die Kunden der Kreditinstitute Chip-Karten erhalten. Anders als bei der Euroscheckkarte wird ein winziger Mikrochip in die Karte eingefügt, der alle erforderlichen Daten, z. B. Name des Kreditinstituts, Geheimcode, Kreditrahmen etc. enthält. Diese Karte könnte zu verschiedenen Zwecken benutzt werden: zum Einkaufen, Telefonieren, Bargeld abheben, zur Nutzung neuester Kommunikationswege. Die Einführung einer solchen Chip-Karte wird jedoch davon abhängen, ob die notwendigen Investitionen zu akzeptablen Kosten durchgeführt werden können. Bisherige Versuche haben sehr hohe Kosten für die technischen Einrichtungen und die Plastikkartenherstellung verursacht.

6. Erstellen Sie ein unterschriftsfertiges Schreiben, indem Sie den folgenden Brief übersetzen. Alle weiteren Angaben finden Sie unter dem Brieftext. Ergänzen Sie selbstständig die Anrede- und Verabschiedungsformel und ggf. Hinweise auf Anlagen. (*Commercial Correspondence: Offer*)

Wir freuen uns den Erhalt Ihres Schreibens bestätigen zu können, das uns am Freitag vergangener Woche erreicht hat. Wie gewünscht, übersenden wir Ihnen unseren neuesten Katalog über Computerausstattungen. Unsere Exportpreisliste für Europa ist ebenfalls beigefügt. Vorausgesetzt, dass größere Mengen bestellt werden, sind wir gern bereit individuelle Lösungen für unsere Kunden zu entwickeln.

Im Falle von Erstaufträgen liefern wir unter der Bedingung eines unwiderruflichen und bestätigten Dokumentenakkreditivs zu unseren Gunsten, zahlbar bei der Handelsbank, Köln. Bei Wiederholungsaufträgen würden wir jedoch Bezahlung auf der Basis CAD akzeptieren.

Die Lieferzeit für die meisten unserer Produkte beträgt zur Zeit ca. 10 Tage nach Auftragserhalt, vorbehaltlich individueller Wünsche, z.B. hinsichtlich Design, Verpackung oder Transport.

Absender:	Braun AG, Kommunikationsentwicklung, Kiefernstr. 44, 50767 Köln
Empfänger:	ComputerLand, 65 North Catalina Ave., Pasadena, CA 91106, USA
Datum:	12. 4. des laufenden Jahres

7. Erstellen Sie ein unterschriftsfertiges Schreiben, indem Sie den folgenden Brief übersetzen. Alle weiteren Angaben finden Sie unter dem Brieftext. Ergänzen Sie selbstständig die Anrede- und Verabschiedungsformel und ggf. Hinweise auf Anlagen. (*Commercial Correspondence: Order*)

> Von unserem gemeinsamen Geschäftsfreund, der Firma ComStar, haben wir erfahren, dass Sie auch Standardversionen von Festplattenlaufwerken herstellen. Wir benötigen dringend 400 Laufwerke, da unser bisheriger Lieferant aufgrund eines Fabrikbrandes nicht in der Lage ist seinen Lieferverpflichtungen nachzukommen.
>
> Gemäß Ihrem gültigen Katalog, den uns ComStar freundlicherweise zur Verfügung gestellt hat, sind wir bereit, 400 Stück des Typs XT 1/34 zum Gesamtpreis von $ 101.200, CIF Hamburg einschließlich Exportverpackung, zu bestellen. Allerdings wird der Auftrag unter der Bedingung erteilt, dass die Lieferung bis spätestens 15. November erfolgt. Bitte teilen Sie uns umgehend mit, ob Sie diesen Auftrag annehmen. Sollte dies der Fall sein und Ihre Produkte sowie die Auftragsausführung unseren Vorstellungen entsprechen, sind wir gerne bereit unseren zukünftigen Bedarf bei Ihrem Unternehmen zu decken.

Absender:	Bladmann GmbH & Co KG, Weststr. 12, 70197 Stuttgart
Empfänger:	Linsey plc, Warbreck Hill Road, Blackpool FY2 OYF, GB
Datum:	2. Oktober des laufenden Jahres

8. Erstellen Sie ein unterschriftsfertiges Schreiben, indem Sie den folgenden Brief übersetzen. Alle weiteren Angaben finden Sie unter dem Brieftext. Ergänzen Sie selbstständig die Anrede- und Verabschiedungsformel und ggf. Hinweise auf Anlagen. (*Commercial Correspondence: Delay in Delivery*)

```
Mit Bezug auf unseren Auftrag Nr. 13476/93
müssen wir Ihnen leider mitteilen, dass die
Lieferung noch nicht eingetroffen ist,
obwohl Sie diese gemäß dem Kaufvertrag für
die erste Oktoberwoche zugesagt hatten. Wir
benötigen die 2000 Drucker, Modell „Print-
Star 5", dringend mit Blick auf das bevor-
stehende Weihnachtsgeschäft. Eine noch
größere Verspätung würde uns in eine
unangenehme Lage bringen, da bereits
Bestellungen langjähriger Kunden unseres
Unternehmens vorliegen.

Wir ersuchen Sie daher, den Auftrag sofort
auszuführen, damit die Drucker uns spätes-
tens nächste Woche Donnerstag zur Verfügung
stehen.

Wenn Sie nicht bereit oder in der Lage sein
sollten Ihren Verpflichtungen nachzukommen,
sehen wir uns gezwungen den Auftrag zu
widerrufen. Wir werden unseren Bedarf dann
bei einem anderen Lieferanten decken. In
Anbetracht der schwierigen Situation beste-
hen wir auf einer sofortigen Antwort mit
Angabe der Gründe für die Lieferverzöge-
rung.
```

Absender:	Zander GmbH, Technik-Center, Holzgartenstr. 103, 75175 Pforzheim
Empfänger:	PrintStar Ltd, PO Box 21, Stanmore, Middlesex HA7 1AY, GB
Datum:	14. Oktober des laufenden Jahres

9. Erstellen Sie ein unterschriftsfertiges Schreiben, indem Sie den folgenden Brief übersetzen. Alle weiteren Angaben finden Sie unter dem Brieftext. Ergänzen Sie selbstständig die Anrede- und Verabschiedungsformel und ggf. Hinweise auf Anlagen. (*Commercial Correspondence:* Enquiry)

> Wir beziehen uns auf das Gespräch, das wir auf der letzten London Office Fair mit Ihrem Verkaufsleiter, Mr Chris Prior, geführt haben. Mr Prior versprach damals, uns Informationen über Ihr neues Diktiergerät "Speak Easy" zuzusenden.
>
> Leider sind die Unterlagen bis heute noch nicht bei uns eingetroffen. Da wir nach wie vor gute Chancen sehen das Gerät erfolgreich auf dem deutschen Markt zu vertreiben, möchten wir Sie heute nochmals um Zusendung der Unterlagen und zugleich eines Angebots über 500 Stück bitten. Fügen Sie bitte Ihrem Angebot vollständige Angaben über Zahlungsbedingungen und Rabatte für regelmäßige Käufe bei.
>
> Darüber hinaus möchten wir anfragen, ob Sie in Ihrem Haus die Möglichkeit haben die englischsprachige Bedienungsanleitung ins Deutsche zu übertragen. Unsere Analyse hat ergeben, dass dies eine wichtige Voraussetzung für den Vertrieb des Geräts auf dem deutschen Markt ist.

Absender:	Mittler GmbH, Bürokommunikation, Gutenbergstr. 5, 71638 Ludwigsburg
Empfänger:	Miles Ltd, Office Equipment, South View Road, Shrewsbury, Shropshire, SY5 7JH, GB
Datum:	21. Mai des laufenden Jahres

Info-Appendix

Language Section
Correspondence Section

Basic Grammar

A. Vollverben

1. Formen der Vollverben

	1. Verbform (infinitive)	2. Verbform (simple past)	3. Verbform (past participle)
a. regelmäßige Vollverben Bsp.: to walk	walk	walked	walked
b. unregelmäßige Vollverben Bsp.: to go	go	went	gone

2. Bildung der Zeiten unter Verwendung der Verbformen

a. in der *simple form:*

Zeit	1. Element	2. Element (Verbform)	Beispiel
present		1. Verbform (*Beachte:* bei *he/she/it* und Personen/Sachen in der Einzahl: Verb mit Endung *s*)	I ask (he asks)
future	will	+ 1. Verbform	I will ask
present conditional	would	+ 1. Verbform	I would ask
past		2. Verbform	I asked
present perfect	have (*Beachte: he/she/it* und alle Personen/Sachen in der Einzahl: has)	+ 3. Verbform	I have asked (he has asked)

Zeit	1. Element	2. Element (Verbform)	Beispiel
past perfect	had	+ 3. Verbform	I had asked
future perfect	will have	+ 3. Verbform	I will have asked
perfect conditional	would have	+ 3. Verbform	I would have asked

b. in der *progressive form:*

Zeit	1. Element	2. Element (Verbform)	Beispiel
present	am/is/are	jeweils + 1. Verbform mit angehängtem -ing (Beachte bei der Schreibung: – take + -ing = taking stummes e entfällt – get + -ing = getting Endkonsonant wird verdoppelt)	I am asking
future	will be		I will be asking
present conditional	would be		I would be asking
past	I/he/she/it was you/we/they were		I was asking we were asking
present perfect	have been (Beachte: he/she/it has been)		I have been asking/he has been asking
past perfect	had been		I had been asking
future perfect	will have been		I will have been asking
perfect conditional	would have been		I would have been asking

3. Verneinung der Vollverben

a. im *present simple:*

mit "do not" (don't) + 1. Form des Vollverbs.
Bsp.: We do not (don't) grant discounts.
[*Beachte:* he/she/it does not (doesn't)]

b. im *past simple:*

mit "did not" (didn't) + 1. Form des Vollverbs.
Bsp.: I did not (didn't) meet him yesterday.

c. *in allen übrigen Zeiten* der simple- und

der progressive-Formen mit "not". Dabei steht das "not" nach dem 1. Element des Vollverbs.
Bsp.: He would not buy that software.

4. Fragebildung mit den Vollverben

a. im *present simple:*
durch Voranstellung von "do"
Bsp.: Do you buy from different suppliers?
Does he do his own printing?
(*Beachte:* bei he/she/it mit "does")

b. im *past simple:*
durch Voranstellung von "did"
Bsp.: Did you meet him yesterday?
Did she speak to Ms Mace?

c. *in allen übrigen Zeiten* der simple- und progressive-Formen durch Voranstellen des 1. Elements des Vollverbs vor das Subjekt.

Bsp.: They will sign the contract.

Will they sign the contract?

1. Element des Vollverbs   Subjekt

5. Bildung des Passivs

a. in den *simple forms:*
Indem man nach dem obigen Muster der progressive-Formen an das 1. Element die 3. Form der Vollverben anhängt.
Bsp.: I am asked a lot of questions by customers.

b. in den *progressive forms:*
Das Passiv existiert nur noch im present und past. Bildung:
present: am/is/are + being + 3. Verbform
Bsp.: The ship is being loaded.
past: was/were + being + 3. Verbform
Bsp.: The goods were being examined when the mistake was discovered.

6. Anwendung der Zeiten

Zeit	*Anwendungshinweise*	*Beispiele*
present – simple	Für Sachverhalte und wiederkehrende Handlungen, die unabhängig vom Zeitpunkt der Äußerung bedeutsam sind.	M & C *is situated* in Birmingham. M & C *regularly buys* hardware in the Far East.
– progressive	Für Vorgänge und Handlungen, die zum Zeitpunkt der Äußerungen stattfinden.	Stephen *is dictating* a letter.
past – simple	Für Situationen, Gewohnheiten und Sachverhalte, die zum Zeitpunkt des Äußerns abgeschlossen sind. Der Zeitpunkt der Vergangenheit kann angegeben werden.	They *met* their new supplier (yesterday/last week/two months ago/ etc.).

Zeit	Anwendungshinweise	Beispiele
– progressive	Für Vorgänge, die stattfanden, als eine neue Handlung hinzutrat.	Stephen *was dictating* a letter when the reporter *came in*.
present perfect – simple	Für Sachverhalte, die in der Vergangenheit stattfanden und noch für die Gegenwart von Bedeutung sind. Der Zeitpunkt der Vergangenheit darf hier nicht angegeben werden.	Jean and Stephen *have often talked* about expanding in Europe.
– progressive	Für Sachverhalte, die in der Vergangenheit begannen und noch andauern in der Gegenwart. Angabe des Zeitpunktes mit "since", Angabe der Zeitdauer mit "for". (*Beachte:* Im Deutschen wird das Präsens verwendet. "Since" und "for" werden mit "seit" übersetzt.)	They *have been dealing* with computers since 1991/for many years. (Seit 1991/vielen Jahren handeln sie mit Computern.)
past perfect – simple	Für Sachverhalte, die vor einem bestimmten Zeitpunkt der Vergangenheit bereits abgeschlossen waren.	Before they *sold* their first product, Jean and Stephen *had solved* a lot of problems.
– progressive	Für Sachverhalte, die zu einem bestimmten Zeitpunkt der Vergangenheit noch andauerten.	Before the reporter *came in*, Stephen *had been dictating* a letter to his secretary.
will-future	Für die Schilderung zukünftiger Sachverhalte, wenn der Schildernde – nicht sicher ist, ob der Sachverhalt eintreten wird, – die Aussage spontan macht.	Our competitors *will* probably *announce* their new series next week. I think I *will phone* him right now.

Zeit	Anwendungshinweise	Beispiele
going to-future	Für Sachverhalte, mit deren Verwirklichung der Schildernde ziemlich sicher rechnet oder die er zu verwirklichen beabsichtigt. Dabei spielt es keine Rolle, ob er selbst auf die Verwirklichung Einfluss hat oder nicht.	We *are not going to accept* your conditions. They *are going to raise* their prices by next June.

B. Modale Hilfsverben

Die Verwendung von modalen Hilfsverben gibt zusätzliche Informationen über die Absichten oder Einstellungen des Schildernden. Der Satz "He pays his bill by cheque" kann von dem Schildernden mittels modaler Hilfsverben variiert werden. Einige Hilfsverben können nicht alle Zeiten bilden, so dass sie ggf. durch bedeutungsähnliche Ausdrücke ersetzt werden müssen.

Hilfsverb	Absicht	Anwendungsbeispiele	Ausdruck mit annähernd gleicher Bedeutung
can	Fähigkeit	He can pay his bill by cheque (because he has an account).	to be able to
must	Zwang / Verpflichtung / Vermutung	He must pay his bill by cheque (because he has forgotten his money). He must have paid by cheque (because he had no money on him).	to have to
may	Erlaubnis	He may pay his bill by cheque (normally they prefer cash).	to be allowed

Hilfsverb	Absicht	Anwendungsbeispiele	Ausdruck mit annähernd gleicher Bedeutung
must not / may not	Verbot	He must not / may not pay his bill by cheque (because he has overdrawn his account). (*Beachte:* deutsch "nicht dürfen")	not to be allowed to
need not	keine Verpflichtung	He need not pay his bill by cheque (but he is free to do so).	not to have to

C. Bedingungssätze

Bedingungssätze beinhalten eine Verknüpfung von Bedingung und Folge. Je nach Verwirklichungsgrad der Folge unterscheidet man verschiedene Typen. Die Bedingung kann vor der Folge stehen oder auch dahinter.

	If-Satz (Bedingung)	Hauptsatz (Folge)	Aussage
Typ 1	If you *do not pay*, present tense	we *will stop* further business. (a) we *can* no longer *do* business with you. (b) future tense (a) oder Hilfsverb im present tense (b)	Die Folge ist möglich oder sogar sehr wahrscheinlich.
Typ 2	If she *was* in the manager's position, past tense	she *would sign* the contract. present conditional	Die Folge ist möglich, aber die Bedingung ist zum Zeitpunkt des Äußerns nicht von Bedeutung.

	If-Satz (Bedingung)	Hauptsatz (Folge)	Aussage
Typ 3	If they *had modernized* earlier, past perfect	they *would have won* more customers. (= damals) (a) they *would be in a better position now.* (= jetzt) (b) perfect conditional (a) oder present conditional (b)	Die Bedingung kann zum Zeitpunkt des Äußerns nicht mehr verwirklicht werden.

Die Typen 1 und 2 beziehen sich auf die Gegenwart, Typ 3 auf die Vergangenheit. Es ist zu beachten, dass die im Englischen verwendeten Zeiten von denen im Deutschen abweichen.

D. Indirekte Rede

Äußerungen von Personen können sowohl in direkter wie auch in indirekter Form wiedergegeben werden.
Steht bei indirekter Wiedergabe der einleitende Satz im *simple past* (z. B. he said, she replied, they wanted to know, etc.), so sind im darauf folgenden Satz Veränderungen unterschiedlicher Art vorzunehmen:

1. Änderung der Zeiten

Die Zeiten ändern sich im Grundsatz wie folgt:

He says:
"We *produce* a lot of software."
    present tense →
"We *bought* from the Far East."
    past tense →
"We *have delivered* wrong material."
    present perfect →
"We *will send* a new shipment."
    future →
"We *will have developed* a new model next year."
    future perfect →

He said (that) …
they *produced* a lot of software.
    past tense
they *had bought* from the Far East.
    past perfect
they *had delivered* wrong material.
    past perfect
they *would send* a new shipment.
    present conditional
they *would have developed* a new model the following year.
    perfect conditional

2. Wiedergabe von Fragen

She asks: "When will more small companies buy our computers?" →
She asked when more small companies would buy their computers.

Die Wortstellung in direkten Fragesätzen entspricht der in Aussagesätzen. Entscheidungsfragen (Ja- oder Nein-Fragen) werden mit "whether" oder "if" eingeleitet:
She asks: "Do they also produce hardware?" →
She asked whether/if they also produced hardware.

3. Wiedergabe von Aufforderungen, Bitten

He asks his secretary: "Please get me the files on this new offer from DataWorld." →
He asked his secretary to get him the files on that new offer from DataWorld.

Dem Einleitungsteil in der indirekten Wiedergabe folgt die Nennung der angeredeten Person (= his secretary) und eine Infinitiv-Konstruktion (= to get …).

4. Wiedergabe von Pronomen (= Personenwechsel)

Die in der direkten Rede verwendeten Pronomen müssen situationsgerecht umgeformt werden (Bsp.: vgl. 1–3).

5. Wiedergabe von Orts- und Zeitangaben

The manager explains: "We started a new project last year which will be presented next year."
The manager explained (that) they had started a new project the year before which would be presented the following year.

Veränderungen häufig benutzter adverbialer Angaben:

now	→	then
today	→	that day
this week	→	that week
yesterday	→	the day before
last week	→	the week before
tomorrow	→	the following / next day
here	→	there

E. Adjektive – Adverbien

1. Adjektive

Funktion:

This is an *interesting* offer.
Don't be *impolite*.
Their offer sounds *attractive*.
Adjektive beschreiben Personen und Sachen (= Substantive) näher.

2. Adverbien

Funktion:

a. They will *surely* accept our offer.
b. *Unfortunately* we cannot accept your proposal.
c. They have sent us some *really* good ideas.
d. Our new product is selling *extremely* well.

Adverbien beschreiben näher:
a. Verben
b. ganze Sätze
c. Adjektive   d. Adverbien.

Stellung:

> Martin answered the job advertisement *quickly*.
> He took a programming course *at school last year*.

Adverbien stehen am häufigsten am Ende des Satzes. Wenn es mehrere Adverbien gibt, ist die Reihenfolge "manner (wie?) – place (wo?) – time (wann?)" zu beachten.

> Martin *often* thinks about his future.
> He has *always* wanted to work with computers.

Eine wichtige Ausnahme bildet die folgende Gruppe von Adverbien: always/never, usually/hardly ever, sometimes/often etc. Diese stehen vor einem Vollverb bzw. nach einem Hilfsverb.

> Martin *gladly* agreed to work overtime.

Auch viele "adverbs of manner" können an dieser Stelle stehen.

> M & C's job offer sounds *really* good.
> M & C has been expanding *extremely* rapidly.

Adverbien stehen vor den Adjektiven und Adverbien, die sie näher bestimmen.

3. Steigerung von Adjektiven und Adverbien

	Adjektive	*Adverbien*
mit -er, -est	a. alle Adjektive mit 1 Silbe z. B.: tall/taller/tallest great/greater/greatest b. Adjektive mit 2 Silben, die auf -ow, -le, -y, -er enden z. B.: simple/simpler/simplest happy/happier/happiest narrow/narrower/narrowest clever/cleverer/cleverest	a. Adverbien, die die gleiche Form wie Adjektive haben z. B.: fast/hard/long/loud b. Adverbien, die nicht von Adjektiven abgeleitet sind. z. B.: soon
mit more, most	a. Adjektive mit der Betonung auf der 1. Silbe z. B.: perfect/more perfect/most perfect b. alle anderen mehrsilbigen Adjektive z. B.: attractive/more attractive/most attractive	alle Adverbien, die gebildet werden aus Adjektiv + ly z. B.: dangerously/more dangerously/most dangerously quickly/more quickly/most quickly

	Adjektive	*Adverbien*
Ausnahmen mit unregelmäßiger Steigerung	good/better/best far/further (farther)/furthest (farthest) bad/worse/worst	well/better/best badly/worse/worst

F. Infinitiv – Gerundium

1. Infinitiv

a. They had the *opportunity to meet* a German partner.
b. We are *happy to send* you our new catalogue.
c. We will *manage to send* the goods in time.
d. We *expect you to deliver* not later than 15 July.
e. They *waited for me to phone* back.

Eine Infinitiv-Konstruktion wird benutzt nach:

a. *Substantiven* (z. B. opportunity, ability, permission, plan, right, wish)
b. *Adjektiven* (z. B. able, keen, happy, glad, likely, pleased, interested, possible, difficult)
c. *Verben* (z. B. agree, aim, ask, choose, claim, decide, demand, expect, fail, hope, manage, offer, plan, prove, promise, refuse, seem, tend, threaten, want)

Eine Infinitiv-Konstruktion wird häufig benutzt nach:

d. *Verben + Objekt* (z. B. advise, allow, ask, encourage, expect, force, help, invite, like, love, order, prefer, persuade, promise, remind, teach, tell, warn, want)
e. *Verben + for + Subjekt des Infinitivsatzes* (z. B. arrange, ask, prepare, wait)

2. Gerundium

a. We must *apologize for sending* the wrong article.
b. M & C is *happy about entering* the German market.
c. They have no *difficulty in developing* new ideas.
d. M & C suggests *developing* individual solutions.

Eine Gerundium-Konstruktion (Verb + -ing) wird benutzt nach:

a. Verben + Präpositionen, z. B.

accuse s.o. of	get around to
admit of/to	keep from
amount to	live by
arrange about	object to
begin by	persist in
benefit by/from	profit by
care about	refrain from
come of/from	rely on
complain about/of	see about
confess to	specialize in
count on	succeed in
decide against	talk about/of
disapprove of	think about/of
dream about/of	vote against
engage in	warn against
escape from	worry about
fail in	

211

b. Adjektiven + Präpositionen, z. B.

accustomed to	fortunate in
alarmed by	frightened of
amazed at	glad about
angry at	guilty of
appropriate for	happy about
ashamed of	hopeful about
astonished at	interested in
available for	keen on
certain of	necessary for
conscious of	nervous about
correct in	optimistic about
crazy about	pessimistic about
delighted at	pleased at
disappointed at	proud of
engaged in	right in
enthusiastic about	serious about
equivalent to	slow in
excited about	suitable for
famous for	used to
fond of	useful for

c. Substantiven + Präpositionen, z. B.

advantage of	death by	hesitation in	(there's no) point in
alternative to	delight in	hope of	possibility of
aversion to	difference between	impression of	preference for
basis for	difficulty in	interest in	privilege of
belief in	dislike for/of	love of	reason for
blame for	excuse for	means of	reputation for/of
choice between	experience in	method of	satisfaction in
compromise between	facility for	necessity for	step of
danger of	fear of	need for	surprise at
(a good) deal of	fondness for	objection to	taste for
		occasion for	tendency towards
		place for	trouble in
		plan for	way of
		pleasure in/of	

d. einer Reihe von Verben, die in der Regel keinen Infinitiv nach sich ziehen, z. B.

admit	mind
advise	miss
advocate	oppose
allow	permit
can't/couldn't stand	practise
deny	prevent
discontinue	recall
encourage	recollect
escape	recommend
favour	regard
finish	require
give up	resume
imagine	risk
involve	suggest
keep (on)	value
leave off	

Important Irregular Verbs

*means that a regular form exists alongside the irregular form.

be – was/were – been
bear – bore – borne/born
beat – beat – beaten
become – became – become
begin – began – begun
bend – bent – bent
bet – bet* – bet*
bind – bound – bound
bite – bit – bitten
blow – blew – blown
break – broke – broken
breed – bred – bred
bring – brought – brought
build – built – built
burn – burnt* – burnt*
burst – burst – burst
buy – bought – bought
catch – caught – caught
choose – chose – chosen
come – came – come
cost – cost – cost
creep – crept – crept
cut – cut – cut
deal – dealt [e] – dealt [e]
dig – dug – dug
do – did – done
draw – drew – drawn
dream – dreamt* [e] – dreamt* [e]
drink – drank – drunk
drive – drove – driven
eat – ate [e] – eaten
fall – fell – fallen
feed – fed – fed

feel – felt – felt
fight – fought – fought
find – found – found
fly – flew – flown
forget – forgot – forgotten
forgive – forgave – forgiven
freeze – froze – frozen
get – got – got
give – gave – given
go – went – gone [ɒ]
grow – grew – grown
hang – hung* – hung*
have – had – had
hear – heard [ɜ] – heard [ɜ:]
hide – hid – hidden
hit – hit – hit
hold – held – held
hurt – hurt – hurt
keep – kept – kept
know – knew – known
lay – laid – laid
lead – led – led
learn – learnt* – learnt*
leave – left – left
lend – lent – lent
let – let – let
lie – lay – lain
light – lit* – lit*
lose – lost [ɒ] – lost [ɒ]
make – made – made
mean – meant [e] – meant [e]
meet – met – met
pay – paid – paid
put – put – put

read – read [e] – read [e]
ride – rode – ridden
ring – rang – rung
rise – rose – risen [ɪ]
run – ran – run
say – said [e] – said [e]
see – saw – seen
seek – sought – sought
sell – sold – sold
send – sent – sent
set – set – set
shake – shook – shaken
shoot – shot – shot
show – showed – shown
shut – shut – shut
sing – sang – sung
sink – sank – sunk
sit – sat – sat
sleep – slept – slept
smell – smelt* – smelt*
speak – spoke – spoken
spell – spelt* – spelt*
spend – spent – spent
split – split – split
spread – spread – spread
stand – stood – stood
steal – stole – stolen
stick – stuck – stuck
strike – struck – struck
swear – swore – sworn
sweep – swept – swept
swim – swam – swum
swing – swung – swung
take – took – taken

213

teach – taught – taught tear – tore – torn tell – told – told think – thought – thought	throw – threw – thrown understand – understood – understood wake – woke – woken	wear – wore – worn win – won [ʌ] – won write – wrote – written

Pronunciation Guide

[ʌ]	bus [bʌs], run [rʌn]
[ɑː]	last [lɑːst], park [pɑːk]
[aɪ]	my [maɪ], nice [naɪs]
[aʊ]	out [aʊt], how [haʊ]
[ãː]	restaurant ['restrãː]
[æ]	back [bæk], stand [stænd]
[e]	egg [eg], best [best]
[eɪ]	late [leɪt], name [neɪm], safe [seɪf], pay [peɪ]
[eə]	air [eə], where [weə]
[ə]	about [ə'baʊt], member ['membə]
[əʊ]	own [əʊn], so [səʊ]
[ɜː]	firm [fɜːm], word [wɜːd]
[ɪ]	it [ɪt], film [fɪlm]
[ɪə]	near [nɪə], here [hɪə]
[iː]	please [pliːz], see [siː]
[ɒ]	not [nɒt], long [lɒŋ]
[ɔɪ]	boy [bɔɪ], noise [nɔɪz]
[ɔː]	all [ɔːl], north [nɔːθ]
[ʊ]	book [bʊk], good [gʊd]
[ʊə]	sure [ʃʊə], tour [tʊə]
[uː]	who [huː], school [skuːl]
[ŋ]	young [jʌŋ], thing [θɪŋ]
[r]	right [raɪt], friend [frend], porridge ['pɒrɪdʒ]
[s]	sir [sɜː], Miss [mɪs]
[z]	busy ['bɪzɪ], please [pliːz]
[θ]	thing [θɪŋ], both [bəʊθ], nothing ['nʌθɪŋ]
[ð]	that [ðæt], with [wɪð], another [ə'nʌðə]
[ʃ]	shop [ʃɒp], fresh [freʃ]
[ʒ]	television ['telɪvɪʒn]
[v]	visit ['vɪzɪt], love [lʌv]
[w]	well [wel], what [wɒt], always ['ɔːlweɪz], quite [kwaɪt]
[tʃ]	chairman
dʒ	Germany
[']	conversation [kɒnvə'seɪʃn]

List of Intentions

Schlüssel	Key
Anbieten 11	Ability 16
Anlagen, Verweisen auf 8	Accompanying mail 9
Aufmerksamkeit 23	Annoyance 25
Bedanken 13	Attention 23
Bedauern 17	Commitment 14
Begleitschreiben 9	Compulsion 24
Bereitschaft 12	Emphasis 21
Bekräftigen 15	Enclosures, Drawing attention to 8
Beziehen auf 6	Expectation 20
Bitten 3	Expectation, positive 5
Drängen 19	Getting in touch 1
Empfang 10	Inability 18
Entschlossenheit 22	Interest 2
Erhalt 10	Mail, accompanying 9
Erwartung 20	Offering 11
Erwartung, positive 5	Pointing out 4
Fähigkeit 16	Receipt 10
Gezwungensein 24	Reconfirm 15
Hinweisen 4	Referring 6
Interesse 2	Regret 17
Kontakt aufnehmen 1	Request 3
Nachdruck 21	Resolution 22
Unvermögen 18	Suggestion 7
Verärgerung 25	Thanks 13
Verpflichtung 14	Urgency 19
Vorschlagen 7	Willingness 12

The numbers refer to the following list of intentions.

1 Getting in touch –
   Kontakt aufnehmen

   we have been given your name by <n>
   we have received your address
      from <n>

   your firm was recommended to us
      by <n>

2 Showing interest – *Interesse zeigen*
   we are very much interested in
      <n>/<vb + -ing>

3 Making requests – *Um etwas bitten*

please <vb>
we would like you <to + vb>
we should appreciate it if you would <vb>
we should be grateful if you would <vb>
it would be appreciated if you could <vb>
<n> would be appreciated

4 Pointing out – *Auf etwas hinweisen*

we should like to point out <that-clause>
we wish to point out <that-clause>

5 Expressing positive expectations – *Positive Erwartungen ausdrücken*

we hope <to + vb>/<that-clause>
we look forward to <n>/<vb + -ing>
we would be (very) happy <to + vb>

6 Referring to s. th. – *Sich auf etwas beziehen*

we refer to <n>
referring to <n>

7 Making suggestions – *Vorschläge machen*

(may) we suggest <vb + -ing>

8 Drawing attention to enclosure(s) – *Auf Anlage(n) verweisen*

please find enclosed <n>
we are also sending you <n>
enclosed (with this letter) we are sending you <n>
at the same time we enclose <n>
we are enclosing <n>
enclosed you will find <n>

9 Drawing attention to accompanying mail – *Auf Begleitschreiben verweisen*

under separate cover we are sending you <n>

10 Acknowledging receipt – *Eingang/Erhalt bestätigen*

we have received <n>
we are in receipt of <n>
we were (very) pleased to receive <n>
it was a pleasure to receive <n>
we wish to confirm receipt of <n>
we acknowledge with thanks <n>

11 Offering something – *Etwas anbieten*

we have the pleasure of <vb + -ing>
we are happy <to + vb>
we are glad <to + vb>

12 Expressing willingness – *Bereitschaft ausdrücken*

we will be glad <to + vb>
we will be pleased <to + vb>
we will be happy <to + vb>
we are prepared <to + vb>

13 Expressing thanks – *Sich bedanken*

(we) thank you (very much) for <n>/<vb + -ing>

14 Expressing commitment – *Sich zu etwas verpflichten*

we assure you <that-clause>
you may be sure <that-clause>

15 Reconfirming statements – *(Bereits gemachte) Aussagen bekräftigen*

we note <that-clause>
we understand <that-clause>

16 Expressing ability – *Fähigkeit ausdrücken*

we are in a position <to + vb>

17 Expressing regret – *Bedauern ausdrücken*

we note with regret <that-clause>
we (very much) regret <that-clause>/<vb + -ing>
we are sorry <that-clause>
much to our regret we <vb>

18 Expressing inability – *Unvermögen ausdrücken*

it is impossible for us <to + vb>
we are unable <to + vb>
we are not in a position <to + vb>

19 Expressing urgency – *Auf etwas drängen*

we must ask you <to + vb>
we must insist on <vb + -ing>
we must insist <that-clause>

20 Expressing expectation – *Erwartung ausdrücken*

we trust <that-clause>
we would hope <that-clause>

21 Expressing emphasis – *Nachdruck verleihen*

you will (certainly) understand <that-clause>
you must realize <that-clause>

22 Expressing resolution – *Entschlossenheit ausdrücken*

we shall have to <vb>
we shall have no alternative other than <to + vb>
we shall be compelled <to + vb>

23 Directing attention to s. th. – *Aufmerksamkeit auf etwas lenken*

we wish to draw your intention to <n>

24 Expressing compulsion – *Gezwungensein ausdrücken*

we have no other choice but <to + vb>
we have no alternative but <to + vb>

25 (Politely) expressing annoyance – *(Höflich) Verärgerung ausdrücken*

we regret <to + vb>/<that-clause>
we are sorry <that-clause>
we are greatly surprised at <n>
we are greatly surprised <that-clause>

Commercial Terms

a. Terms of Delivery

EXW	ex works	*ab Werk*
FAS	free alongside ship	*frei Längsseite Seeschiff*
FOB	free on board	*frei an Bord*
FCA	free carrier	*frei Frachtführer*
CFR	cost and freight	*Kosten und Fracht*
CIF	cost, insurance, freight	*Kosten, Versicherung, Fracht*
CPT	carriage paid to	*frachtfrei*
CIP	carriage and insurance paid to	*frachtfrei versichert*
DES	delivered ex ship	*geliefert ab Schiff*
DEQ	delivered ex quay	*geliefert ab Kai*
DAF	delivered at frontier	*geliefert Grenze*
DDP	delivered duty paid	*geliefert verzollt*
DDU	delivered duty unpaid	*geliefert unverzollt*

Note:

The terms can be classified E, F, C and D terms. You can see which category the term falls into from the first letter of the abbreviation. If the terms are listed in the order E, F, C, D, it can be said that with the 'E' term, the seller bears the fewest responsibilities, and with the 'D' terms, the seller bears the most responsibilities.

'E terms': The seller makes the goods available to the buyer at his (the seller's) works.

'F terms': The seller has to deliver the goods into the hands of the carrier.

'C terms': The seller has to deliver the goods into the hands of the carrier and also to contract for the main carriage.s

'D terms': The seller has to deliver the goods into the hands of the carrier to contract for the main carriage, and to bear the risk of transport necessary to convey the goods to the country of destination.

b. Terms of Payment

cash in advance	Vorauszahlung/Vorauskasse
cash with order (CWO)	Barzahlung bei Auftragserteilung

payment on receipt of invoice/payment on invoice	Zahlung bei Rechnungserhalt
payment by bank draft on London against pro-forma invoice	Zahlung durch Bankscheck auf London sofort nach Eingang der Proforma-Rechnung
one-third with order, one-third on delivery, and one-third within two months after delivery	$1/3$ bei Auftragserteilung, $1/3$ bei Lieferung und $1/3$ innerhalb von zwei Monaten nach Lieferung
cash on delivery (COD)	gegen Nachnahme
payment on receipt of goods	Zahlung bei Erhalt der Waren
payment within 60 days from date of invoice	Zahlung innerhalb von 60 Tagen nach Rechnungsdatum
30 days net	30 Tage netto
two months' credit	2 Monate Ziel
strictly net	rein netto
2% for cash	2% Skonto bei Barzahlung
... less 2% cash discount for payment within ... days	... abzüglich 2% Skonto für Zahlung innerhalb ... Tagen
10 days 2%, 30 days net (2/10, net 30)	Zahlung innerhalb 10 Tagen abzüglich 2% Skonto oder innerhalb 30 Tagen netto
2/10 E. O. M. (*end of month*)/ R. O. G. (*receipt of goods*)	2% Skonto für Zahlung innerhalb von 10 Tagen nach Ende des Liefermonats/nach Erhalt der Waren
against three months' acceptance	gegen Dreimonatsakzept
documents against payment (D/P)/cash against documents (CAD)	Kasse gegen Dokumente
documents against acceptance (D/A)	Dokumente gegen Akzept
The shipping documents will be surrendered against bank acceptance.	Übergabe der Versanddokumente erfolgt gegen Bankakzept.
payment by (ir)revocable and (un)confirmed documentary (letter of) credit	Zahlung durch (un)widerrufliches und (un)bestätigtes Dokumentenakkreditiv

c. International Dispatch Documents

Pro-forma Invoice

A pro-forma invoice (sometimes also called "commercial invoice") may serve as a quotation or a request for payment in advance. It is also used when goods are sent on approval or consigned to an agent for sale.

Consular Invoice

When country A imports goods from country B, it may first be necessary to have this special commercial invoice signed by a representative of A's government (i.e. by a consular representative) who lives in B. This gives A better control over the amounts of goods it imports. A consular invoice also prevents "dumping", i.e. the selling of goods in foreign countries at very low prices.

Bill of Lading (B/L)

An important document issued for shipment by sea. It has three functions:

a) it is a formal receipt issued by the carrier for the goods question,
b) it is a document giving the importer the right to claim the goods on arrival,
c) it is a document giving evidence of the contract between the exporter and the shipper.

A document stating that the goods are in "apparent good order and condition" is a "clean" bill of lading; if it contains a clause indicating any defect in the condition of the packages, it is called a "foul" ("dirty" or "claused") bill of lading.

An "airway bill", on the other hand, accompanies goods sent by air.

Insurance Certificate

An exporter who wants proof of insurance for a shipment has to obtain an insurance certificate. The insurance covers theft and damage during the shipment.

Certificate of Origin

A document showing the origin of goods. It is prepared by the exporter and signed by a Chamber of Commerce or customs officer in the exporting country.

Proof of origin may be necessary because the treatment of foreign goods by the importing country differs according to the country in which the goods originate.

For example, although Britain might charge import duty on goods from Brazil, it does not do so on goods from Germany. (EU member states do not charge duty on each other's goods.)

Other Documents

Inspection certificate (Prüfungszertifikat)
Weight certificate (Gewichtszertifikat)
Packing list (Packliste, Versandliste)

Abbreviations

a. Common English/American Abbreviations

ad (advt) advertisement
am (ante meridiem) before noon
av 1) average 2) avenue
BA Bachelor of Arts (= university degree)
B/E bill of exchange
b/f brought forward
B/L bill of lading
Bros brothers
BSc AE: BS Bachelor of Science (= university degree)
C Celsius; Centigrade
c 1) circa (c 1778 = about 1778) 2) cent(s)
CA chartered accountant (= BE: an accountant who has passed the official examinations of the Institute of Chartered Accountants)
C/A current account
cat catalogue
cc 1) carbon copy 2) cubic centimetre(s)
C/FwD carried forward
co company
c/o care of
CV curriculum vitae
deg degree
dep 1) departure 2) depart
dept department
doz dozen
Dr 1) doctor 2) drive (in addresses)
E east
E & OE errors and omissions excepted (= often included at the end of an invoice to safeguard the creditor against clerical mistakes)
EU European Union
eg (exempli gratia) for example
enc(l) (encls) enclosure(s)

est estimated
etc (et cetera) and so on
ext(n) extension
F Fahrenheit
ft foot (feet) (1 ft = 30.480 centimetres)
gal gallon (AE: 1 gal = 3.785 litres; BE: 1 gal = 4.545 litres)
GMT Greenwich Mean Time
h 1) hour 2) half 3) high
hp 1) horsepower 2) hire purchase
hwy AE: highway
ie (id est) that is
IMO international money order
in(s) inch(es) (1 in = 2.540 centimetres)
Inc incorporated
incl 1) including 2) inclusive
info information
int international
intercom intercommunication system
inv invoice
K 1) thousand (salary $30K+ = a salary of $30,000 or more) 2) kilo(byte)
lb(s) pound(s) (1 lb = 0.453 kilograms)
Ltd limited
M 1) BE: motorway 2) Clothes etc.: medium
m million (£300m = three hundred million pounds)
MA Master of Arts (= university degree)
memo memorandum (= informal written note)
Messrs (messieurs) plural of Mr
mfg manufacturing
mi mile(s) (1 mi = 1.609 kilometres)
min 1) minute 2) minimum

MO money order
MP member of parliament
mph miles per hour
Ms (= today often used instead of Miss or Mrs)
MSc AE: MS Master of Science (= university degree)
N north
N/C no charge
NE northeast
no (numero) number
NW northwest
oz ounce(s) (1 oz = 28.348 grams)
p 1) BE: pence; penny 2) page
pa per annum (= per year)
pc(t) per cent
per pro (per procurationem) on behalf of
PLC public limited company
pm (post meridiem) after noon
PO Box post office box
p & p postage and packing
pp 1) → per pro 2) pages
PR public relations
PS (postscriptum) postscript
pto please turn over
qty quantity
Rd road
ref reference
reg 1) regular 2) regulation 3) registered
regd registered
req required
sae stamped addressed envelope
RSVP (répondez s'il vous plaît) please reply
S south
SE southeast
Sq square
St street
SW southwest

tel telephone
t 1) time 2) ton (tonne)
TV television
UK United Kingdom of Great Britain and Northern Ireland
US United States (of America)
USA → US
USPS United States Postal Service
VAT value added tax
VIP very important person
viz (videlicet) namely; that is
vol volume
vs versus (= against)
W west
wt weight
y 1) year 2) yard(s)
yd(s) yard(s) (1 yd = 0.9144 metres)
yr 1) year 2) your
Zip code (zone improvement plan) (= fivedigit number that identifies each postal delivery area in the US)

& (ampersand) and
&c et cetera; and so forth
@ at; each (three apples @5¢ = three apples at five cents each)
¢ cent(s)
© copyrighted
20° twenty degrees
" ditto marks
$ dollar
# 1) number (if used in front of a figure: the train leaves at 12.25, track #14) 2) pounds (if it follows a figure: here is a 10# sack of flour)
£ pound Sterling
® registered trademark
8' 1) eight feet 2) eight minutes
8" 1) eight inches 2) eight seconds

b. Abbreviations of English Counties and American States

Beds	Bedfordshire	Herts	Hertfordshire	Oxon	Oxfordshire
Berks	Berkshire	Lancs	Lancashire	S. Yorkshire	South Yorkshire
Bucks	Buckinghamshire	Leics	Leicestershire	Staffs	Staffordshire
Cambs	Cambridgeshire	Lincs	Lincolnshire	Tyne & Wear	Tyne and Wear
Co. Durham	County Durham	Northants	Northamptonshire	W. Midlands	West Midlands
E. Sussex	East Sussex	Northd	Northumberland	W. Sussex	West Sussex
Glos	Gloucestershire	N. Yorkshire	North Yorkshire	W. Yorkshire	West Yorkshire
Hants	Hampshire	Notts	Nottinghamshire	Wilts	Wiltshire

Alabama	AL	Indiana	IN	Nebraska	NE	Rhode Island	RI
Alaska	AK	Iowa	IA	Nevada	NV	South Carolina	SC
Arizona	AZ	Kansas	KS	New Hampshire	NH	South Dakota	SD
Arkansas	AR	Kentucky	KY	New Jersey	NJ	Tennessee	TN
California	CA	Louisiana	LA	New Mexico	NM	Texas	TX
Colorado	CO	Maine	ME	New York	NY	Utah	UT
Connecticut	CT	Maryland	MD	North Carolina	NC	Vermont	VT
Delaware	DE	Massachusetts	MA	North Dakota	ND	Virginia	VA
Florida	FL	Michigan	MI	Ohio	OH	Washington	WA
Georgia	GA	Minnesota	MN	Oklahoma	OK	West Virginia	WV
Hawaii	HI	Mississippi	MS	Oregon	OR	Wisconsin	WI
Idaho	ID	Missouri	MO	Pennsylvania	PA	Wyoming	WY
Illinois	IL	Montana	MT				

(District of Columbia DC)

Vocabulary

Unit by Unit

The following abbreviations are used in the vocabulary list:
IC = Introductory Course
MC = Main Course
Sec.A. = Secretarial Activities
Com.C. = Commercial Correspondence

Within the individual units, the words appear in alphabetical order.

IC 1: Technologies Mean Opportunities

agent ['eɪdʒənt]   *Vertreter/in, Handelnde/r*
all over [ɔːl'əʊvə]   *überall*
at the latest [æt ðə 'leɪtɪst]   *spätestens*
to boom into [buːm 'ɪntʊ]   *sich schnell entwickeln zu*
brilliant ['brɪljənt]   *hervorragend, brillant*
builder ['bɪldə]   *Bauunternehmer/in*
classmate ['klɑːsmeɪt]   *Klassenkamerad/in*
confidential [ˌkɒnfɪ'denʃl]   *vertraulich*
contract proposal ['kɒntrækt prə'pəʊzl]   *Vertragsentwurf*
corporation [ˌkɔːpə'reɪʃn]   *Handelsgesellschaft*
customer ['kʌstəmə]   *Kunde/Kundin*
to deal with ['diːl 'wɪð]   *sich befassen mit*
decorator ['dekəreɪtə]   *Innenarchitekt/in*
desperately ['despərətli]   *hier: dringend*
during the course of ['djʊərɪŋ ðə 'kɔːs əv]   *hier: im Verlauf von*
emancipated [ɪ'mænsɪpeɪtɪd]   *emanzipiert*
emergency [ɪ'mɜːdʒənsi]   *Notfall*
habit ['hæbɪt]   *Gewohnheit*
hardware ['hɑːdweə]   *Hardware*
to look after ['lʊk 'ɑːftə]   *sich kümmern um*
to look forward to ['lʊk 'fɔːwəd]   *sich freuen auf*
permanent ['pɜːmənənt]   *(an)dauernd, permanent*
plumber ['plʌmə]   *Installateur/in*
proper ['prɒpə]   *geeignet, korrekt*
rather than ['rɑːðə ðən]   *eher als*
to react [riː'ækt]   *reagieren*
responsibilities [rɪˌspɒnsə'bɪlətɪz]   *Pflichten, Aufgaben*
to run [rʌn]   *(eine Firma) führen/betreiben*
to share [ʃeə]   *teilen*
software ['sɒftweə]   *Software*
solution [sə'luːʃn]   *Lösung*
space [speɪs]   *hier: Zeitspanne*
to specialize in ['speʃəlaɪz ɪn]   *sich spezialisieren auf*
to stand for ['stænd fɔː]   *stehen für*
state of affairs ['steɪt əv ə'feəz]   *Sachverhalt*
strength [streŋθ]   *Stärke*
to supply [sə'plaɪ]   *liefern, zur Verfügung stellen*
tailor-made ['teɪləmeɪd]   *maßgeschneidert*
temporary ['tempərəri]   *vorübergehend*

IC 2: A Company in the Making

abroad [ə'brɔːd]   *im/ins Ausland*
to afford [ə'fɔːd]   *sich leisten können*
applications software [ˌæplɪ'keɪʃənz 'sɒftweə]   *anwenderorientierte Software*
aspect ['æspekt]   *Gesichtspunkt, Aspekt*
to assemble [ə'sembl]   *zusammensetzen, montieren*
to do business with s.o. [duː 'bɪznɪs]   *mit jmndm. Geschäfte abwickeln/tätigen*
to collect [kə'lekt]   *sammeln*
component [kəm'pəʊnənt]   *Bauteil, Komponente*
to establish contacts [ɪ'stæblɪʃ 'kɒntækts]   *Kontakte anbahnen*
correspond to [ˌkɒrɪ'spɒnd tuː]   *entsprechen*
to meet s.o.'s demands ['miːt 'sʌmwʌns dɪ'mɑːndz]   *jmnds. Nachfrage befriedigen*

Info — Vocabulary: Unit by Unit

to dive [daɪv]   *tauchen*
duration [djʊəˈreɪʃn]   *Dauer*
equipment [ɪˈkwɪpmənt]   *Ausstattung*
to expand [ɪkˈspænd]   *ausdehnen, expandieren*
favourable [ˈfeɪvərəbl]   *günstig*
to fit (into) [fɪt ˈɪntʊ]   *passen (in)*
focus (n) [ˈfəʊkəs]   *Augenmerk*
to increase [ɪnˈkriːs]   *steigern*
to indicate [ˈɪndɪkeɪt]   *angeben, anzeigen, markieren*
mainly [ˈmeɪnlɪ]   *hauptsächlich, in erster Linie*
to market [ˈmɑːkɪt]   *vertreiben, auf den Markt bringen, vermarkten*
nowadays [ˈnaʊədeɪz]   *heutzutage, heute*
particular [pəˈtɪkjʊlə]   *hier: jeweilig*
practically [ˈpræktɪkəlɪ]   *praktisch*
to purchase [ˈpɜːtʃəs]   *kaufen, erwerben*
rapid [ˈræpɪd]   *sehr schnell, rapide*
recently [ˈriːsntlɪ]   *kürzlich, vor kurzem*
specific [spɪˈsɪfɪk]   *speziell*
supplier [səˈplaɪə]   *Lieferant*

(ever) since then [ˈevə ˌsɪns ˈðen]   *seitdem*
to keep a keen eye on [ˈkiːp ə ˈkiːn ˈaɪ ɒn]   *etw. mit großem Interesse verfolgen*
to found [faʊnd]   *(be)gründen*
to gain [geɪn]   *gewinnen, erhalten*
independent [ˌɪndɪˈpəndənt]   *unabhängig*
to introduce [ˌɪntrəˈdjuːs]   *einführen*
to involve [ɪnˈvɒlv]   *beinhalten, einschließen*
to make it [ˈmeɪk ɪt]   *es schaffen*
to manage to do s.th. [ˈmænɪdʒ tə ˈduː]   *gelingen etw. zu tun*
period [ˈpɪərɪəd]   *Zeit(spanne)*
to prove [pruːv]   *sich erweisen als*
to rely on [rɪˈlaɪ ɒn]   *sich verlassen auf*
risk (n) [rɪsk]   *Wagnis, Risiko*
scientist [ˈsaɪəntɪst]   *(Natur-)Wissenschaftler/in*
slight [slaɪt]   *gering(fügig)*
so far [səʊ fɑː]   *bislang, bis jetzt*
to have in store [ˈhæv ɪn ˈstɔː]   *bereithalten*
surprising [səˈpraɪzɪŋ]   *überraschend*
training course [ˈtreɪnɪŋ kɔːs]   *Ausbildung*
unusual [ʌnˈjuːʒʊəl]   *unüblich*

IC 3: A Business Career

to apply for [əˈplaɪ fɔː]   *sich bewerben um/für*
basis [ˈbeɪsɪs]   *Grundlage, Basis*
career [kəˈrɪə]   *Karriere, Laufbahn*
chip [tʃɪp]   *(Computer-)Chip*
column [ˈkɒləm]   *Spalte*
to come across [kʌm əˈkrɒs]   *begegnen*
to come true [kʌm truː]   *wahr werden, verwirklicht werden*
to concern [kənˈsɜːn]   *angehen, (an)betreffen*
to have s.th. under control [kənˈtrəʊl]   *etw. unter Kontrolle haben*
to attend courses [əˈtend ˈkɔːsɪz]   *Kurse belegen/besuchen*
despite [dɪˈspaɪt]   *trotz*
drastically [ˈdræstɪkəlɪ]   *drastisch*
EU (European Union) [ˈiːˈjuː(ˌjʊərəˈpiːən ˈjuːnjən)]   *EU (Europäische Union)*
to read economics [iːkəˈnɒmɪks]   *Wirtschaftswissenschaften studieren*
even [ˈiːvn]   *sogar*

IC 4: The Computer – a Man-Made Device

absent [ˈæbsənt]   *abwesend*
to accompany [əˈkʌmpənɪ]   *begleiten*
to admit [ədˈmɪt]   *zugeben, sich eingestehen*
alike [əˈlaɪk]   *gleichermaßen*
among [əˈmʌŋ]   *unter, inmitten von*
area [ˈeərɪə]   *hier: Bezirk*
to arrange [əˈreɪndʒ]   *einrichten, arrangieren*
basic [ˈbeɪsɪk]   *grundsätzlich*
to be in charge of [bi ɪn ˈtʃɑːdʒ əv]   *verantwortlich sein für*
colleague [ˈkɒliːg]   *Kollege/Kollegin*
computerized [kəmˈpjuːtəraɪzd]   *computererstellt*
to confess [kənˈfes]   *bekennen, gestehen*
to consider [kənˈsɪdə]   *erachten*
considerable [kənˈsɪdərəbl]   *beträchtlich*
a couple of [ə ˈkʌpl əv]   *ein paar*
to take o.'s course [ˈteɪk wʌns ˈkɔːs]   *seinen Gang gehen*

data protection [ˈdeɪtə prəˈtekʃn] *Datenschutz*
demand [dɪˈmɑːnd] *Nachfrage, Forderung*
device [dɪˈvaɪs] *Vorrichtung*
digital [ˈdɪdʒɪtl] *digital*
to dislike [dɪsˈlaɪk] *nicht mögen*
to drop [drɒp] *absetzen*
event [ɪˈvent] *Ereignis*
except (for) [ɪkˈsept fɔː] *außer*
to fail [feɪl] *versagen*
to feed (irr) [fiːd] *füttern*
time frame [freɪm] *Zeitrahmen*
headmistress [ˌhedˈmɪstrɪs] *Schulleiterin*
s.o. can't help doing s.th. [ˈkɑːnt ˈhelp] *jmnd. kann nicht anders als*
humans [ˈhjuːmənz] *Menschen*
information sheet [ˌɪnfəˈmeɪʃn ˈʃiːt] *Informationsblatt*
to make s.th. known [ˈmeɪk ˈsʌmθɪŋ ˈnəʊn] *etw. bekanntmachen*
labour [ˈleɪbə] *Arbeitskräfte*
to give s.o. a lecture [ˈlektʃə] *jmndm. die Leviten lesen*
to stretch s.th. to its limits [stretʃ] *etw. auf die Spitze treiben*
to link [lɪŋk] *verbinden*
to locate [ləʊˈkeɪt] *ansiedeln*
to mean well [miːn wel] *es gut meinen*
mess [mes] *Durcheinander*
on principle [ɒn ˈprɪnsəpl] *aus Prinzip*
to operate [ˈɒpəreɪt] *in Betrieb nehmen*
to perplex [pəˈpleks] *verwirren*
to persuade [pəˈsweɪd] *überreden*
Primary School [ˈpraɪmərɪ skuːl] *Grundschule*
principle [ˈprɪnsəpl] *Grundsatz, Prinzip*
to process [prəˈses] *verarbeiten*
publicly [ˈpʌblɪklɪ] *öffentlich, in der Öffentlichkeit*
reliable [rɪˈlaɪəbl] *zuverlässig*
to record [rɪˈkɔːd] *aufzeichnen, speichern*
to require [rɪˈkwaɪə] *benötigen, erfordern*
to store [stɔː] *speichern*
to succeed [səkˈsiːd] *erfolgreich sein*
to suspect [səˈspekt] *den Verdacht haben*
first day of term [tɜːm] *1. Schultag*
to play a trick on s.o. [ˈpleɪ ə ˈtrɪk ɒn] *jmndm. einen Streich spielen*

IC 5: Opening Up New Markets

to act as [ækt] *handeln als*
assembly shop [əˈsemblɪ ʃɒp] *Montagehalle*
to attend to [əˈtend] *sich kümmern um*
basically [ˈbeɪsɪkəlɪ] *grundsätzlich*
but [bʌt] *hier: außer, mit Ausnahme von*
canteen [kænˈtiːn] *Kantine*
to celebrate [ˈselɪbreɪt] *feiern*
certainty [ˈsɜːtntɪ] *Gewissheit, Sicherheit*
to comply with [kəmˈplaɪ wɪð] *entsprechen*
to deal in [diːl ɪn] *handeln mit*
decoration [ˌdekəˈreɪʃn] *Dekoration*
to decrease [diːˈkriːs] *abnehmen*
efficient [ɪˈfɪʃənt] *tüchtig, wirksam, effizient*
essential [ɪˈsenʃl] *grundsätzlich*
facility [fəˈsɪlətɪ] *Einrichtung, Anlage*
factory-like [ˈfæktərɪ ˌlaɪk] *wie eine Fabrik*
figures [ˈfɪgəz] *Zahlen*
flight [flaɪt] *Flug*
in fact [ɪn fækt] *hier: sogar*
incoming [ˈɪnˌkʌmɪŋ] *eingehend*
to insist on [ɪnˈsɪst ɒn] *bestehen auf*
keen competition [ˈkiːn ˌkɒmpɪˈtɪʃn] *scharfer Wettbewerb*
latest [ˈleɪtɪst] *neuest*
likely [ˈlaɪklɪ] *wahrscheinlich, möglich*
market research [ˈmɑːkɪt rɪˈsɜːtʃ] *Marktforschung, Markterhebung*
merely [ˈmɪəlɪ] *lediglich, bloß, nur*
to slip o.'s mind [ˈslɪp wʌns ˈmaɪnd] *es ist jmndm. entfallen*
to modify [ˈmɒdɪfaɪ] *anpassen, modifizieren*
outdoors [ˈaʊtdɔːz] *im Freien*
to place s.o. in a difficult position [ˈdɪfɪkəlt pəˈzɪʃn] *jmndn. in eine schwierige Lage bringen*
to post [pəʊst] *versenden*
to prefer [prɪˈfɜː] *bevorzugen, vorziehen*
promising [ˈprɒmɪsɪŋ] *vielversprechend*
to recheck [ˌriːˈtʃek] *erneut überprüfen*
as regards [æz rɪˈgɑːdz] *hinsichtlich, bezüglich, betreffend*
regulation [ˌregjʊˈleɪʃn] *Vorschrift, Bestimmung*
reply (n) [rɪˈplaɪ] *Antwort*

representative [ˌreprɪˈzentətɪv]   Vertreter/in, Repräsentant/in
to rush into s.th. [ˈrʌʃ ˈɪntʊ]   etw. überstürzen
sales outlet [ˈseɪlz ˈaʊtlet]   Absatzgebiet
sales set-up [ˈseɪlz ˈsetʌp]   Vertriebsorganisation
serious [ˈsɪərɪəs]   ernst(haft)
shift [ʃɪft]   (Arbeits-)Schicht
to sort out [ˈsɔːt ˈaʊt]   klären
staff [stɑːf]   Personal
storage capacity [ˈstɔːrɪdʒ kəˈpæsətɪ]   Lagerkapazität

IC 6: Applying for a Job

ability [əˈbɪlətɪ]   Fähigkeit
to address [əˈdres]   sich wenden an
applicant [ˈæplɪkənt]   Bewerber/in
appointment [əˈpɔɪntmənt]   Termin
to be bored [biː ˈbɔːd]   sich langweilen
bit [bɪt]   ein wenig, ein bisschen
committee [kəˈmɪtɪ]   Vorstand, Komitee
current [ˈkʌrənt]   gegenwärtig
dozen [ˈdʌzn]   Dutzend
flexible [ˈfleksəbl]   anpassungsfähig, flexibel
to hang around [hæŋ əˈraʊnd]   sich herumtreiben
inconvenient [ˌɪnkənˈviːnjənt]   ungünstig
to lead s.o. to do s.th. [liːd]   jmndn. dazu bringen etw. zu tun
occasional [əˈkeɪʒənl]   gelegentlich
to work overtime [ˌwɜːk ˈəʊvətaɪm]   Überstunden machen
to proceed [prəˈsiːd]   vorgehen
provided (that) [prəˈvaɪdɪd]   vorausgesetzt (, dass)
public transport [ˈpʌblɪk ˈtrænspɔːt]   öffentliche Verkehrsmittel
to recommend [ˌrekəˈmend]   empfehlen
to review [rɪˈvjuː]   nochmals überprüfen
roughly [ˈrʌflɪ]   ungefähr, in groben Zügen
skilled labour [ˈskɪld ˈleɪbə]   Facharbeiter/in
to specify [ˈspesɪfaɪ]   genau angeben, spezifizieren
straightaway [ˌstreɪtəˈweɪ]   direkt, sofort
trend [trend]   Entwicklung, Trend
up-to-date [ˈʌptʊdeɪt]   zeitgemäß, modern

IC 7: Technologies in Everyday Life

adequate [ˈædɪkwət]   angemessen, adäquat
to adjust [əˈdʒʌst]   einstellen, regulieren, abstimmen
appliance [əˈplaɪəns]   Gerät
available [əˈveɪləbl]   verfügbar
carafe [kəˈræf]   hier: Glaskanne
cash dispenser [ˈkæʃ dɪˈspensə]   Geldautomat
claim [kleɪm]   Anspruch, Klage, Behauptung
colony [ˈkɒlənɪ]   Kolonie
Commonwealth [ˈkɒmənwelθ]   Commonwealth
community [kəˈmjuːnətɪ]   Gemeinschaft
credit indication [ˈkredɪt ɪnˈdɪkeɪʃn]   hier: Kartenwert
credit limit [ˈkredɪt ˈlɪmɪt]   hier: Kartenwert
department store [dɪˈpɑːtmənt ˈstɔː]   Kaufhaus
dial tone [ˈdaɪəl təʊn]   Wählton
to dial [ˈdaɪəl]   wählen
digit [ˈdɪdʒɪt]   Ziffer
disadvantage [ˌdɪsədˈvɑːntɪdʒ]   Nachteil
to display [dɪˈspleɪ]   zeigen, ausstellen
to drip [drɪp]   tropfen
earphones [ˈɪəfəʊnz]   Kopfhörer
to be endangered [ɪnˈdeɪndʒəd]   gefährdet sein
to establish [ɪˈstæblɪʃ]   gründen
European Union [ˌjʊərəˈpiːən ˈjuːnjən]   Europäische Union
frequency [ˈfriːkwənsɪ]   hier: Frequenz
gradual [ˈgrædʒʊəl]   allmählich
to grant [grɑːnt]   gewähren
to insert [ɪnˈsɜːt]   einführen
to install [ɪnˈstɔːl]   einrichten, installieren
joint-stock company [ˈdʒɔɪnt ˈstɒk ˈkʌmpənɪ]   in GB: Aktiengesellschaft
to key in [kiː ɪn]   eingeben, eintasten
to withdraw money [wɪðˈdrɔː ˈmʌnɪ]   Geld abheben
to notify [ˈnəʊtɪfaɪ]   informieren
to observe [əbˈzɜːv]   beachten
opportunity [ˌɒpəˈtjuːnətɪ]   Gelegenheit
to overheat [ˌəʊvəˈhiːt]   überhitzen
phonecard phone [ˈfəʊnˌkɑːd ˈfəʊn]   Kartentelefon
to prevent [prɪˈvent]   vermeiden
procedure [prəˈsiːdʒə]   Vorgang, Vorgehen

queue(n) [kju:] *Schlange*
rationalization [ˌræʃnəlaɪˈzeɪʃn] *Rationalisierung*
to recognize [ˈrekəgnaɪz] *halten für, anerkennen*
to reduce [rɪˈdju:s] *verringern, reduzieren*
service sector [ˈsɜːvɪs ˈsektə] *Dienstleistungsbereich, -sektor*
electric shaver [ɪˈlektrɪk ˈʃeɪvə] *elektrischer Rasierapparat*
slot [slɒt] *Schlitz*
target [ˈtɑːgɪt] *Ziel*
to trim [trɪm] *schneiden*
long-hair trimmer [ˈlɒŋ heə ˈtrɪmə] *Langhaarschneider*
up to [ʌp tu:] *bis zu*
widely [ˈwaɪdlɪ] *weithin*

IC 8: Planning One's Career

to think in terms of alternatives [ɔːlˈtɜːnətɪvz] *an Alternativen denken*
ambition [æmˈbɪʃn] *Streben, Ambition*
to arise (irr) [əˈraɪz] *aufkommen*
attraction [əˈtrækʃn] *Reiz*
brochure [ˈbrəʊʃə] *Broschüre*
circumstances [ˈsɜːkəmstənsɪz] *Umstände*
diligent [ˈdɪlɪdʒənt] *fleißig, sorgfältig*
dislikes [dɪsˈlaɪks] *Abneigungen*
employer [ɪmˈplɔɪə] *Arbeitgeber/in*
enjoyable [ɪnˈdʒɔɪəbl] *angenehm*
ever [ˈevə] *jemals*
to execute [ˈeksɪkju:t] *ausführen*
extensive [ɪkˈstensɪv] *ausgedehnt, umfangreich*
to face [feɪs] *sich gegenübersehen*
to impose [ɪmˈpəʊz] *auferlegen, erfordern*
inflexible [ɪnˈfleksəbl] *unflexibel*
to invest [ɪnˈvest] *investieren*
job hunting [ˈdʒɒb ˈhʌntɪŋ] *Arbeitsplatzsuche*
jobcentre [ˈdʒɒbsentə] *Arbeitsvermittlung*
likes [laɪks] *Vorlieben*
to limit o.s. to s.th. [ˈlɪmɪt] *sich auf etw. beschränken*
to have in mind [maɪnd] *im Sinn haben*
to pick up [pɪk ˈʌp] *hier: aufnehmen, machen*
to plump for [ˈplʌmp fɔː] *sich entscheiden für*

probable [ˈprɒbəbl] *wahrscheinlich*
to reflect on [rɪˈflekt ɒn] *nachdenken über*
relevant [ˈreləvənt] *wichtig, bedeutsam, relevant*
satisfactory [ˌsætɪsˈfæktərɪ] *zufriedenstellend*
school-leaving qualification [ˈsku:l ˌli:vɪŋ ˌkwɒlɪfɪˈkeɪʃn] *Schulabschluss*
signpost [ˈsaɪnpəʊst] *Hinweis*
skill [skɪl] *Fertigkeit*
source [sɔːs] *Quelle*
spare-time [ˈspeətaɪm] *Freizeit-*
to stretch [stretʃ] *hier: ausreichen*
substantial [səbˈstænʃl] *beträchtlich*
theoretically-minded [θɪəˈretɪkəlɪ ˈmaɪndɪd] *theoretisch interessiert/orientiert*
to give s.th. thought [θɔːt] *etw. in Betracht ziehen*
trade association [ˈtreɪd əˌsəʊsɪˈeɪʃn] *Arbeitgeberverband*
uncertain [ʌnˈsɜːtn] *unsicher*
unfortunately [ʌnˈfɔːtʃnətlɪ] *unglücklicherweise*
to be used to doing s.th. [ju:st] *gewohnt sein etw. zu tun*

MC 1: Banking and Savings

statement of account [ˈsteɪtmənt əv əˈkaʊnt] *Kontoauszug*
affair [əˈfeə] *Angelegenheit*
agreed [əˈgri:d] *vereinbart*
allowance [əˈlaʊəns] *hier: Vergütung*
altogether [ˌɔːltəˈgeðə] *insgesamt*
amount [əˈmaʊnt] *Betrag*
apart from [əˈpɑːt frɒm] *abgesehen von*
at random [æt ˈrændəm] *nach dem Zufallsprinzip*
attitude [ˈætɪtjuːd] *Einstellung, Haltung*
auxiliary (verb) [ɔːgˈzɪljərɪ (vɜːb)] *Hilfsverb*
average (adj) [ˈævərɪdʒ] *durchschnittlich*
balance [ˈbæləns] *Saldo*
balance forward [ˈbæləns ˈfɔːwəd] *Saldovortrag*
banking [ˈbæŋkɪŋ] *Bankwesen*
blank [blæŋk] *Leerstelle*
board [bɔːd] *an Bord (des Schiffes)*
both ... and [bəʊθ ... ænd] *sowohl ... als auch*
building society [ˈbɪldɪŋ səˈsaɪətɪ] *Bausparkasse*

to calculate ['kælkjʊleɪt] *berechnen, kalkulieren*
caption ['kæpʃn] *Bildunterschrift*
charging period ['tʃɑːdʒɪŋ 'pɪərɪəd] *Abrechnungszeitraum*
chart [tʃɑːt] *Schaubild*
to claim [kleɪm] *beanspruchen*
to contain [kən'teɪn] *enthalten*
convenience [kən'viːnjəns] *Annehmlichkeit*
to cover ['kʌvə] *abdecken, umfassen, beinhalten*
to be in credit ['kredɪt] *in den schwarzen Zahlen sein, über ein Guthaben verfügen*
current account ['kʌrənt ə'kaʊnt] *Girokonto*
to deduct from [dɪ'dʌkt frɒm] *abbuchen von*
deposit account [dɪ'pɒzɪt ə'kaʊnt] *Sparkonto*
direct debiting [dɪ'rekt 'debɪtɪŋ] *Lastschriftverfahren*
draw date ['drɔː 'deɪt] *Ziehungstermin*
to enter s.th. ['entə] *hier: gutschreiben*
entry charge ['entrɪ tʃɑːdʒ] *Buchungsgebühr*
to exceed [ɪk'siːd] *übersteigen, überschreiten*
expenditure [ɪk'spendɪtʃə] *(Geld-)Ausgabe*
fancy dress party ['fænsɪ 'dres 'pɑːtɪ] *Maskenball, Kostümfest*
fee [fiː] *Gebühr*
final total ['faɪnl 'təʊtl] *Saldo*
flat charge ['flæt 'tʃɑːdʒ] *Grundgebühr*
form (n) [fɔːm] *hier: Formular*
government-owned ['gʌvnmənt 'əʊnd] *staatlich*
in return [ɪn rɪ'tɜːn] *im Gegenzug*
in s.o.'s favour ['feɪvə] *zu jmnds. Gunsten*
to instruct [ɪn'strʌkt] *anweisen*
insurance [ɪn'ʃʊərəns] *Versicherung*
to insure [ɪn'ʃʊə] *versichern*
interest ['ɪntrəst] *hier: Zinsen*
irrevocable [ˌɪrɪ'vəʊkəbl] *unwiderruflich*
to issue ['ɪʃuː] *ausgeben*
item ['aɪtəm] *hier: Punkt*
leaflet ['liːflɪt] *Prospekt*
less [les] *abzüglich*
letter of credit ['letə əv 'kredɪt] *Dokumentenakkreditiv*
manufacturer [ˌmænjʊfæktʃərə] *Hersteller*
to match [mætʃ] *passend zusammenstellen*
to miss [mɪs] *fehlen*
money order ['mʌnɪ 'ɔːdə] *Zahlungsanweisung*
to move [muːv] *hier: umziehen*

net charge ['net 'tʃɑːdʒ] *Nettobelastung*
notice of withdrawal ['nəʊtɪs əv wɪð'drɔːəl] *Kündigungsfrist*
on board ship [ɒn ˌbɔːd 'ʃɪp] *an Bord (des Schiffes)*
permission [pə'mɪʃn] *Erlaubnis*
to provide [prə'vaɪd] *gewährleisten, ermöglichen*
to qualify for ['kwɒlɪfaɪ] *hier: berechtigt sein zu*
quantity ['kwɒntətɪ] *Menge, Quantität*
quarter year ['kwɔːtə jɜː] *Vierteljahr*
quarterly ['kwɔːtəlɪ] *vierteljährlich*
to reclaim [rɪ'kleɪm] *zurückfordern*
saving habit ['seɪvɪŋ 'hæbɪt] *Sparverhalten*
savings ['seɪvɪŋz] *Sparen*
seller ['selə] *Verkäufer/in*
separate ['seprət] *gesonderte(r/s)*
spare part [ˌspeə 'pɑːt] *Ersatzteil*
spending habit ['spendɪŋ 'hæbɪt] *Ausgabeverhalten*
statement of account ['steɪtmənt əv ə'kaʊnt] *Kontoauszug*
transaction [træn'zækʃn] *Transaktion, Vorgang*
to transfer [træns'fɜː] *überweisen*
trusted ['trʌstɪd] *bewährt, zuverlässig*
until further notice [ən'tɪl 'fɜːðə 'nəʊtɪs] *bis auf Widerruf*
variety [və'raɪətɪ] *Vielfalt*
vital ['vaɪtl] *wesentlich, (lebens)wichtig*
willingness ['wɪlɪŋnɪs] *Bereitschaft*

MC 2: Investment and the Stock Exchange

above [ə'bʌv] *obige(r/s)*
additional [ə'dɪʃənl] *zusätzlich*
to administer [əd'mɪnɪstə] *ausüben*
to advise s.o. [əd'vaɪz] *jmndm. raten*
to arrange [ə'reɪndʒ] *anordnen, einordnen*
badly ['bædlɪ] *hier: dringend*
to go bankrupt [gəʊ 'bæŋkrʌpt] *Bankrott machen*
benefit ['benɪfɪt] *Ertrag, Vorteil, Nutzen*
board of directors ['bɔːd əv dɪ'rektəz] *Vorstand*
broker ['brəʊkə] *Makler/in*

capital growth [ˈkæpɪtl ˌgrəʊθ] *Kapitalzuwachs*
chairman [ˈtʃeəmən] *Vorsitzender*
climate [ˈklaɪmɪt] *Klima*
collective [kəˈlektɪv] *gemeinsam, kollektiv*
to have in common [ˈhæv ɪn ˈkɒmən] *etw. gemeinsam haben*
debt [det] *(Geld) Schuld*
to define [dɪˈfaɪn] *bestimmen*
to delay [dɪˈleɪ] *verschieben, zurückstellen*
to deny [dɪˈnaɪ] *leugnen, abstreiten*
diplomatically [ˌdɪpləˈmætɪkəlɪ] *diplomatisch*
dividend [ˈdɪvɪdend] *Dividende*
earnings [ˈɜːnɪŋz] *Ertrag*
economic [ˌiːkəˈnɒmɪk] *wirtschaftliche(r/s)*
economy [ɪˈkɒnəmɪ] *Wirtschaft*
edge [edʒ] *Rand*
to elect [ɪˈlekt] *wählen*
to enquire [ɪnˈkwaɪə] *sich erkundigen*
fertiliser [ˈfɜːtɪlaɪzə] *Düngemittel*
fixed [fɪkst] *festgelegt, festgeschrieben*
fund [fʌnd] *Fond*
further to [ˈfɜːðə tuː] *in Ergänzung zu*
generally [ˈdʒenərəlɪ] *im allgemeinen, generell*
gilts [gɪltz] *see "gilt-edged securities"*
gilt-edged securities (pl) [ˈgɪltedʒd sɪˈkjʊərətɪz] *mündelsichere (Wert-)Papiere*
to guarantee [ˌgærənˈtiː] *garantieren*
guide [gaɪd] *Führer, Ratgeber*
to have s.th. handy [ˈhændɪ] *etw. bereit/verfügbar haben, zur Hand haben*
illustration [ˌɪləˈstreɪʃn] *Abbildung*
imaginary [ɪˈmædʒɪnərɪ] *hier: erfunden, eingebildet*
in proportion to [ɪn prəˈpɔːʃn tuː] *im Verhältnis zu*
income [ˈɪnkʌm] *Einkommen*
income tax [ˈɪnkʌm ˌtæks] *Einkommenssteuer*
instead of [ɪnˈsted ɒv] *anstatt*
Investment Trust Company [ɪnˈvestmənt ˈtrʌst ˈkʌmpənɪ] *Investmentgesellschaft*
investor [ɪnˈvestə] *Investor*
liability [ˌlaɪəˈbɪlətɪ] *Haftung*
liable [ˈlaɪəbl] *haftbar*
loan [ləʊn] *Darlehen*
major [ˈmeɪdʒə] *bedeutend*
to make clear [ˈmeɪk ˈklɪə] *klarmachen/-stellen*

managing director [ˈmænɪdʒɪŋ dɪˈrektə] *geschäftsführender Direktor*
National Savings Bonds [ˈnæʃnl ˈseɪvɪŋz ˈbɒndz] *Staatsanleihen*
National Savings Certificates [ˈnæʃnl ˈseɪvɪŋz səˈtɪfɪkəts] *Sparzertifikate*
ordinary [ˈɔːdnrɪ] *einfach*
to be overdue [ˌəʊvəˈdjuː] *überfällig sein*
to own [əʊn] *besitzen*
paragraph [ˈpærəgrɑːf] *(Text) Absatz, Paragraph*
part owner [ˈpɑːt ˈəʊnə] *Teilhaber/in*
pattern [ˈpætən] *Muster*
plastics [ˈplæstɪks] *hier: Kunststoffwerte*
policy [ˈpɒləsɪ] *hier: Politik*
to pool [puːl] *vereinen, zusammenlegen*
possession [pəˈzeʃn] *Eigentum*
property [ˈprɒpətɪ] *Eigentum*
to put s.th. into practice [ˈpræktɪs] *etw. in die Tat umsetzen*
private limited company (Ltd) [ˈpraɪvɪt ˈlɪmɪtɪd ˈkʌmpənɪ] *etwa: Gesellschaft mit beschränkter Haftung (GmbH)*
profit [ˈprɒfɪt] *Ertrag, Profit*
proprietor [prəˈpraɪətə] *Eigentümer/in*
public limited company (plc) [ˈpʌblɪk ˈlɪmɪtɪd ˈkʌmpənɪ] *etwa: Aktiengesellschaft (AG)*
publicity brochure [pʌbˈlɪsətɪ ˈbrəʊʃə] *Werbebroschüre*
purchase [ˈpɜːtʃəs] *Kauf*
purpose [ˈpɜːpəs] *Zweck*
to keep records [ˈkiːp ˈrekɔːdz] *Akten führen*
reluctant [rɪˈlʌktənt] *unwillig, zurückhaltend*
to reply [rɪˈplaɪ] *antworten*
to reveal [rɪˈviːl] *darlegen, zum Vorschein bringen, enthalten, aufzeigen*
reward [rɪˈwɔːd] *hier: Ertrag*
to rewrite [ˌriːˈraɪt] *umschreiben, neu schreiben*
to carry a risk [ˈkærɪ ə ˌrɪsk] *ein Risiko tragen*
to take a risk [ˈteɪk ə ˌrɪsk] *ein Risiko eingehen*
to select [sɪˈlekt] *auswählen*
share (n) [ʃeə] *Aktie, Anteil*
shareholder [ˈʃeəˌhəʊldə] *Aktionär/in, Anteilseigner/in*
sharp fall [ˈʃɑːp ˈfɔːl] *drastischer Rückgang/ Verfall*

sleeping partner ['sli:pɪŋ 'pɑ:tnə] *stille/r Teilhaber/in*
sole [səʊl] *alleinig*
spectacular [spek'tækjʊlə] *aufsehenerregend, spektakulär*
stock exchange ['stɒk ɪks'tʃeɪndʒ] *Börse*
tactful ['tæktfʊl] *höflich, taktvoll*
Unit Trusts ['ju:nɪt 'trʌsts] *Investmenttrusts*
unlikely [ʌn'laɪklɪ] *unwahrscheinlich*
unlimited [ʌn'lɪmɪtɪd] *unbegrenzt, unbeschränkt*
until then [ən'tɪl ðen] *bis dahin*
to keep a watch on ['ki:p ə 'wɒtʃ ɒn] *(scharf) beobachten*

MC 3: Advertising and Publicity

to adopt [ə'dɒpt] *hier: einführen*
to advertise ['ædvətaɪz] *werben für, Werbung machen für*
advertisement [əd'vɜ:tɪsmənt] *Anzeige*
advertising slogan ['ædvətaɪzɪŋ 'sləʊgən] *Werbeslogan*
affluent ['æflʊənt] *wohlhabend*
to aim [eɪm] *zielen*
ancient ['eɪnʃənt] *altertümlich*
annual ['ænjʊl] *jährlich*
to appeal to [ə'pi:l] *ansprechen, anziehen*
association [ə,səʊsɪ'eɪʃn] *hier: Gedankenverbindung, Assoziation*
bait [beɪt] *Köder*
brake lining ['breɪk 'laɪnɪŋ] *Bremsbelag*
breakthrough ['breɪkθru:] *Durchbruch*
breathless ['breθlɪs] *atemlos*
broadcast(ing) ['brɔ:dkɑ:st(ɪŋ)] *Rundfunk*
bustling ['bʌslɪŋ] *geschäftig*
celebrity [se'lebrətɪ] *Berühmtheit*
to keep a check on ['ki:p ə 'tʃek ɒn] *kontrollieren*
claim (n) [kleɪm] *hier: Klage*
to combine ['kɒmbaɪn] *verbinden*
commercial (n) [kə'mɜ:ʃl] *Werbespot*
comparison [kəm'pærɪsn] *Vergleich*
competition [,kɒmpɪ'tɪʃn] *Wettbewerb*
complaint [kəm'pleɪnt] *Beschwerde, Reklamation*

consumer [kən'sju:mə] *Verbraucher/in*
contentment [kən'tentmənt] *Zufriedenheit*
convention [kən'venʃn] *Versammlung*
to convince [kən'vɪns] *überzeugen*
cosmopolitan [,kɒzmə'pɒlɪtən] *kosmopolitisch, weltbürgerlich*
cuisine [kwi:'zi:n] *Küche*
currency entry charges ['kʌrənsɪ 'entrɪ 'tʃɑ:dʒɪz] *Wechselgebühren*
decent ['di:snt] *anständig*
desirable [dɪ'zaɪərəbl] *begehrenswert, wünschenswert*
to differ ['dɪfə] *voneinander abweichen*
to direct at [dɪ'rekt æt] *richten an*
to disagree [,dɪsə'gri:] *nicht zustimmen/übereinstimmen*
dishonest [dɪs'ɒnɪst] *unehrlich*
dull [dʌl] *langweilig*
effort ['efət] *Bemühung, Anstrengung*
to eliminate [ɪ'lɪmɪneɪt] *ausschließen, eliminieren*
to endorse [ɪn'dɔ:s] *hier: sich stark machen für*
entrepreneur [,ɒntrəprə'nɜ:] *Unternehmer/in*
escape (n) [ɪ'skeɪp] *Flucht, Ausweg*
to exaggerate [ɪg'zædʒəreɪt] *übertreiben*
excitement [ɪk'saɪtmənt] *Aufregung*
extent [ɪk'stent] *Ausmaß*
fairytale ['feərɪteɪl] *Märchen*
false [fɔ:ls] *falsch*
to feature ['fi:tʃə] *hier: hervorheben, in den Vordergrund rücken*
floodlight ['flʌdlaɪt] *Flutlicht*
folklore ['fəʊklɔ:] *Folklore*
free-enterprise country ['fri: 'entəpraɪz 'kʌntrɪ] *Land mit freier Marktwirtschaft*
frequent ['fri:kwənt] *häufig*
furniture removal ['fɜ:nɪtʃə ri:'mu:vl] *Möbelspedition*
to gather ['gæðə] *sammeln*
gift [gɪft] *Geschenk*
half-board [,hɑ:f 'bɔ:d] *Halbpension*
hassle ['hæsəl] *hier: "Zirkus", "Theater"*
honest ['ɒnɪst] *ehrlich*
ideally [aɪ'dɪəlɪ] *idealerweise*
to identify with [aɪ'dentɪfaɪ wɪð] *sich identifizieren mit*

to imitate ['ɪmɪteɪt]   nachahmen, imitieren
immoral [ɪ'mɒrəl]   unmoralisch
to improve [ɪm'pruːv]   (sich) (ver)bessern
insulting [ɪn'sʌltɪŋ]   beleidigend
to invent [ɪn'vent]   erfinden
jealousy ['dʒeləsɪ]   Eifersucht
large-scale ['lɑːdʒ 'skeɪl]   Massen-, in großem Umfang
licence ['laɪsəns]   Lizenz
liqueur [lɪ'kjʊə]   Likör
logo ['ləʊgəʊ]   Firmenzeichen, -logo
male [meɪl]   männliche(r/s)
medieval [ˌmedɪ'iːvl]   mittelalterlich
memorable ['memərəbl]   denkwürdig
misleading [ˌmɪs'liːdɪŋ]   irreführend
motto ['mɒtəʊ]   Schlagwort, Motto
objectionable [əb'dʒekʃnəbl]   anstößig
obvious ['ɒbvɪəs]   hier: naheliegend
offensive [ə'fensɪv]   ärgerniserregend, anstößig
onwards ['ɒnwədz]   weiter
to pair [peə]   hier: zusammenstellen (von zwei Elementen)
pavement café ['peɪvmənt 'kæfeɪ]   Straßencafé
perfume [pə'fjuːm]   Parfüm
personality [ˌpɜːsə'nælətɪ]   Persönlichkeit
plastic surgery ['plæstɪk 'sɜːdʒərɪ]   plastische Chirurgie
to police [pə'liːs]   kontrollieren, überwachen
psychologist [saɪ'kɒlədʒɪst]   Psychologe/-gin
publicity [pʌb'lɪsətɪ]   Werbung
quaint [kweɪnt]   hier: malerisch
to quote [kwəʊt]   (Preis) angeben/mitteilen
regardless of [rɪ'gɑːdlɪs əv]   ohne Rücksicht auf
to register ['redʒɪstə]   registrieren
resort [rɪ'zɔːt]   hier: Urlaubsort
to respect [rɪ'spekt]   achten, respektieren
ridiculous [rɪ'dɪkjʊləs]   lächerlich
rigorous ['rɪgərəs]   rigoros, rücksichtslos
rolling ['rəʊlɪŋ]   dahinfließend
to safeguard ['seɪfgɑːd]   sichern
scientific [ˌsaɪən'tɪfɪk]   wissenschaftlich
score [skɔː]   hier: Punktzahl
sentimental [ˌsentɪ'mentl]   sentimental
sexism ['seksɪzəm]   Sexismus
slogan ['sləʊgən]   Slogan
sophisticated [sə'fɪstɪkeɪtɪd]   anspruchsvoll
to sponsor ['spɒnsə]   fördern, sponsern
Surgeon General ['sɜːdʒən 'dʒenərəl]   Leiter der US Gesundheitsbehörde
surroundings (pl) [sə'raʊndɪŋz]   Umgebung
syllable ['sɪləbl]   Silbe
tar [tɑː]   Teer
technique [tek'niːk]   Technik, Arbeitsweise
to tempt [tempt]   versuchen
tremendous [trɪ'mendəs]   enorm
truthful ['truːθfʊl]   hier: wahrheitsliebend
untruthful [ˌʌn'truːθfʊl]   unwahr
vigilance committee ['vɪdʒɪləns kə'mɪtɪ]   Bürgerwehr, Selbstschutzgruppe
watchdog ['wɒtʃdɒg]   Wachhund
wilderness ['wɪldənɪs]   Wildnis
to wink at [wɪŋk æt]   zuzwinkern
women's rights movement ['wɪmɪnz 'raɪts 'muːvmənt]   Frauenrechtsbewegung

MC 4:   Credit

accuracy ['ækjʊrəsɪ]   Richtigkeit, Genauigkeit
to acquire [ə'kwaɪə]   erhalten
alcoholic [ˌælkə'hɒlɪk]   Alkoholiker/in
to be annoyed [ə'nɔɪd]   verärgert sein
Annual Percentage Rate ['ænjʊl pə'sentɪdʒ reɪt]   etwa: effektiver Jahreszins
arithmetic [ə'rɪθmətɪk]   Arithmetik
assessment [ə'sesmənt]   Einschätzung
bank overdraft [bæŋk 'əʊvədrɑːft]   Überziehungskredit
deck of cards ['dek əv 'kɑːdz]   Kartenspiel
cartoon [kɑː'tuːn]   Witzzeichnung, Karikatur
cautious ['kɔːʃəs]   vorsichtig
Consumer Advice [kən'sjuːmə əd'vaɪs]   Verbraucherberatung
consumer protection [kən'sjuːmə prə'tekʃn]   Verbraucherschutz
credit reference agency ['kredɪt 'refrəns 'eɪdʒənsɪ]   Kreditauskunftei
currency ['kʌrənsɪ]   Währung
dispute [dɪ'spjuːt]   Auseinandersetzung
to ease [iːz]   hier: vermindern
eligible ['elɪdʒəbl]   berechtigt, in Frage kommend
to estimate ['estɪmeɪt]   schätzen

Fair Trading ['feə 'treɪdɪŋ]   *lauterer Wettbewerb*
to fall behind [fɔːl bɪ'haɪnd]   *in Verzug geraten*
faulty ['fɔːltɪ]   *fehlerhaft*
to fear [fɪə]   *fürchten*
fitness [fɪtnɪs]   *Eignung, Tauglichkeit*
goal [gəʊl]   *Ziel*
growth [grəʊθ]   *Wachstum*
high street bank ['haɪ ˌstriːt 'bæŋk]   *Bank/Sparkasse für Jedermann*
to hire ['haɪə]   *vermieten*
hire purchase ['haɪə 'pɜːtʃəs]   *Mietkauf*
in advance [ɪn əd'vɑːns]   *im Voraus*
in the meantime [ɪn ðə 'miːntaɪm]   *in der Zwischenzeit*
invasion [ɪn'veɪʒn]   *Eingriff, Invasion*
to investigate [ɪn'vestɪgeɪt]   *aufspüren, nachspüren*
label ['leɪbl]   *Aufschrift, Kennzeichnung*
Loan Guarantee Scheme ['ləʊn ˌgærən'tɪ 'skiːm]   *Staatliches Förderungsprogramm für kleine Betriebe*
loan company ['ləʊn ˌkʌmpənɪ]   *Kreditunternehmen*
loyal ['lɔɪəl]   *treu, loyal*
misery ['mɪzərɪ]   *Elend*
network ['netwɜːk]   *Netz*
nought [nɔːt]   *Null*
to overspend [ˌəʊvə'spend]   *zu viel ausgeben*
to overuse [ˌəʊvə'juːz]   *über Gebühr beanspruchen*
to owe [əʊ]   *schulden*
to predict [prɪ'dɪkt]   *voraussagen*
privacy ['prɪvəsɪ]   *Geheimhaltung*
to refuse [rɪ'fjuːz]   *sich weigern, ablehnen*
to be reluctant [biː rɪ'lʌktənt]   *wenig geneigt sein, ungern wollen*
remedy ['remɪdɪ]   *Heilmittel*
renovation [ˌrenəʊ'veɪʃn]   *Renovierung*
repayment [riː'peɪmənt]   *Rückzahlung*
saturation [ˌsætʃə'reɪʃn]   *Sättigung*
spending ['spendɪŋ]   *(finanzielle) Ausgaben*
to stack [stæk]   *Karten betrügerisch mischen*
sympathetic [ˌsɪmpə'θetɪk]   *verständnisvoll*
tax office ['tæks 'ɒfɪs]   *Finanzamt*
trader ['treɪdə]   *Kaufmann*
vehicle ['viːɪkl]   *hier: Träger, Vehikel*

MC 5: International Trade Organizations

to abandon [ə'bændən]   *aufgeben*
to abolish [ə'bɒlɪʃ]   *abschaffen*
to conclude agreements [kən'kluːd ə'griːmənts]   *Abkommen schließen*
at this stage [æt ðɪs 'steɪdʒ]   *an diesem Punkt*
to benefit from ['benɪfɪt frɒm]   *profitieren von*
binding [baɪndɪŋ]   *verpflichtend, bindend*
to boast [bəʊst]   *hier: sein Eigen nennen*
citizen ['sɪtɪzn]   *Bürger/in*
to collapse [kə'læps]   *zusammenbrechen*
to compete [kəm'piːt]   *in Wettbewerb stehen*
complex ['kɒmpleks]   *kompliziert, komplex*
to conduct a meeting [kən'dʌkt ə 'miːtɪŋ]   *eine Besprechung führen*
consequently ['kɒnsɪkwəntlɪ]   *folglich*
to co-ordinate [kəʊ'ɔːdɪneɪt]   *koordinieren*
to create [kriː'eɪt]   *(er)schaffen*
criminal records ['krɪmɪnl 'rekɔːdz]   *Kriminalstatistik*
currency union ['kʌrənsɪ 'juːnjən]   *Währungsunion*
damage (n) ['dæmɪdʒ]   *Beschädigung*
decade ['dekeɪd]   *Jahrzehnt*
delighted [dɪ'laɪtɪd]   *erfreut, begeistert*
deposit [dɪ'pɒzɪt]   *hier: Anzahlung*
to devote [dɪ'vəʊt]   *sich widmen*
to direct [dɪ'rekt]   *(zu)leiten*
discrimination [dɪˌskrɪmɪ'neɪʃn]   *Benachteiligung, Diskriminierung*
duty ['djuːtɪ]   *Zoll(abgabe)*
eightfold ['eɪtfəʊld]   *um das Achtfache*
to engage in [ɪn'geɪdʒ]   *beteiligen an*
entirely [ɪn'taɪəlɪ]   *gänzlich, ganz und gar*
European Coal and Steel Community Fund [ˌjʊərə'piːən kəʊl ənd stiːl kə'mjuːnətɪ]   *Europäische Gemeinschaft für Kohle und Stahl*
to make explicit ['meɪk ɪk'splɪsɪt]   *klarstellen*
foreign policy ['fɒrən 'pɒləsɪ]   *Außenpolitik*
fundamental [ˌfʌndə'mentl]   *grundsätzlich, fundamental*
grant (n) [grɑːnt]   *Subvention, Zuschuss*
Gross National Product (GNP) ['grəʊs 'næʃnl 'prɒdʌkt]   *Bruttosozialprodukt (BSP)*

to prepare ground for [prɪˈpeə ˈgraʊnd fɔː]
    den Boden bereiten für
handsome [ˈhænsəm]   gut aussehend
home affairs [ˈhəʊm əˈfeəz]   Innenpolitik
huge [hjuːdʒ]   riesig
to incorporate [ɪnˈkɔːpəreɪt]   einbauen
infrastructure [ˈɪnfrəˌstrʌktʃə]   Infrastruktur
inhabitant [ɪnˈhæbɪtənt]   Einwohner/in
internally [ɪnˈtɜːnəli]   intern
interpreter [ɪnˈtɜːprɪtə]   Dolmetscher/in
justice affairs [ˈdʒʌstɪs əˈfeəz]   Rechtspolitik
legal value [ˈliːgl ˈvæljuː]   Rechtscharakter
loss [lɒs]   Verlust
modernization grants [ˌmɒdənaɪˈzeɪʃn ˈgrɑːnts]
    Modernisierungshilfe
monetary union [ˈmʌnɪtəri ˈjuːnjən]
    Währungsunion
noble [ˈnəʊbl]   ehrenvoll, nobel
non-repayable [nɒn riːˈpeɪəbl]   nicht rückzahlbar
North Atlantic Treaty Organization (NATO)
    [ˈnɔːθ ətˈlæntɪk ˈtriːti ˌɔːgənaɪˈzeɪʃn]   Nordatlantikvertrag (NATO)
to obey [əˈbeɪ]   befolgen
platinum [ˈplætɪnəm]   Platin
pre-established [ˌpriːɪˈstæblɪʃt]   vorformuliert
to progress [prəʊˈgres]   hier: sich entwickeln
to provoke [prəˈvəʊk]   provozieren
raw material [ˌrɔː məˈtɪərɪəl]   Rohstoff
rules of conduct [ˈruːlz əv ˈkɒndʌkt]   Verhaltensregeln
to secure [sɪˈkjʊə]   sichern
security policy [sɪˈkjʊərəti ˈpɒləsi]   Sicherheitspolitik
to seek [siːk]   suchen
to be self-sufficient [ˌselfsəˈfɪʃnt]   Selbstversorger sein
smash [smæʃ]   hier: Schlag, Schmetterball
sound (adj) [saʊnd]   stark, solide
stomach ache [ˈstʌmək eɪk]   Magenschmerzen
tariff [ˈtærɪf]   Zolltarif
tin [tɪn]   Zinn
trade terms [ˈtreɪd ˈtɜːmz]   Handelsbedingungen
underdeveloped [ˌʌndədɪˈveləpt]   unterentwickelt
to unify [ˈjuːnɪfaɪ]   vereinigen, vereinheitlichen

unity [ˈjuːnəti]   Einigkeit, Einheit
usage [ˈjuːzɪdʒ]   Gebrauch
virtually [ˈvɜːtʃʊəli]   praktisch, eigentlich, im Grunde genommen
volume of trade [ˈvɒljuːm əv ˈtreɪd]   Handelsvolumen
to yawn [jɔːn]   gähnen
zone [zəʊn]   Zone

MC 6: Computerization and Technology

to abbreviate [əˈbriːvɪeɪt]   abkürzen
to adapt to [əˈdæpt tuː]   sich anpassen an
beyond [bɪˈjɒnd]   über ... hinaus
binary code [ˈbaɪnəri kəʊd]   Binärcode
bits and pieces [bɪts ən ˈpiːsɪz]   Teile
bookkeeping [ˈbʊkˌkiːpɪŋ]   Buchführung
brake [breɪk]   hier: Hemmnis
brief [briːf]   kurz
calculator [ˈkælkjʊleɪtə]   Rechner
to capture [ˈkæptʃə]   erobern
compatible [kəmˈpætəbl]   kompatibel
to conceive [kənˈsiːv]   planen, konzipieren
to confirm [kənˈfɜːm]   bestätigen
competitor [kəmˈpetɪtə]   Wettbewerber/in, Mitbewerber/in
currency conversion [ˈkʌrənsi kənˈvɜːʃn]
    Währungsumrechnung/-konvertierung
data [ˈdeɪtə]   Daten
to download [ˈdaʊnləʊd]   hier: übertragen
to drive (irr) [draɪv]   hier: antreiben
elevator [ˈelɪveɪtə]   Aufzug, Lift
eventually [ɪˈventʃʊəli]   schließlich
facial expression [ˈfeɪʃl ɪkˈspreʃn]   Gesichtsausdruck
graphics [ˈgræfɪks]   Grafik
immigrant [ˈɪmɪgrənt]   Einwanderer/-derin
largely [ˈlɑːdʒli]   hier: hauptsächlich
lecture [ˈlektʃə]   Vortrag, Vorlesung
mass [mæs]   Masse
to master [ˈmɑːstə]   beherrschen
to put it in a nutshell [ˈnʌt-ʃel]   um es kurz und bündig zu sagen
patent [ˈpeɪtənt]   Patent

235

physical ['fɪzɪkl] *physikalisch*
punch-card ['pʌntʃkɑːd] *Lochkarte*
to purify ['pjʊərɪfaɪ] *aufbereiten, reinigen*
to push out of [ˌpʊʃ 'aʊt əv] *verdrängen*
recording machine [rɪ'kɔːdɪŋ mə'ʃiːn] *Aufnahmegerät*
to reject [rɪ'dʒekt] *zurückweisen*
to resemble [rɪ'zembl] *ähneln*
to sink (irr) [sɪŋk] *sinken*
tabulating machine ['tæbjʊleɪtɪŋ mə'ʃiːn] *Rechenmaschine*
training manual ['treɪnɪŋ ˌmænjʊəl] *Benutzerhandbuch, Software-Leitfaden*
via ['vaɪə] *über, mittels*
to wink [wɪŋk] *zwinkern*

MC 7: The Development of a Product

advanced [əd'vɑːnst] *fortschrittlich*
advisability [ədˌvaɪzə'bɪlətɪ] *Rat, Empfehlung*
assets ['æsets] *Vermögenswerte*
in bulk (quantities) [bʌlk] *in großen Mengen*
charge [tʃɑːdʒ] *hier: Forderung*
commerce ['kɒmɜːs] *Handel*
competitive market [kəm'petətɪv 'mɑːkɪt] *Markt mit starker Konkurrenz*
conclusion [kən'kluːʒn] *Schlussfolgerung*
consignment [kən'saɪnmənt] *(Waren)Sendung*
controller [kən'trəʊlə] *Leiter/in des Rechnungswesens*
conventional [kən'venʃənl] *konventionell, herkömmlich*
conversely [ˌkɒn'vɜːslɪ] *umgekehrt*
courteous ['kɜːtjəs] *höflich*
daring ['deərɪŋ] *gewagt*
darts [dɑːts] *Pfeilwerfen*
deadline ['dedlaɪn] *letzter Termin*
distribution [ˌdɪstrɪ'bjuːʃn] *Vertrieb*
diversified [daɪ'vɜːsɪfaɪd] *unterschiedlich*
flow chart ['fləʊtʃɑːt] *Flussdiagramm*
flow of goods ['fləʊ əv 'gʊds] *Güterfluss*
forecast ['fɔːkɑːst] *Voraussage*
forwarding agent ['fɔːwədɪŋ ˌeɪdʒənt] *Spediteur/in*
foundation [faʊn'deɪʃn] *hier: Grundlagen*
freight service ['freɪt ˌsɜːvɪs] *Frachtdienst*

to fulfil [fʊl'fɪl] *erfüllen*
guideline ['gaɪdlaɪn] *Leitlinie*
inference ['ɪnfərəns] *Folgerung, Rückschluss*
intermediate [ˌɪntə'miːdjət] *mittleres Niveau*
to launch [lɔːntʃ] *einführen, lancieren*
long-range [ˌlɒŋ 'reɪndʒ] *weitreichend*
manual ['mænjʊəl] *manuell, mit der Hand*
manpower ['mænˌpaʊə] *menschliche Arbeitskraft*
necessity [nɪ'sesətɪ] *Notwendigkeit*
obligation [ˌɒblɪ'geɪʃn] *Verpflichtung*
old-fashioned [ˌəʊld'fæʃnd] *altmodisch*
outdoor season ['aʊtdɔː 'siːzn] *Freiluftsaison*
to overestimate [ˌəʊvər'estɪmeɪt] *überschätzen*
packaging ['pækɪdʒɪŋ] *Verpackung*
parent company ['peərənt 'kʌmpənɪ] *Muttergesellschaft*
percentage [pə'sentɪdʒ] *Prozentsatz*
pick-up ['pɪkʌp] *Warenaufnahme*
probability [ˌprɒbə'bɪlətɪ] *Wahrscheinlichkeit*
to promote [prə'məʊt] *fördern, werben für*
to regulate ['regjʊleɪt] *regulieren*
to reinvest [ˌriːɪn'vest] *reinvestieren*
retailer [riː'teɪlə] *Einzelhändler/in*
to satisfy conditions ['sætɪsfaɪ kən'dɪʃnz] *Bedingungen erfüllen*
Secretary-Treasurer ['sekrətrɪ 'treʒərə] *Leiter/in der Finanzabteilung*
shop floor [ˌʃɒp 'flɔː] *Produktionsstätte*
short-term ['ʃɔːttɜːm] *kurzfristig*
to sign up [saɪn 'ʌp] *verpflichten*
snooker ['snuːkə] *Lochbilliard*
steady ['stedɪ] *ständig*
stock [stɒk] *Lager(bestand)*
subsidiary [səb'sɪdjərɪ] *Tochtergesellschaft*
supervision [ˌsuːpə'vɪʒn] *Aufsicht, Überwachung*
tennis racket ['tenɪs ˌrækɪt] *Tennisschläger*
tenpin bowling ['tenpɪn 'bəʊlɪŋ] *Bowling*
unfavourable [ˌʌn'feɪvərəbl] *ungünstig*
valve [vælv] *Ventil*
wholesaler ['həʊlˌseɪlə] *Großhändler/in*

MC 8: Employment and Unemployment

access ['ækses] *Zugang*
accreditation [əˈkredɪtɪʃn] *hier: Teilnahmeberechtigung*
administration [ədˌmɪnɪˈstreɪʃn] *Verwaltung*
administrative [ədˈmɪnɪstrətɪv] *administrativ, Verwaltungs-*
apparent [əˈpærənt] *offensichtlich*
to assess [əˈses] *bewerten*
associated with [əˈsəʊʃieɪtɪd wɪð] *im Zusammenhang mit*
to attain [əˈteɪn] *erlangen*
to be attracted [bi: əˈtræktɪd] *hier: interessiert sein an*
beneficial [ˌbenɪˈfɪʃl] *vorteilhaft*
on campus [ɒn ˈkæmpəs] *hier: im Seminar*
client [ˈklaɪənt] *Kunde/-din*
client evidence [ˈklaɪənt ˈevɪdəns] *hier: Lernfortschritt*
college [ˈkɒlɪdʒ] *Bildungsgang zwischen höherer Schule und Universität*
to commit o.s. [kəˈmɪt] *sich verpflichten*
complicated [ˈkɒmplɪkeɪtɪd] *kompliziert*
to cut [kʌt] *reduzieren*
CV (curriculum vitae) [ˈsiːˈviː (kəˌrɪkjələmˈviːtaɪ)] *Lebenslauf*
to deceive [dɪˈsiːv] *täuschen*
to declare [dɪˈkleə] *erklären*
to distort [dɪˈstɔːt] *verzerren*
to dominate [ˈdɒmɪneɪt] *beherrschen, dominieren*
downward [ˈdaʊnwəd] *abnehmend*
drop [drɒp] *Rückgang*
electronic transmission [ˌɪlekˈtrɒnɪk trænzˈmɪʃn] *Datenübertragung*
entry requirements [ˈentri rɪˈkwaɪəmənts] *Eingangsvoraussetzungen*
evidence [ˈevɪdəns] *Nachweis*
to extend [ɪkˈstend] *erweitern*
external verifier [ɪkˈstɜːnl ˈverɪfaɪə] *Fremdgutachter/in*
extract [ˈekstrækt] *Auszug*
failure [ˈfeɪljə] *Fehlschlag*
filing [ˈfaɪlɪŋ] *Aktenverwaltung*

full-time [ˌfʊlˈtaɪm] *Vollzeit-*
guidance [ˈgaɪdns] *Anleitung, Unterweisung*
jobclub [ˈdʒɒbklʌb] *Staatliche Einrichtung zur Bekämpfung der Jugendarbeitslosigkeit*
literacy skill [ˈlɪtərəsi ˈskɪl] *Lese- und Schreibfertigkeit*
measure [ˈmeʒə] *Maßnahme*
medium-sized [ˈmiːdjəm ˌsaɪzd] *mittelgroß*
near-abandonment [ˈnɪə əˈbændənmənt] *Fast-Aufgabe*
to neglect [nɪˈglekt] *vernachlässigen*
nicknamed [ˈnɪkneɪmd] *mit dem Spitznamen*
numeracy skill [ˈnjuːmərəsi ˈskɪl] *Rechenfertigkeit*
opposition party [ˌɒpəˈzɪʃn ˈpɑːti] *Oppositionspartei*
painful [ˈpeɪnfʊl] *schmerzhaft*
partial [ˈpɑːʃl] *teilweise*
to participate in [pɑːˈtɪsɪpeɪt ɪn] *teilnehmen an*
pre-vocational [ˌpriːvəʊˈkeɪʃənl] *vorberuflich*
realistic [ˌrɪəˈlɪstɪk] *realistisch*
recognition [ˌrekəgˈnɪʃn] *Anerkennung*
recognized [ˈrekəgnaɪzd] *anerkannt*
red tape [ˌredˈteɪp] *Papierkrieg*
to reform [ˌriːˈfɔːm] *reformieren*
to relate to [rɪˈleɪt tuː] *hier: sich beziehen auf*
relief [rɪˈliːf] *Entlastung*
reprographics [ˌriːprəˈgræfɪks] *Vervielfältigung*
to respond to [rɪˈspɒnd] *antworten auf, reagieren auf*
to reverse [rɪˈvɜːs] *umkehren, umdrehen*
review (n) [rɪˈvjuː] *Überprüfung*
to run down [ˈrʌn ˈdaʊn] *hier: abbauen*
to sample [sɑːmpl] *hier: feststellen*
schoolleaver [ˈskuːlliːvə] *Schulabgänger/in*
sector [ˈsektə] *Bereich*
shameful [ˈʃeɪmfʊl] *schmählich*
shipyard [ˈʃɪpjɑːd] *Werft*
skill [skɪl] *Fertigkeit*
skilled job [ˈskɪld ˈdʒɒb] *qualifizierte Tätigkeit*
spokesman [ˈspəʊksmən] *Sprecher*
state of ferment [ˈsteɪt əv fəˈment] *Unruhe*
statistics [stəˈtɪstɪks] *Statistik*
steel mill [ˈstiːl ˌmɪl] *Stahlwerk*
strings [strɪŋz] *hier: Bedingungen*

study skills ['stʌdɪ ˌskɪlz] *für das Lernen wichtige Fertigkeiten*
to be suited [bi: su:tɪd] *geeignet sein*
supervisory work ['su:pəvaɪzərɪ 'wɜ:k] *hier: Leitungsaufgaben*
to take on [teɪk ɒn] *übernehmen, annehmen*
to trail behind (vb) [treɪl bɪ'haɪnd] *zurückliegen, zurückfallen*
trainee [treɪ'ni:] *Auszubildende/r*
to undertake [ˌʌndə'teɪk] *übernehmen*
unqualified [ˌʌn'kwɒlɪfaɪd] *ohne Abschluss*
unskilled [ˌʌn'skɪld] *ungelernt*
untrained [ˌʌn'treɪnd] *ohne Ausbildung*
vocational training [vəʊ'keɪʃənl 'treɪnɪŋ] *Berufsausbildung*
weakness ['wi:knɪs] *Schwäche*
well-educated [ˌwel'edju:keɪtɪd] *hier: gut ausgebildet*
to worsen ['wɜ:sn] *sich verschlimmern*
worthwhile [ˌwɜ:θ'waɪl] *lohnend*

MC 9: Resources and the Environment

to be affected [ə'fektɪd] *beeinflusst werden*
air inlet ['eə ˌɪnlet] *Lufteinlass*
artery ['ɑ:tərɪ] *Arterie*
to blend in with [ˌblend 'ɪn wɪð] *hier: anpassen an*
cloth [klɒθ] *Stoff, Tuch*
concrete ['kɒnkri:t] *Beton*
to conserve [kən'sɜ:v] *erhalten, konservieren*
to consume [kən'sju:m] *verbrauchen, konsumieren*
to contaminate [kən'tæmɪneɪt] *verunreinigen, vergiften*
controversy ['kɒntrəvɜ:sɪ] *Streit, Kontroverse*
to convert [kən'vɜ:t] *umwandeln*
Council for the Protection of Rural England ['kaʊnsl fɔ: ðə prə'tekʃn əv 'rʊərəl 'ɪŋglənd] *Kuratorium für die Erhaltung des ländlichen Englands*
to deplete [dɪ'pli:t] *sich erschöpfen*
derelict ['derɪlɪkt] *verlassen, aufgegeben*

desalting plant [dɪ'sɔ:ltɪŋ 'plɑ:nt] *Entsalzungsanlage*
developer [dɪ'veləpə] *Grundstückserschließer/in*
domestic [dəʊ'mestɪk] *häuslich, Haushalts-*
draught [drɑ:ft] *(Luft-)Zug*
to drill [drɪl] *bohren*
dry cement ['draɪ sɪ'ment] *Trockenzement*
eager ['i:gə] *hier: ungeduldig wartend*
evaporation [ɪˌvæpə'reɪʃn] *Verdunstung, Verdampfung*
flap [flæp] *Verschlussklappe*
fraction ['frækʃn] *Bruchteil*
to freshen ['freʃn] *aufbereiten*
fuel [fjʊəl] *Treibstoff, Brennstoff*
gap [gæp] *Lücke*
glass sheet ['glɑ:s 'ʃi:t] *Glasplatte*
Green Belt ['gri:n ˌbelt] *Grüngürtel*
habitat ['hæbɪtæt] *Lebensraum*
handicap ['hændɪkæp] *Nachteil*
to hold on tight to ['həʊld ɒn ˌtaɪt tu:] *festhalten an*
housing ['haʊzɪŋ] *Wohnraum*
human race ['hju:mən 'reɪs] *Menschheit*
impasse [æm'pɑ:s] *Sackgasse*
impure [ɪm'pjʊə] *unsauber*
in turn [ˌɪn'tɜ:n] *wiederum, im Gegenzug*
irrigation [ˌɪrɪ'geɪʃn] *Bewässerung*
key phrase ['ki: ˌfreɪz] *Schlüsselbegriff*
leisure ['leʒə] *Freizeit*
meadow ['medəʊ] *Wiese*
musician [mju:'zɪʃn] *Musiker/in*
natural resources ['nætʃrəl rɪ'sɔ:sɪz] *Naturschätze*
navigation [ˌnævɪ'geɪʃn] *Navigation*
nuclear power ['nju:klɪə 'paʊə] *Atomenergie*
oil well ['ɔɪlwel] *Ölquelle*
pesticide ['pestɪsaɪd] *Pestizid*
pollution [pə'lu:ʃn] *Verschmutzung*
to preserve [prɪ'zɜ:v] *bewahren*
priority [praɪ'ɒrətɪ] *Vorrang, Priorität*
to prohibit [prə'hɪbɪt] *verbieten*
prosperous ['prɒspərəs] *blühend, wohlhabend*
rear [rɪə] *Rückseite*
to recirculate [rɪ'sɜ:kjʊleɪt] *umwälzen*
to release [rɪ'li:s] *freigeben*

reservoir ['rezəvwɑː]   Staubecken, Talsperre
residential area [ˌrezɪ'denʃl 'eərɪə]   Wohngebiet
to restore [rɪ'stɔː]   wiederherstellen
to reuse [ˌriː'juːz]   wiederverwenden
the reverse [rɪ'vɜːs]   das Umgekehrte
rock [rɒk]   Gestein
to run short [ˌrʌn 'ʃɔːt]   knapp werden
severe [sɪ'vɪə]   hier: in starkem Maße
sewage ['sjuːɪdʒ]   Abwässer
shaded ['ʃeɪdɪd]   beschattet, schattig
shortage ['ʃɔːtɪdʒ]   Mangel
spacious ['speɪʃəs]   hier: weitläufig
to be at stake [steɪk]   auf dem Spiel stehen
sufficient [sə'fɪʃnt]   ausreichend
survival [sə'vaɪvl]   überleben
tap [tæp]   Wasserhahn
tidal power ['taɪdl 'paʊə]   Gezeitenenergie
timber ['tɪmbə]   Holz
underused agricultural land [ˌʌndə'juːzd ˌægrɪ'kʌltʃərəl 'lænd]   Grenzertragsböden
uranium [jʊ'reɪnjəm]   Uran
urban sprawl ['ɜːbən 'sprɔːl]   Zersiedlung
useable ['juːzəbl]   gebrauchsfähig
vein [veɪn]   Vene
to vent [vent]   hier: abziehen
wasteful ['weɪstfʊl]   verschwenderisch
water supply ['wɔːtə sə,plaɪ]   Wasserversorgung

MC 10: Graphs, Charts and Tables

to be attached to [ə'tætʃt tuː]   verbunden sein mit
bar chart ['bɑːtʃɑːt]   Balken-, Säulendiagramm
buying pattern ['baɪɪŋ 'pætən]   Kaufverhalten
cruise ['kruːz]   Kreuzfahrt
decline [dɪ'klaɪn]   Rückgang
to be due to s.th. [djuː]   auf etw. zurückzuführen sein
to enable s.o. to do s.th. [ɪ'neɪbl]   jmndn. in die Lage versetzen etw. zu tun
graph [grɑːf]   grafische Darstellung
heading ['hedɪŋ]   Überschrift
inferior [ɪn'fɪərɪə]   hier: weniger qualifiziert
to raise an issue ['reɪz ən 'ɪʃuː]   einen Sachverhalt anschneiden

to level off ['levl ɒf]   sich ausgleichen
mortgage ['mɔːgɪdʒ]   Hypothek
option ['ɒpʃn]   Wahl(möglichkeit)
peak [piːk]   Höhepunkt
pie chart ['paɪtʃɑːt]   Torten-, Kreisdiagramm
premises (pl) ['premɪsɪz]   Gebäude, Gelände
proportion [prə'pɔːʃn]   Anteil
prospects (pl) ['prɒspekts]   Aussichten
recommendation [ˌrekəmen'deɪʃn]   Empfehlung
to reconcile ['rekənsaɪl]   hier: in Übereinstimmung bringen
recovery [rɪ'kʌvərɪ]   Erholung
reference ['refrəns]   Verweis, Bezug
significant [sɪg'nɪfɪkənt]   bedeutend
steeply ['stiːplɪ]   steil
substantially [səb'stænʃəlɪ]   wesentlich, beträchtlich
to survey [sə'veɪ]   hier: untersuchen
to be in full swing [biː ɪn fʊl 'swɪŋ]   auf dem Höhepunkt sein
table [teɪbl]   Tabelle
travel habits ['trævl 'hæbɪts]   Reisegewohnheiten
whereas [weər'æz]   während

Sec. A. 1: Telephoning in Business

answerphone ['ɑːnsəfəʊn]   Anrufbeantworter
apron ['eɪprən]   Schürze
assurance [ə'ʃʊərəns]   Versicherung, Bestätigung
on behalf of [ɒn bɪ'hɑːf ɒv]   im Namen von
conference call ['kɒnfərəns kɔːl]   Konferenzschaltung
confirmation [ˌkɒnfə'meɪʃn]   Bestätigung
convenient [kən'viːnjənt]   zweckmäßig, günstig
to deliver [dɪ'lɪvə]   liefern
delivery [dɪ'lɪvərɪ]   Lieferung
discrepancy [dɪ'skrepənsɪ]   Diskrepanz, Abweichung
distribute [dɪ'strɪbjuːt]   verteilen
extension [ɪk'stenʃn]   Nebenanschluss, Nebenstelle
glove [glʌv]   Handschuh
to put a matter right ['pʊt ə 'mætə 'raɪt]   etw. richtigstellen

method of dispatch ['meθəd əv dɪ'spætʃ]
    Versandart
on time [ˌɒn 'taɪm]   rechtzeitig
outlet ['aʊtlet]   hier: Verkaufsstelle
to put through [pʊt 'θruː]   (telefonisch) verbinden, durchstellen
terms of payment ['tɜːmz əv 'peɪmənt]   Zahlungsbedingungen
trading regulations ['treɪdɪŋ ˌregjʊ'leɪʃnz]
    Handelsbestimmungen
Yours sincerely ['jɔːz sɪn'sɪəlɪ]   etwa: Mit freundlichen Grüßen

Sec. A. 2: Appointments

appointments book/calendar/diary [ə'pɔɪntmənts 'bʊk/'kælɪndə/'daɪərɪ]   Terminkalender
appropriate [ə'prəʊprɪət]   geeignet, angemessen
to assume [ə'sjuːm]   annehmen, vermuten
completion [kəm'pliːʃn]   Vervollständigung
owing to ['əʊɪŋ ˌtuː]   aufgrund, wegen
provisional [ˌprə'vɪʒənl]   vorläufig, einstweilig
reception desk [rɪ'sepʃn ˌdesk]   Empfang, Rezeption
self-employed [ˌselfɪm'plɔɪd]   selbstständig
unavoidable [ˌʌnə'vɔɪdəbl]   unvermeidbar

Sec. A. 3: Travelling Arrangements

accommodation [əˌkɒmə'deɪʃn]   Unterkunft, Quartier
compartment [kəm'pɑːtmənt]   Abteil
connecting service [kə'nektɪŋ 'sɜːvɪs]   Anschluss
sales contract ['seɪlz ˌkɒntrækt]   Kaufvertrag
sleeping berth ['sliːpɪŋ bɜːθ]   Liegewagenplatz
with ... hours to spare [wɪð ... 'aʊəz tə'speə]   mit einem Zeitgewinn von ... Stunden

Sec. A. 4: Room Reservations

approximately [ə'prɒksɪmətlɪ]   ungefähr, circa
central heating ['sentrəl 'hiːtɪŋ]   Zentralheizung
to commence [kə'mens]   beginnen
disabled [dɪs'eɪbld]   Behinderte/r
double bed ['dʌbl bed]   Doppelbett
invoice ['ɪnvɔɪs]   Rechnung
licensed bar ['laɪsənst 'bɑː]   Bar mit Alkoholausschank
lounge [laʊndʒ]   Gesellschaftsraum, Hotelhalle
slide projector ['slaɪd prə'dʒektə]   Diaprojektor
twin bed [ˌtwɪn 'bed]   zwei (gleiche) Einzelbetten
walking stick ['wɔːkɪŋstɪk]   Gehstock

Sec. A. 5: Invitations

to be acquainted with [ə'kweɪntɪd]   vertraut sein mit
agency ['eɪdʒənsɪ]   Agentur
agenda [ə'dʒendə]   Tagesordnung
distributorship [dɪ'strɪbjʊtəʃɪp]   Vertrieb
expense [ɪk'spens]   Auslage
fashion ['fæʃn]   Mode
lightweight ['laɪtweɪt]   leicht

Sec. A. 6: Visitors to the Company

to brush up [ˌbrʌʃ 'ʌp]   sich frisch machen
compromise ['kɒmprəmaɪz]   Kompromiss
to depart [dɪ'pɑːt]   abreisen, abfahren
folder ['fəʊldə]   Mappe
host [həʊst]   Gastgeber/in
schedule ['ʃedjuːl]   Programm

Sec. A. 7: Socializing

actually ['æktʃʊəlɪ]   eigentlich, tatsächlich
bred [bred]   aufgewachsen
daily grind ['deɪlɪ 'graɪnd]   etwa: tägliches Einerlei
German cuisine ['dʒɜːmən kwɪ'ziːn]   deutsche Küche
to slave away ['sleɪv ə'weɪ]   sich abrackern
to socialize with s.o. ['səʊʃəlaɪz wɪð]   mit jmndm. geselligen Umgang pflegen
topic ['tɒpɪk]   Thema, Gesprächsgegenstand
touchdown ['tʌtʃdaʊn]   Landung

to cure s.o. ['kjʊə]   *jmndn. heilen*
inhibition [ɪnɪ'bɪʃn]   *Hemmung*

Com. C. 1: English – the Language of Business Communication

advantage [əd'vɑːntɪdʒ]   *Vorteil*
agreement [ə'griːmənt]   *Vereinbarung*
to apply to [ə'plaɪ]   *zutreffen auf*
at least [ət 'liːst]   *mindestens, wenigstens*
background knowledge ['bækgraʊnd 'nɒlɪdʒ]   *Hintergrundwissen*
to be based on [beɪst]   *beruhen auf, sich gründen auf*
in case of conflict ['keɪs əv 'kɒnflɪkt]   *im Falle eines Konfliktes*
common ['kɒmən]   *gemeinsam*
communication [kə,mjuːnɪ'keɪʃn]   *Kommunikation*
to contact s.o. ['kɒntækt]   *mit jmndm. in Kontakt treten, mit jmndm. Kontakt aufnehmen*
co-operation [kəʊ,ɒpə'reɪʃn]   *Zusammenarbeit*
diagram ['daɪəgræm]   *Diagramm*
embarrassing [ɪm'bærəsɪŋ]   *peinlich*
equally ['iːkwəlɪ]   *gleichermaßen*
essentially [ɪ'senʃəlɪ]   *in hohem Maße, ganz besonders*
exchange [ɪks'tʃeɪndʒ]   *Austausch*
to expect [ɪk'spekt]   *erwarten*
to provide evidence [prə'vaɪd 'evɪdəns]   *Beweise sichern*
fax [fæks]   *Fax*
for further use [fɔː 'fɜːðə ,juːs]   *zur weiteren Verwendung*
in general [ɪn 'dʒenərəl]   *im Allgemeinen*
instant ['ɪnstənt]   *unmittelbar*
key word ['kiːwɜːd]   *Schlüsselwort*
limited to ['lɪmɪtɪd]   *beschränkt auf*
long-standing [,lɒŋ'stændɪŋ]   *seit langer Zeit bestehend*
to maintain [meɪn'teɪn]   *behaupten, aufrechterhalten*
means (pl) [miːnz]   *Mittel*
moreover [mɔː'rəʊvə]   *darüber hinaus*
necessarily ['nesəsərəlɪ]   *notwendigerweise*

to make notes ['meɪk 'nəʊts]   *Notizen anfertigen (für einen Vortrag)*
orally ['ɔːrəlɪ]   *mündlich*
to be plain to see [pleɪn]   *auf der Hand liegen*
to prepare for [prɪ'peə fɔː]   *sich vorbereiten auf*
to provide [prə'vaɪd]   *hier: ermöglichen*
record ['rekɔːd]   *Aufzeichnung*
role [rəʊl]   *Rolle*
telecommunications [telɪkə,mjuːnɪ'keɪʃnz]   *Tele(=Fern)kommunikation*
trading and commercial power ['treɪdɪŋ ən kə'mɜːʃl 'paʊə]   *Handels- und Wirtschaftsmacht*
upsetting [ʌp'setɪŋ]   *hier: unangenehm*
to welcome ['welkəm]   *hier: empfangen*

Com. C. 2: Layout of the Business Letter

addressee [,ædre'siː]   *Empfänger/in*
advisable [əd'vaɪzəbl]   *ratsam, angebracht*
to draw attention to s.th. [,drɔː ə'tenʃn]   *Aufmerksamkeit auf etw. lenken*
body of the letter ['bɒdɪ əv ðə 'letə]   *Brieftext, Textteil*
capital letter ['kæpɪtl 'letə]   *Großbuchstabe*
common ['kɒmən]   *hier: gebräuchlich, üblich*
complimentary close [,kɒmplɪ'mentərɪ 'kləʊz]   *Höflichkeitsschlussformel*
contents ['kɒntents]   *Inhalt*
to cover ['kʌvə]   *umfassen, beinhalten*
delay (in delivery) [dɪ'leɪ (ɪn dɪ'lɪvərɪ)]   *Lieferverzug*
enclosure [ɪn'kləʊʒə]   *Anlage (zu einem Schreiben)*
enquiry, inquiry [ɪn'kwaɪərɪ]   *Anfrage*
figure ['fɪgə]   *Ziffer*
file number ['faɪl ,nʌmbə]   *Aktenzeichen*
for the attention of [ə'tenʃn]   *zu Händen von, z. Hd.*
impersonal title [ɪm'pɜːsənl 'taɪtl]   *hier: Firmenname, der ein Sachname ist*
indented [ɪn'dentɪd]   *eingerückt, eingezogen*
individual (n) [,ɪndɪ'vɪdjʊəl]   *Einzelperson*
initials [ɪ'nɪʃlz]   *Anfangsbuchstaben, Initialen*
to be intended for s.o. [ɪn'tendɪd]   *für jmndn. gedacht sein*

to be intended to [ɪn'tendɪd] *hier: beabsichtigt sein*
italics [ɪ'tælɪks] *Kursivschrift*
job title ['dʒɒbtaɪtl] *Funktionsbezeichnung (einer Person in einer Firma)*
layout ['leɪaʊt] *(äußere) Gestaltung*
letter-head ['letəhed] *Briefkopf*
to be made up of ['meɪd ˌʌp əv] *bestehen aus*
Messrs ['mesəz] *(die) Herren*
mixed-up ['mɪkst ʌp] *völlig durcheinander gebracht*
Mmes ['meɪdæm] *(die) Damen*
order ['ɔːdə] *Reihenfolge*
postcode ['pəʊstkəʊd] *Postleitzahl*
to be common practice ['kɒmən 'præktɪs] *allgemein üblich sein*
previous ['priːvjəs] *vorherig, vorhergehend*
to reorganize [ˌriːˈɔːgənaɪz] *hier: wieder in die ursprüngliche Form bringen*
responsible [rɪ'spɒnsəbl] *verantwortlich*
salutation [ˌsæljuː'teɪʃn] *Anrede (in einem Schreiben)*
semi ['semi] *Halb-*
to sign [saɪn] *unterzeichnen, unterschreiben*
signature ['sɪgnətʃə] *Unterschrift*
specimen letter ['spesɪmən 'letə] *Musterbrief*
subject heading ['sʌbdʒɪkt 'hedɪŋ] *Betreff*
trusted friendship ['trʌstɪd 'frendʃɪp] *hier: vertrauensvolle Zusammenarbeit*
Yours faithfully ['jɔːz 'feɪθfʊli] *etwa: Mit freundlichen Grüßen*

Com. C. 3: Enquiry

above-mentioned [ə'bʌv 'menʃnd] *oben genannt*
background ['bækgraʊnd] *Hintergrund*
catalogue ['kætəlɒg] *Katalog*
to make a decision [dɪ'sɪʒn] *eine Entscheidung treffen*
drawing ['drɔːɪŋ] *Zeichnung*
enquirer [ɪn'kwaɪərə] *der/die Anfragende*
expectation [ˌekspek'teɪʃn] *Erwartung*
intention [ɪn'tenʃn] *Intention, Absicht*
kind (n) [kaɪnd] *Art*

legal obligation ['liːgl ˌɒblɪ'geɪʃn] *rechtliche Verbindlichkeit*
nevertheless [ˌnevəðə'les] *trotzdem, nichtsdestoweniger*
to obtain [əb'teɪn] *sich verschaffen, bekommen, erhalten*
phrase [freɪz] *(mehrwortiger) Ausdruck*
to put o.s. into s.o.'s place [pleɪs] *sich in jmnds. Lage versetzen*
potential [pəʊ'tenʃl] *möglich, potenziell*
quotation of prices [kwəʊ'teɪʃn əv 'praɪsɪz] *Preisangabe*
relationship [rɪ'leɪʃnʃɪp] *Beziehung, Verbindung*
request for [rɪ'kwest fɔː] *Bitte um*
to make a request [rɪ'kwest] *eine Bitte äußern*
respective [rɪ'spektɪv] *jeweilig*
routine [ruː'tiːn] *Routine*
sample ['sɑːmpl] *Muster*
terms of delivery ['tɜːmz əv dɪ'lɪvəri] *Lieferbedingungen*

Com. C. 4: Offer

to announce [ə'naʊns] *ankündigen*
to acknowledge [ək'nɒlɪdʒ] *bestätigen*
be bound by s.th. [baʊnd] *an etw. gebunden sein*
to enter into business (relations) ['entə ɪntə 'bɪznɪs (riː'leɪʃns)] *eine Geschäftsverbindung eingehen*
clause [klɔːz] *Klausel, Zusatz*
to declare as [dɪ'kleə əz] *ausweisen als*
to mail [meɪl] *(mit der Post) aufgeben/verschicken)*
offer (n) ['ɒfə] *Angebot*
readiness ['redɪnɪs] *Bereitschaft*
reasonable ['riːznəbl] *hier: angemessen*
receipt [rɪ'siːt] *Empfang, Erhalt, Eingang*
to remind s.o. of s.th. [rɪ'maɪnd] *jmnd. an etw. erinnern*
to meet requirements [rɪ'kwaɪəmənts] *Anforderungen entsprechen*
to serve a purpose ['sɜːv ə 'pɜːpəs] *einem Zweck dienen*
service ['sɜːvɪs] *Dienstleistung*

solicited offer [sə'lɪsɪtɪd 'ɒfə] *verlangtes Angebot*
subject to prior sale ['sʌbdʒɪkt tʊ 'praɪə 'seɪl] *Zwischenkauf vorbehalten*
unsolicited offer [ˌʌnsə'lɪsɪtɪd 'ɒfə] *unverlangtes Angebot*
voluntary offer ['vɒləntəri 'ɒfə] *unverlangtes Angebot*
to withdraw [wɪð'drɔː] *widerrufen*
withdrawal [wɪð'drɔːəl] *Zurücknahme, Widerruf*
without engagement [ɪn'geɪdʒmənt] *unverbindlich*

Com. C. 5: Order

according to [ə'kɔːdɪŋ] *gemäß, entsprechend*
to compare [kəm'peə] *vergleichen*
to establish a contract [ɪ'stæblɪʃ ə 'kɒntrækt] *einen Vertrag schließen*
firm offer ['fɜːm 'ɒfə] *verbindliches Angebot*
in writing [ɪn 'raɪtɪŋ] *schriftlich*
initial order [ɪ'nɪʃl 'ɔːdə] *Erstauftrag*
interval ['ɪntəvl] *(zeitlicher) Abstand, Intervall*
order form/sheet ['ɔːdə fɔːm/ʃiːt] *Auftragsformular*
to place an order (with s.o.) ['pleɪs ən 'ɔːdə] *(jmndm.) einen Auftrag erteilen*
to point out [pɔɪnt 'aʊt] *hinweisen auf*
preceding [ˌpriː'siːdɪŋ] *vorhergehend*
reliability [rɪˌlaɪə'bɪləti] *Zuverlässigkeit*
repeat order [rɪ'piːt 'ɔːdə] *Nachbestellung*
sales contract ['seɪlz 'kɒntrækt] *Kaufvertrag*
specifications [ˌspesɪfɪ'keɪʃnz] *hier: Angaben*
to standardize ['stændədaɪz] *standardisieren, vereinheitlichen*
standing order ['stændɪŋ 'ɔːdə] *Dauerauftrag*
trial order [ˌtraɪəl 'ɔːdə] *Probeauftrag*

Com. C. 6: Acknowledgement of Order

to accept [ək'sept] *akzeptieren, annehmen*
acceptance [ək'septəns] *Annahme*
acknowledgement [ək'nɒlɪdʒmənt] *Bestätigung*
commitment [kə'mɪtmənt] *Verpflichtung*
to constitute ['kɒnstɪtjuːt] *bilden, darstellen*
counter-offer [ˌkaʊntə'ɒfə] *Gegenangebot*
delivery date [dɪ'lɪvəri deɪt] *Liefertermin*
to desire [dɪ'zaɪə] *wünschen*
to dispatch [dɪ'spætʃ] *versenden*
instruction [ɪn'strʌkʃn] *Anweisung, Instruktion*
misunderstanding [ˌmɪsʌndə'stændɪŋ] *Missverständnis*
mode of dispatch ['məʊd əv dɪ'spætʃ] *Versandart*
to precede [ˌpriː'siːd] *vorausgehen*
to request [rɪ'kwest] *erbitten, bitten um*
sales negotiations ['seɪlz nɪˌgəʊʃɪ'eɪʃnz] *Verkaufsverhandlungen*
to stipulate ['stɪpjʊleɪt] *festlegen, vereinbaren*
to submit [səb'mɪt] *unterbreiten*

Com. C. 7: Delay in Delivery

to accommodate [ə'kɒmədeɪt] *entgegenkommen*
act of God [ækt əv gɒd] *höhere Gewalt*
behaviour [bɪ'heɪvjə] *Verhalten*
continuation [kənˌtɪnjʊ'eɪʃn] *Fortsetzung*
to cope with ['kəʊp wɪð] *fertig werden mit, gewachsen sein*
to depend heavily on s.th. [dɪ'pend 'hevɪli] *auf etw. sehr angewiesen sein*
to be entitled to do s.th. [ɪn'taɪtld] *einen Anspruch auf etw. haben*
in accordance with [ɪn ə'kɔːdəns wɪð] *in Übereinstimmung mit*
to incur [ɪn'kɜː] *hier: entstehen*
part shipment ['pɑːt ˌʃɪpmənt] *Teilsendung*
punctual ['pʌŋktjʊəl] *pünktlich*
reduction [rɪ'dʌkʃn] *Reduzierung, Herabsetzung*
to refer to [rɪ'fɜː] *sich beziehen auf*
reminder [rɪ'maɪndə] *Mahnung*
resolution [ˌrezə'luːʃn] *Entschlossenheit*
to withdraw from [wɪð'drɔː] *zurücktreten von*

Com. C. 8: Complaints and their Adjustments

adjustment [əˈdʒʌstmənt] *Beilegung*
apology [əˈpɒlədʒɪ] *Entschuldigung*
compensation [ˌkɒmpenˈseɪʃn] *Entschädigung*
to complain [kəmˈpleɪn] *reklamieren, sich beschweren*
to settle a complaint [ˈsetl ə kəmˈpleɪnt] *eine Reklamation beilegen*
condition [kənˈdɪʃn] *Zustand*
to damage [ˈdæmɪdʒ] *beschädigen*
execution [ˌeksɪˈkjuːʃn] *Ausführung, Durchführung*
faultless [ˈfɔːltlɪs] *fehlerfrei*
to be forced to [fɔːst] *gezwungen sein*
furious [ˈfjʊərɪəs] *wütend*
if requested [ɪf rɪˈkwestɪd] *falls gewünscht*
in view of [ɪn ˈvjuː əv] *im Hinblick auf*
to include [ɪnˈkluːd] *einschließen*
involved [ɪnˈvɒlvd] *betreffend*
to justify [ˈdʒʌstɪfaɪ] *rechtfertigen*
regret [rɪˈgret] *Bedauern*
replacement [rɪˈpleɪsmənt] *Ersatz*
to fail in o.'s responsibilities [ˈfeɪl ɪn wʌnz rɪˌspɒnsəˈbɪlətɪz] *seiner Verantwortung nicht gerecht werden*
to result from [rɪˈzʌlt frəm] *sich ergeben aus*
to substantiate [səbˈstænʃɪeɪt] *stärken, festigen*
terms [tɜːmz] *Bedingungen*
trading partner [ˈtreɪdɪŋ ˌpɑːtnə] *Geschäftspartner/in*
to be up to s.th. [biː ˈʌp tʊ] *einer Sache entsprechen*
with care [wɪð ˈkeə] *sorgfältig, mit Sorgfalt*

Alphabetical Vocabulary List

The numbers refer to the corresponding units of the book.

to abandon *MC5*
to abbreviate *MC6*
ability *IC6*
to abolish *MC5*
above *MC2*
above-mentioned *Com. C.3*
abroad *IC2*
absent *IC4*
accept *Com. C.6*
acceptance *Com. C.6*
to access *MC8*
to accommodate *Com. C.7*
accommodation *Sec. A.3*
to accompany *IC4*
in accordance with *Com. C.7*
according to *Com. C.5*
statement of account *MC1*
accredition *MC8*
accuracy *MC4*
to acknowledge *Com. C.4*
acknowledgement *Com. C.6*
to be acquainted with *Sec. A.5*
to acquire *MC4*
to act as *IC5*
act of God *Com. C.7*
actually *Sec. A.7*
to adapt to *MC6*
additional *MC2*
to address *IC6*
addressee *Com. C.2*
adequate *IC7*
to adjust *IC7*
adjustment *Com. C.8*
to administer *MC2*
administration *MC8*
administrative *MC8*
to admit *IC4*
to adopt *MC3*
advance *MC4*
advanced *MC7*
advantage *Com. C.1*
to advertise *MC3*
advertisement *MC3*
advertising slogan *MC3*
advisability *MC7*
advisable *Com. C.2*

to advise s.o. *MC2*
affair *MC1*
state of affairs *IC1*
to be affected *MC9*
affluent *MC3*
to afford *IC2*
agency *Sec. A.5*
agenda *Sec. A.5*
agent *IC1*
agreed *MC1*
agreement *Com. C.1*
to conclude agreements *MC5*
to aim *MC3*
air inlet *MC9*
alcoholic *MC4*
alike *IC4*
all over *IC1*
allowance *MC1*
to think in terms of alternatives *IC8*
altogether *MC1*
ambition *IC8*
among *IC4*
amount *MC1*
ancient *MC3*
to announce *Com. C.4*
to be annoyed *MC4*
annual *MC3*
Annual Percentage Rate *MC4*
answerphone *Sec. A.1*
apart from *MC1*
apology *Com. C.8*
apparent *MC8*
to appeal to *MC3*
appliance *IC7*
applicant *IC6*
applications software *IC2*
to apply for *IC3*
to apply to *Com. C.1*
appointment *IC6*
appointments book/calendar/diary *Sec. A.2*
appropriate *Sec. A.2*
approximately *Sec. A.4*
apron *Sec. A.1*

area *IC4*
to arise (irr) *IC8*
arithmetic *MC4*
to arrange *MC2*
to arrange for *IC4*
artery *MC9*
aspect *IC2*
to assemble *IC2*
assembly shop *IC5*
to assess *MC8*
assessment *MC4*
assets *MC7*
associated with *MC8*
association *MC3*
to assume *Sec. A.2*
assurance *Sec. A.1*
at least *Com. C.1*
at random *MC1*
to be attached to *MC10*
to attain *MC8*
to attend courses/classes *IC3*
to attend to *IC5*
to draw attention to s.th. *Com. C.2*
for the attention of *Com. C.2*
attitude *MC1*
to be attracted to *MC8*
attraction *IC8*
auxiliary (verb) *MC1*
available *IC7*
average (adj) *MC1*
background *Com. C.3*
background knowledge *Com. C.1*
badly *MC2*
bait *MC3*
balance *MC1*
balance forward *MC1*
bank overdraft *MC4*
banking *MC1*
to go bankrupt *MC2*
bar chart *MC10*
to be based on *Com. C.1*
basic *IC4*
basically *IC5*
basis *IC3*
on behalf of *Secr. A.1*
behaviour *Com. C.7*
beneficial *MC8*
benefit *MC2*
to benefit from *MC5*
beyond *MC6*
binary code *MC6*
binding *MC5*
bit *IC6*

bits and pieces *MC6*
blank *MC1*
to blend in with *MC9*
board *MC1*
board of directors *MC2*
on board ship *MC1*
to boast *MC5*
body of the letter *Com. C.2*
bookkeeping *MC6*
to boom into *IC1*
to be bored *IC6*
both ... and *MC1*
be bound by s.th. *Com. C.4*
brake *MC6*
brake lining *MC3*
breakthrough *MC3*
breathless *MC3*
bred *Secr. A.7*
brief *MC6*
brilliant *IC1*
broadcast(ing) *MC3*
brochure *IC8*
broker *MC2*
to brush up *Sec. A.6*
builder *IC1*
building society *MC1*
in bulk (quantities) *MC7*
to enter into business (relations) *Com. C.4*
to do business with s.o. *IC2*
bustling *MC3*
but *IC5*
buying pattern *MC10*
to calculate *MC1*
calculator *MC6*
on campus *MC8*
canteen *IC5*
capital growth *MC2*
capital letter *Com. C.2*
caption *MC1*
to capture *MC6*
carafe *IC7*
deck of cards *MC4*
with care *Com. C.8*
career *IC3*
cartoon *MC4*
cash dispenser *IC7*
catalogue *Com. C.3*
cautious *MC4*
to celebrate *IC5*
celebrity *MC3*
central heating *Sec. A.4*
certainty *IC5*
chairman *MC2*
to be in charge of *IC4*
charge *MC7*

245

Alphabetical Vocabulary List

charging period *MC1*
chart *MC1*
to keep a check on *MC3*
chip *IC3*
circumstances *IC8*
citizen *MC5*
claim *IC7*
to claim *MC1*
classmate *IC1*
clause *Com. C.4*
client *MC8*
client evidence *MC8*
climate *MC2*
cloth *MC9*
to collapse *MC5*
colleague *IC4*
to collect *IC2*
collective *MC2*
college *MC8*
colony *IC7*
column *IC3*
to combine *MC3*
to come across *IC3*
to come true *IC3*
to commence *Sec. A.4*
commerce *MC7*
commercial (n) *MC3*
to commit o.s. *MC8*
commitment *Com. C.6*
committee *IC6*
common *Com. C.1*
to have in common *MC2*
Commonwealth *IC7*
communication *Com. C.1*
community *IC7*
to compare *Com. C.5*
comparison *MC3*
compartment *Sec. A.3*
compatible *MC6*
compensation *Com. C.8*
to compete *MC5*
competiton *MC3*
keen competition *IC5*
competitive market *MC7*
competitor *MC6*
to complain *Com. C.8*
complaint *MC3*
completion *Sec. A.2*
complex *MC5*
complicated *MC8*
complimentary close *Com. C.2*
to comply with *IC5*
component *IC2*
compromise *Sec. A.6*
computerized *IC4*

to conceive *MC6*
concern *IC3*
conclusion *MC7*
concrete *MC9*
condition *Com. C.8*
to conduct a meeting *MC5*
conference call *Sec. A.1*
to confess *IC4*
confidential *IC1*
to confirm *MC6*
confirmation *Sec. A.1*
in case of conflict *Com. C.1*
connecting service *Sec. A.3*
consequently *MC5*
to conserve *MC9*
to consider *IC4*
considerable *IC4*
consignment *MC7*
to constitute *Com. C.6*
to consume *MC9*
consumer *MC3*
Consumer Advice *MC4*
consumer protection *MC4*
to contact s.o. *Com. C.1*
to establish contacts *IC2*
to contain *MC1*
to contaminate *MC9*
contentment *MC3*
contents *Com. C.2*
continuation *Com. C.7*
contract proposal *IC1*
to have s.th. under control *IC3*
controller *MC7*
controversy *MC9*
convenience *MC1*
convenient *Sec. A.1*
convention *MC3*
conventional *MC7*
conversely *MC7*
to convert *MC9*
to convince *MC3*
to co-ordinate *MC5*
co-operation *Com. C.1*
to cope with *Com. C.7*
corporation *IC1*
to correspond to *IC2*
cosmopolitan *MC3*
Council for the Protection of Rural England *MC9*
counter-offer *Com. C.6*
a couple of *IC4*
during the course of *IC1*
to take o.'s course *IC4*
to attend courses *IC3*
courteous *MC7*

to cover *MC1*
to create *MC5*
to be in credit *MC1*
credit indication *IC7*
credit limit *IC7*
credit reference agency *MC4*
criminal records *MC5*
cruise *MC10*
cuisine *MC3*
currency *MC4*
currency conversion *MC6*
currency entry charges *MC3*
currency union *MC5*
current *IC6*
current account *MC1*
customer *IC1*
to cut *MC8*
CV (curriculum vitae) *MC8*
daily grind *Sec. A.7*
to damage *Com. C.8*
damage (n) *MC5*
daring *MC7*
darts *MC7*
data *MC6*
data protection *IC4*
deadline *MC7*
to deal in *IC5*
to deal with *IC1*
debt *MC2*
decade *MC5*
to deceive *MC8*
decent *MC3*
to make a decision *Com. C.3*
to declare *MC8*
to declare as *Com. C.4*
decline *MC10*
decoration *IC5*
decorator *IC1*
to decrease *IC5*
to deduct from *MC1*
to define *MC2*
delay (in delivery) *Com. C.2*
to delay *MC2*
delighted *MC5*
to deliver *Sec. A.1*
delivery *Sec. A.1*
delivery date *Com. C.6*
demand *IC4*
to meet s.o.'s demands *IC2*
to deny *MC2*
to depart *Sec. A.6*
department store *IC7*
to depend heavily on s.th. *Com. C.7*
to deplete *MC9*
deposit *MC5*

deposit account *MC1*
derelict *MC9*
desalting plant *MC9*
desirable *MC3*
to desire *Com. C.6*
desperately *IC1*
despite *IC3*
developer *MC9*
device *IC4*
to devote *MC5*
diagram *Com. C.1*
dial tone *IC7*
to dial *IC7*
to differ *MC3*
digit *IC7*
digital *IC4*
diligent *IC8*
diplomatically *MC2*
to direct *MC5*
to direct at *MC3*
direct debiting *MC1*
disabled *Sec. A.4*
disadvantage *IC7*
to disagree *MC3*
discrepancy *Sec. A.1*
discrimination *MC5*
dishonest *MC3*
to dislike *IC4*
dislikes *IC8*
to dispatch *Com. C.6*
mode of dispatch *Com. C.6*
to display *IC7*
dispute *MC4*
to distort *MC8*
distribute *Sec. A.1*
distribution *MC7*
distributorship *Sec. A.5*
to dive *IC2*
diversified *MC7*
dividend *MC2*
domestic *MC9*
to dominate *MC8*
double bed *Sec. A.4*
to download *MC6*
downward *MC8*
dozen *IC6*
drastically *IC3*
draught *MC9*
draw date *MC1*
drawing *Com. C.3*
to drill *MC9*
to drip *IC7*
to drive (irr) *MC6*
drop *MC8*
to drop *IC4*
dry cement *MC9*

Alphabetical Vocabulary List | Info

to be due to s.th. *MC10*
dull *MC3*
duration *IC2*
duty *MC5*
eager *MC9*
earnings *MC2*
earphones *IC7*
to ease *MC4*
economic *MC2*
to read economics *IC3*
economy *MC2*
edge *MC2*
efficient *IC5*
effort *MC3*
eightfold *MC5*
to elect *MC2*
electronic transmission *MC8*
elevator *MC6*
eligible *MC4*
to eliminate *MC3*
emancipated *IC1*
embarrassing *Com. C.1*
emergency *IC1*
employer *IC8*
to enable s.o. to do s.th. *MC10*
enclosure *Com. C.2*
to be endangered *IC7*
to endorse *MC3*
to engage in *MC5*
engagement *Com. C.4*
enjoyable *IC8*
entrepreneur *MC3*
to enquire *MC2*
enquirer *Com. C.3*
enquiry, inquiry *Com. C.2*
to enter s.th. *MC1*
entirely *MC5*
to be entitled to do s.th. *Com. C.7*
entry charge *MC1*
entry requirements *MC8*
equally *Com. C.1*
equipment *IC2*
escape (n) *MC3*
essential *IC5*
essentially *Com. C.1*
to establish *IC7*
to establish a contract *Com. C.5*
to estimate *MC4*
EU (European Union) *IC3*
European Coal and Steel Community Fund *MC5*
European Union (EU) *IC7*
evaporation *MC9*

even *IC3*
event *IC4*
eventually *MC6*
ever *IC8*
ever since then *IC3*
evidence *MC8*
to provide evidence *Com. C.1*
to exaggerate *MC3*
to exceed *MC1*
except (for) *IC4*
exchange *Com. C.1*
excitement *MC3*
to execute *IC8*
execution *Com. C.8*
to expand *IC2*
to expect *Com. C.1*
expectation *Com. C.3*
expenditure *MC1*
expense *Sec. A.5*
to make explicit *MC5*
to extend *MC8*
extensive *IC8*
extent (n) *MC3*
extention *Sec. A.1*
external verifier *MC8*
extract *MC8*
to face *IC8*
facial expression *MC6*
facility *IC5*
in fact *IC5*
factory-like *IC5*
to fail *IC4*
failure *MC8*
Fair Trading *MC4*
fairytale *MC3*
to fall behind *MC4*
false *MC3*
fancy dress party *MC1*
fashion *Sec. A.5*
faultless *Com. C.8*
faulty *MC4*
in s.o.'s favour *MC1*
favourable *IC2*
fax *Com. C.1*
to fear *MC4*
to feature *MC3*
fee *MC1*
to feed (irr) *IC4*
fertiliser *MC2*
figure *Com. C.2*
figures *IC5*
file number *Com. C.2*
filing *MC8*
final total *MC1*
firm offer *Com. C.5*

to fit (into) *IC2*
fitness *MC4*
fixed *MC2*
flap *MC9*
flat charge *MC1*
flexible *IC6*
flight *IC5*
floodlight *MC3*
flow chart *MC7*
flow of goods *MC7*
focus (n) *IC2*
folder *Sec. A.6*
folklore *MC3*
for further use *Com. C.1*
to be forced to *Com. C.8*
forecast *MC7*
foreign policy *MC5*
form (n) *MC1*
forwarding agent *MC7*
to found *IC3*
foundation *MC7*
fraction *MC9*
time frame *IC4*
free-enterprise country *MC3*
freight service *MC7*
frequency *IC7*
frequent *MC3*
to freshen *MC9*
fuel *MC9*
to fulfil *MC7*
full-time *MC8*
fund *MC2*
fundamental *MC5*
furious *Com. C.8*
furniture removal *MC3*
further to *MC2*
to gain *IC3*
gap *MC9*
to gather *MC3*
in general *Com. C.1*
generally *MC2*
German cuisine *Sec. A.7*
gift *MC3*
gilts *MC2*
gilt-edged securities (pl) *MC2*
glass sheet *MC9*
glove *Sec. A.1*
goal *MC7*
government-owned *MC1*
gradual *IC7*
to grant *IC7*
graph *MC10*
graphics *MC6*
Green Belt *MC9*

Gross National Product (GNP) *MC5*
to prepare ground for *MC5*
growth *MC4*
to guarantee *MC2*
guidance *MC8*
guide *MC2*
guideline *MC7*
habit *IC1*
habitat *MC9*
half-board *MC3*
handicap *MC9*
handsome *MC5*
handy *MC2*
to hang around *IC6*
hardware *IC1*
hassle *MC3*
heading *MC10*
headmistress *IC4*
s.o. can't help doing s.th. *IC4*
high street bank *MC4*
to hire *MC4*
hire purchase *MC4*
to hold on tight to *MC9*
home affairs *MC5*
honest *MC3*
host *Sec. A.6*
housing *MC9*
huge *MC5*
human race *MC9*
humans *IC4*
ideally *MC3*
to identify with *MC3*
if requested *Com. C.8*
illustration *MC2*
imaginary *MC2*
to imitate *MC3*
immigrant *MC6*
immoral *MC3*
impasse *MC9*
impersonal title *Com. C.2*
to impose *IC8*
to improve *MC3*
impure *MC9*
in turn *MC9*
to include *Com. C.8*
income *MC2*
income tax *MC2*
incoming *IC5*
inconvenient *IC6*
to incorporate *MC5*
to increase *IC2*
to incur *Com. C.7*
indented *Com. C.2*
independent *IC3*
to indicate *IC2*

247

Info — Alphabetical Vocabulary List

individual (n) *Com. C.2*
inference *MC7*
inferior *MC10*
inflexible *IC8*
information sheet *IC4*
infrastructure *MC5*
inhabitant *MC5*
inhibition *Sec. A.7*
initial order *Com. C.5*
initials *Com. C.2*
to insert *IC7*
to insist on *IC5*
to install *IC7*
instant *Com. C.1*
instead of *MC2*
to instruct *MC1*
instruction *Com. C.6*
insulting *MC3*
insurance *MC1*
to insure *MC1*
to be intended for s.o. *Com. C.2*
to be intended to *Com. C.2*
intention *Com. C.3*
interest *MC1*
intermediate *MC7*
internally *MC5*
interpreter *MC5*
interval *Com. C.5*
to introduce *IC3*
invasion *MC4*
to invent *MC3*
to invest *IC8*
investigate *MC4*
Investment Trust Company *MC2*
investor *MC2*
invoice *Sec. A.4*
to involve *IC3*
involved *Com. C.8*
irrevocable *MC1*
irrigation *MC9*
to raise an issue *MC10*
to issue *MC1*
italics *Com. C.2*
item *MC1*
jealousy *MC3*
job hunting *IC8*
job title *Com. C.2*
Jobcentre *IC8*
jobclub *MC8*
joint-stock company *IC7*
justice affairs *MC5*
to justify *Com. C.8*
to keep a check on *MC3*
to keep a keen eye on *IC3*

to key in *IC7*
key phrase *MC9*
key word *Com. C.1*
kind (n) *Com. C.3*
to make s.th. known *IC4*
label *MC4*
labour *IC4*
largely *MC6*
large-scale *MC3*
latest *IC1*
to launch *MC7*
layout *Com. C.2*
to lead s.o. to do s.th. *IC6*
leaflet *MC1*
lecture *MC6*
to give s.o. a lecture *IC4*
legal obligation *Com. C.3*
legal value *MC5*
leisure *MC9*
less *MC1*
letter of credit *MC1*
letter-head *Com. C.2*
to level off *MC10*
liability *MC2*
liable *MC2*
licence *MC3*
licensed bar *Sec. A.4*
lightweight *Sec. A.5*
likely *IC5*
likes *IC8*
to limit o.s. to s.th. *IC8*
limited to *Com. C.1*
to stretch s.th. to its limits *IC4*
to link *IC4*
liqueur *MC3*
literacy skill *MC8*
loan *MC2*
loan company *MC4*
Loan Guarantee Scheme *MC4*
to locate *IC4*
logo *MC3*
long-hair trimmer *IC7*
long-range *MC7*
long-standing *Com. C.1*
to look after *IC1*
to look forward to *IC1*
loss *MC5*
lounge *Sec. A.4*
loyal *MC4*
to be made up of *Com. C.2*
to mail *Com. C.4*
mainly *IC2*
to maintain *Com. C.1*
major *MC2*

to make clear *MC2*
to make it *IC3*
male *MC3*
to manage to do s.th. *IC3*
managing director *MC2*
manpower *MC7*
manual *MC7*
manufacturer *MC1*
market research *IC5*
to market *IC2*
mass *MC6*
to master *MC6*
to match *MC1*
to put a matter right *Sec. A.1*
meadow *MC9*
to mean well *IC4*
means (pl) *Com. C.1*
measure *MC8*
medieval *MC3*
medium-sized *MC8*
memorable *MC3*
merely *IC5*
mess *IC4*
Messrs *Com. C.2*
method of dispatch *Sec. A.1*
to have in mind *IC8*
to slip o.'s mind *IC5*
misery *MC4*
misleading *MC3*
to miss *MC1*
misunderstanding *Com. C.6*
mixed-up *Com. C.2*
Mmes *Com. C.2*
mode of dispatch *Com. C.6*
modernization grants *MC5*
to modify *IC5*
monetary union *MC5*
money order *MC1*
moreover *Com. C.1*
mortgage *MC10*
motto *MC3*
to move *MC1*
musician *MC9*
National Savings Bonds *MC2*
National Savings Certificates *MC2*
natural resources *MC9*
navigation *MC9*
near-abandonment *MC8*
necessarily *Com. C.1*
necessity *MC7*
to neglect *MC8*
sales negotiations *Com. C.6*
net charge *MC1*
network *MC4*

nevertheless *Com. C.3*
nicknamed *MC8*
noble *MC5*
non-repayable *MC5*
North Atlantic Treaty Organization (NATO) *MC5*
to make notes *Com.C1*
until further notice *MC1*
notice of withdrawal *MC1*
to notify *IC7*
nought *MC4*
nowadays *IC2*
nuclear power *MC9*
numeracy skill *MC8*
to put it in a nutshell *MC6*
to obey *MC5*
objectionable *MC3*
obligation *MC7*
to observe *IC7*
to obtain *Com. C.3*
obvious *MC3*
occasional *IC6*
offensive *MC3*
offer (n) *Com. C.4*
unsolicited offer *Com. C.4*
voluntary offer *Com. C.4*
oil well *MC9*
old-fashioned *MC7*
on behalf of *Sec. A.1*
on principle *IC4*
onwards *MC3*
to operate *IC4*
opportunity *IC7*
opposition party *MC8*
option *MC10*
orally *Com. C.1*
order *Com. C.2*
order form/sheet *Com. C.5*
to place an order (with s.o.) *Com. C.5*
ordinary *MC2*
outdoor season *MC7*
outdoors *IC5*
outlet *Sec. A.1*
to be overdue *MC2*
to overestimate *MC7*
to overheat *IC7*
to overspend *MC4*
to work overtime *IC6*
to overuse *MC4*
to owe *MC4*
owing to *Sec. A.2*
to own *MC2*
packaging *MC7*
painful *MC8*
to pair *MC3*

248

Alphabetical Vocabulary List

paragraph *MC2*
parent company *MC7*
part owner *MC2*
part shipment *Com. C.7*
partial *MC8*
to participate in *MC8*
particular *IC2*
patent *MC6*
pattern *MC2*
pavement café *MC3*
peak *MC10*
percentage *MC7*
perfume *MC3*
period *IC3*
permanent *IC1*
permission *MC1*
to perplex *IC4*
personality *MC3*
to persuade *IC4*
pesticide *MC9*
phonecard phone *IC7*
phrase *Com. C.3*
physical *MC6*
to pick up *IC8*
pick-up *MC7*
pie chart *MC10*
to put o.s. into s.o.'s place *Com. C.3*
to be plain to see *Com. C.1*
plastic surgery *MC3*
plastics *MC2*
platinum *MC5*
plumber *IC1*
to plump for *IC8*
to point out *Com. C.5*
to police *MC3*
policy *MC2*
pollution *MC9*
to pool *MC2*
to post *IC5*
to place s.o. in a difficult position *IC5*
possession *MC2*
postcode *Com. C.2*
potential *Com. C.3*
practically *IC2*
to be common practice *Com. C.2*
to put s.th. into practice *MC2*
pre-established *MC5*
pre-vocational *MC8*
to precede *Com. C.6*
preceding *Com. C.5*
to predict *MC4*
to prefer *IC5*

premises (pl) *MC10*
to prepare for *Com. C.1*
to preserve *MC9*
to prevent *IC7*
previous *Com. C.2*
Primary School *IC4*
principle *IC4*
priority *MC9*
privacy *MC4*
private limited company (Ltd) *MC2*
probability *MC7*
probable *IC8*
procedure *IC7*
to proceed *IC6*
to process *IC4*
profit *MC2*
to progress *MC5*
to prohibit *MC9*
promising *IC5*
to promote *MC7*
proper *IC1*
property *MC2*
proportion *MC10*
in proportion to *MC2*
contract proposal *IC1*
proprietor *MC2*
prosperous *MC9*
prospects (pl) *MC10*
data protection *IC4*
to prove *IC3*
to provide *MC1*
to provide evidence *Com. C.1*
provided (that) *IC6*
provisional *Sec. A.2*
to provoke *MC5*
psychologist *MC3*
public limited company (plc) *MC2*
public transport *IC6*
publicity *MC3*
publicity brochure *MC2*
publicly *IC4*
punch-card *MC6*
punctual *Com. C.7*
purchase *MC2*
to purchase *IC2*
to purify *MC6*
to serve a purpose *Com. C.4*
purpose *MC2*
to push out of *MC6*
to put a matter right *Sec. A.1*
to put through *Sec. A.1*
quaint *MC3*
to qualify for *MC1*

quantity *MC1*
quarter year *MC1*
quarterly *MC1*
queue (n) *IC7*
quotation of prices *Com. C.3*
to quote *MC3*
rapid *IC2*
rather than *IC1*
rationalization *IC7*
raw material *MC5*
to react *IC1*
readiness *Com. C.4*
realistic *MC8*
rear *MC9*
reasonable *Com. C.4*
receipt *Com. C.4*
recently *IC2*
reception desk *Sec. A.2*
to recheck *IC5*
recirculate *MC9*
to reclaim *MC1*
recognition *MC8*
recognized *MC8*
to recognize *IC7*
to recommend *IC6*
recommendation *MC10*
to reconcile *MC10*
to keep records *MC2*
record *Com. C.1*
to record *IC4*
recording machine *MC6*
recovery *MC10*
red tape *MC8*
to reduce *IC7*
reduction *Com. C.7*
to refer to *Com. C.7*
reference *MC10*
to reflect on *IC8*
to reform *MC8*
to refuse *MC4*
as regards *IC5*
regardless of *MC3*
to register *MC3*
regret *Com. C.8*
to regulate *MC7*
regulation *IC5*
reinvest *MC7*
to reject *MC6*
to relate to *MC8*
relationship *Com. C.3*
to release *MC9*
relevant *IC8*
reliability *Com. C.5*
reliable *IC4*
relief *MC8*
reluctant *MC2*

to rely on *IC3*
remedy *MC4*
to remind s.o. of s.th. *Com. C.4*
reminder *Com. C.7*
renovation *MC4*
to reorganize *Com. C.2*
repayment *MC4*
repeat order *Com. C.5*
replacement *Com. C.8*
reply *IC5*
to reply *MC2*
representative *IC5*
reprographics *MC8*
request for *Com. C.3*
to make a request *Com. C.3*
to request *Com. C.6*
to require *IC4*
to meet requirements *Com. C.4*
research *IC5*
to resemble *MC6*
reservoir *MC9*
residential area *MC9*
resolution *Com. C.7*
resort *MC3*
to respect *MC3*
respective *Com. C.3*
to respond to *MC8*
responsibilities *IC1*
to fail in o.'s responsibilities *Com. C.8*
responsible *Com. C.2*
to restore *MC9*
to result from *Com. C.8*
retailer *MC7*
in return *MC1*
to reuse *MC9*
to reveal *MC2*
the reverse *MC9*
to reverse *MC8*
review (n) *MC8*
to review *IC6*
reward *MC2*
to rewrite *MC2*
ridiculous *MC3*
rigorous *MC3*
risk (n) *IC3*
to carry/take a risk *MC2*
rock *MC9*
role *Com. C.1*
rolling *MC3*
roughly *IC6*
routine *Com. C.3*
rules of conduct *MC5*
to run *IC1*

Info — Alphabetical Vocabulary List

to run down *MC8*
to run short *MC9*
to rush into s.th. *IC5*
to safeguard *MC3*
sale *Com. C.5*
sales contract *Sec. A.3*
sales negotiations *Com. C.6*
sales outlet *IC5*
sales set-up *IC5*
salutation *Com. C.2*
sample *Com. C.3*
to sample *MC8*
satisfactory *IC8*
to satisfy conditions *MC7*
saturation *MC4*
saving habit *MC1*
savings *MC1*
schedule *Sec. A.6*
schoolleaver *MC8*
school-leaving qualification *IC8*
scientific *MC3*
scientist *IC3*
score *MC3*
Secretary-Treasurer *MC7*
sector *MC8*
to secure *MC5*
security policy *MC5*
to seek *MC5*
to select *MC2*
self-employed *Sec. A.2*
to be self-sufficient *MC5*
seller *MC1*
semi *Com. C.2*
sentimental *MC3*
separate *MC1*
serious *IC5*
to serve a purpose *Com. C.4*
service *Com. C.4*
service sector *IC7*
to settle a complaint *Com. C.8*
severe *MC9*
sewage *MC9*
sexism *MC3*
shaded *MC9*
shameful *MC8*
share (n) *MC2*
to share *IC1*
shareholder *MC2*
sharp fall *MC2*
electric shaver *IC7*
shift *IC5*
shipyard *MC8*
shop floor *MC7*

shortage *MC9*
short-term *MC7*
to sign *Com. C.2*
to sign up *MC7*
signature *Com. C.2*
significant *MC10*
signpost *IC8*
since then *IC3*
to sink (irr) *MC6*
skilled job *MC8*
skilled labour *IC6*
to slave away *Sec. A.7*
sleeping berth *Sec. A.3*
sleeping partner *MC2*
slide projector *Sec. A.4*
slight *IC3*
to slip one's mind *IC5*
slogan *MC3*
slot *IC7*
smash *MC5*
snooker *MC7*
to socialize with s.o. *Sec. A.7*
so far *IC3*
software *IC1*
sole *MC2*
solicited offer *Com. C.4*
solution *IC1*
sophisticated *MC3*
to sort out *IC5*
sound (adj) *MC5*
source *IC8*
space *IC1*
spacious *MC9*
spare part *MC1*
with ... hours to spare *Sec. A.3*
spare-time *IC8*
to specialize in *IC1*
specific *IC2*
specifications *Com. C.5*
to specify *IC6*
specimen letter *Com. C.2*
spectacular *MC2*
spending *MC4*
spending habit *MC1*
spokesman *MC8*
to sponsor *MC3*
to stack *MC4*
staff *IC5*
at this stage *MC5*
to be at stake *MC9*
to stand for *IC1*
to standardize *Com. C.5*
standing order *Com. C.5*
state of affairs *IC1*

state of ferment *MC8*
statement of account *MC1*
statistics *MC8*
steady *MC7*
steel mill *MC8*
steeply *MC10*
to stipulate *Com. C.6*
stock *MC7*
stock exchange *MC2*
stomach ache *MC5*
storage capacity *IC5*
to have in store *IC3*
to store *IC4*
straightaway/straight away *IC6*
strength *IC1*
to stretch *IC8*
to stretch s.th. to its limits *IC4*
strings *MC8*
study skills *MC8*
subject heading *Com. C.2*
subject to prior sale *Com. C.4*
to submit *Com. C.6*
subsidiary *MC7*
substantial *IC8*
substantially *MC10*
to substantiate *Com. C.8*
to succeed *IC4*
sufficient *MC9*
to be suited *MC8*
supervision *MC7*
supervisory work *MC8*
supplier *IC2*
to supply *IC1*
Surgeon General *MC3*
surprising *IC3*
surroundings (pl) *MC3*
survey *MC10*
survival *MC9*
to suspect *IC4*
to be in full swing *MC10*
syllable *MC3*
sympathetic *MC4*
table *MC10*
tabulating machine *MC6*
tactful *MC2*
tailor-made *IC1*
to take on *MC8*
tap *MC9*
tar *MC3*
target *IC7*
tariff *MC5*
tax office *MC4*
technique *MC3*

telecommunications *Com. C.1*
temporary *IC1*
to tempt *MC3*
tennis racket *MC7*
tenpin bowling *MC7*
term *IC4*
terms *Com. C.8*
terms of delivery *Com. C.3*
terms of payment *Sec. A.1*
theoretically-minded *IC8*
thought *IC8*
tidal power *MC9*
timber *MC9*
on time *Sec. A.1*
time frame *IC4*
tin *MC5*
topic *Sec. A.7*
touchdown *Sec. A.7*
trade association *IC8*
trade terms *MC5*
trader *MC4*
trading *Com. C.1*
trading and commercial power *Com. C.1*
trading partner *Com. C.8*
trading regulations *Sec. A.1*
to trail behind *MC8*
trainee *MC8*
training course *IC3*
training manual *MC6*
transaction *MC1*
to transfer *MC1*
travel habits *MC10*
tremendous *MC3*
trend *IC6*
trial order *Com. C.5*
to play a trick on s.o. *IC4*
to trim *IC7*
long-hair trimmer *IC7*
trusted *MC1*
trusted friendship *Com. C.2*
truthful *MC3*
twin bed *Sec. A.4*
unavoidable *Sec. A.2*
uncertain *IC8*
underdeveloped *MC5*
to undertake *MC8*
underused agricultural land *MC9*
unfavourable *MC7*
unfortunately *IC8*
to unify *MC5*
Unit Trusts *MC2*
unity *MC5*
unlikely *MC2*

250

Alphabetical Vocabulary List

unlimited *MC2*
unqualified *MC8*
unskilled *MC8*
unsolicited offer *Com. C.4*
until further notice *MC1*
until then *MC2*
untrained *MC8*
untruthful *MC3*
unusual *IC3*
to be up to s.th. *Com. C.8*
up to *IC7*
up-to-date *IC6*
upsetting *Com. C.1*
uranium *MC9*
urban sprawl *MC9*

usage *MC5*
useable *MC9*
to be used to doing s.th. *IC8*
valve *MC7*
variety *MC1*
vehicle *MC4*
vein *MC9*
to vent *MC9*
via *MC6*
in view of *Com. C.8*
vigilance committee *MC3*
virtually *MC5*
vital *MC1*
vocational training *MC8*
volume of trade *MC5*

voluntary offer *Com. C.4*
walking stick *Sec. A.4*
wasteful *MC9*
to keep a watch on *MC2*
watchdog *MC3*
water supply *MC9*
weakness *MC8*
to welcome *Com. C.1*
well-educated *MC8*
whereas *MC10*
wholesaler *MC7*
widely *IC7*
wilderness *MC3*
willingness *MC1*
to wink at *MC3*

to withdraw *IC7*
to withdraw from *Com. C.7*
withdrawal *Com. C.4*
women's rights movement *MC3*
to worsen *MC8*
worthwhile *MC8*
in writing *Com. C.5*
to yawn *MC5*
Yours faithfully *Com. C.2*
Yours sincerely *Sec. A.1*
zone *MC5*

Quellenverzeichnis

Wir danken den folgenden Personen, Institutionen, Unternehmen und Verlagen für die freundliche Genehmigung zum Abdruck von Copyright-Material, soweit sie erreicht werden konnten.

3. Umschlagseite:	Georg Philip & Son Ltd., London
Seite 10:	Keystone Pressedienst, Hamburg
Seite 17:	Peter Guest, München
Seite 20:	Peter Guest, München
Seite 21:	Deutsches Museum, München
Seite 22:	Copyrightholder konnte nicht ermittelt werden
Seite 28:	Peter Guest, München
Seite 29:	C. R. Snowdon, Shrewsbury
Seite 30:	C. R. Snowdon, Shrewsbury
Seite 31:	Cartoon Features Syndicate, Boston
Seite 35:	links/rechts: Crown copyright reproduced with the permission of the Controller of Her Majesty's Stationery Office, Sheffield Mitte: The Department of Employment and the Welsh Office, Sheffield
Seite 38:	links: Liverpool Victoria Friendly Society, London rechts: Nationwide Anglia Building Society, London
Seite 43:	Tony Husband, Cheshire; Terence Green, Langenhagen (2×); Drawing by Maslin; © 1989 The NewYorker Magazine, Inc.
Seite 45:	The National Lottery, Watford
Seite 47:	The Image Bank, München (1 + 3)
Seite 54:	Private Eye, London
Seite 64:	Bavaria Bildagentur, Gauting
Seite 65:	Sunday Telegraph, London
Seite 71/73:	Reproduced by permission of the Office of Fair Trading, London
Seite 75:	Wolfgang Ammer, Cartoon – Caricature – Contor, München
Seite 78:	Terence Green, Langenhagen
Seite 82:	The Image Bank, München
Seite 85:	Peter Guest, München
Seite 87:	The Image Bank, München
Seite 88:	The Image Bank, München
Seite 92:	Regents Publishing Comp., New York
Seite 95:	The Department of Employment, London
Seite 99:	The Institute of Careers Officers, West Midlands
Seite 100:	Bournville Business School; Crown copyright reproduced with the permission of the Controller of Her Majesty's Stationery Office, Sheffield
Seite 101:	Private Eye, London
Seite 103:	The Image Bank, München
Seite 108:	Cartoon Features Syndicate, Boston (1×) Private Eye, London (2×) links oben: The Energy Question by Gerald Foley, Penguin Books Ltd., London
Seite 109:	New Statesman 9/85, London
Seite 110:	Countryside, Cheltenham, Council for the Protection of Rural England, London
Seite 111:	dpa
Seite 112:	Gerhard Merfer, Cartoon – Caricature – Contor, München
Seite 114:	Peter Guest, München
Seite 116:	links: Marion Schweizer, München/Rex Features rechts: Horst von Irmer, München
Seite 117:	dpa
Seite 118:	Daily Telegraph, London Jobfinder, Bury St Edmunds
Seite 122:	Punch, London
Seite 125:	Cartoon Features Syndicate, Boston
Seite 126:	Peter Guest, München
Seite 131:	Peter Guest, München
Seite 133:	Peter Guest, München
Seite 135:	Peter Guest, München
Seite 137:	Daten basieren auf: Statistisches Jahrbuch 1989, Statistisches Bundesamt, Wiesbaden
Seite 139:	Frank Hoffmann, Cartoon – Caricature – Contor, München
Seite 142:	Peter Guest, München
Seite 151:	Peter Guest, München
Seite 157:	Peanuts: PIB · Copenhagen
Seite 160:	Punch, London
Seite 175:	Cartoon Features Syndicate, Boston
Seite 182:	Drawing by Modell; © 1983 The New Yorker Magazine, Inc.